Henry Turner Davis

Solitary Places Made Glad

Henry Turner Davis

Solitary Places Made Glad

ISBN/EAN: 9783337168155

Printed in Europe, USA, Canada, Australia, Japan

Cover: Foto ©ninafisch / pixelio.de

More available books at **www.hansebooks.com**

Solitary Places Made Glad:

BEING

OBSERVATIONS AND EXPERIENCES FOR THIRTY-TWO YEARS IN NEBRASKA;

WITH

SKETCHES AND INCIDENTS TOUCHING THE DISCOVERY, EARLY SETTLEMENT, AND DEVELOPMENT OF THE STATE.

BY THE

REV. HENRY T. DAVIS,

OF THE NEBRASKA CONFERENCE.

The wilderness and the solitary place shall be glad for them; and the desert shall rejoice, and blossom as the rose.
—ISAIAH XXXV, 1.

CINCINNATI:
PRINTED FOR THE AUTHOR BY CRANSTON & STOWE.
1890.

To the Ministers and their Families,

who have been, and are now,
engaged in laying the foundations and building up the
Church of Christ on the frontier, is this
book dedicated by

THE AUTHOR.

PREFACE.

SOME time before his death, the late Dr. W. B. Slaughter had in contemplation the writing of a book on Nebraska. He requested me, as I was one of the first pioneers, to furnish him material touching the early settlement of the Territory. The request was complied with, and a limited amount furnished. He afterward said: "You have not furnished me the tithe of what I expected; I shall expect a great deal more from you." Soon after this remark he was called to his heavenly home.

Later, one of the leading members of the Nebraska Conference said to me: "You owe it to the Church and posterity to leave in permanent form your early experiences and observations in Nebraska." A leading pastor in a sister denomination of the State suggested the same thing, and similar suggestions have been made by others. These remarks impressed me with the thought that perhaps I did owe it to the

Church and the world to follow out their suggestions; hence this volume.

I give this unpretentious book to the world, earnestly praying the blessing of God upon every one who may chance to read its pages. If it shall be the means, in the hands of God, of leading a soul to Christ, or a believer up to a higher plane of religious experience or to more active service for the Master, my labor shall not be in vain.

H. T. DAVIS.

LINCOLN, NEBRASKA, June 4, 1890.

CONTENTS.

CHAPTER I.
THE "GREAT AMERICAN DESERT" A MYTH.

Early Views of the West—The Sahara of the United States disappears before the March of Civilization, ... PAGE 15

CHAPTER II.
DISCOVERY OF NEBRASKA.

Coronado's Expedition in 1540–41—De Soto discovers the Mississippi—Father Marquette and La Salle—Nebraska twice owned by Spain, and twice by France—Ceded to the United States in 1803—Organized as a Territory in 1854—Admitted as a State in 1867—Prosperity, . 26

CHAPTER III.
TOPOGRAPHY AND RESOURCES OF NEBRASKA.

Position—Area—Elevation — Climate— Soil— Resources—Intelligence of the People, ... 38

CHAPTER IV.
CALIFORNIA GOLD EXCITEMENT IN 1848–50.

Gold discoverd—Anxious to go—"Outfit" obtained—Farewell to Friends—Trip from South Bend to Old Fort Kearney—Perilous Passage -over the "Big Muddy"—First Night in Nebraska—Beautiful Scene, 46

CHAPTER V.

ACROSS THE PLAINS.

Old Fort Kearney—Nebraska City—Platte River—Indians—New Fort Kearney—Wolves—Midnight Alarm—Chimney Rock—Court-house Rock—Buffaloes—Sweet Water—Summit of the Rocky Mountains—Green River—Bear River—Humboldt—Desert—Carson River—Summit of the Sierra Nevadas—Journey Ended, ... PAGE 56

CHAPTER VI.

CALIFORNIA IN 1850-52.

Disappointed Gold-seekers—Long Illness—Doctor-bill—Wickedness Rampant—Lynch-law—Summary Punishment the Palladium of the People—Vigilance Committees—Bold Robery—The Victim captured and hung, ... 83

CHAPTER VII.

RETURN HOME BY WAY OF THE ISTHMUS.

San Francisco—San Diego—"Wonders of the Deep"—Acapulco—Terrible Storm—Panama—Crossing the Isthmus—From Aspinwall to New York—Home, . 94

CHAPTER VIII.

PERSONAL RECOLLECTIONS.

Memorable City and Church—John Brownfield—David Stover—Conversion—Parental Influence—Call to Preach—Attend Asbury University—Licensed to Preach—Join Conference—First Circuit—Second Circuit—Two Gracious Revivals—First Convert's Triumphant Death—Ordained Deacon—Bishop Waugh, ... 108

CONTENTS.

CHAPTER IX.
ATTENTION TURNED TO THE WEST.

Fascinations of the West—Bellevue Mission offered Us—Acceptance—Adieu to Friends—We reach St. Louis—Up the "Big Muddy"—Arrive in Omaha, . PAGE 122

CHAPTER X.
THE PIONEER EVANGEL.

Methodism Cosmopolitan—Missionaries sent to Oregon in 1834—Planning to capture Kansas and Nebraska for Christ—The Territories organized—The Bishops send out W. H. Goode as a Scout—Our Superintendency an Element of Power—Kansas and Nebraska Conference organized—Quantrell burns the City of Lawrence—Second Conference—Bishop Ames and Dr. Poe on the Missouri River—A Heroine—A Sermon instead of a Dance—The Third Conference, . . . 128

CHAPTER XI.
FIRST WORK IN NEBRASKA.

Crude Ideas of Nebraska—Bellevue—Story of a Diamond—How the People viewed Us—Hunting for a Town without Houses—First Sermon in Nebraska—Wild Speculation—Its Demoralizing Effects—First Quarterage received—Glad of Green Pumpkins—Thankful for Potatoes and Salt—Hospitality of Friends, . . 147

CHAPTER XII.
OMAHA.

When Founded—Indian Tradition of the Name—Amusing and Thrilling Incidents—George Francis Train—Moving in an Ox-wagon—Indians—First Methodist Episcopal Church—Ride on Horseback Two Hundred Miles to

Conference — Falls City in 1860—John Brown—The
Conference divided, ... PAGE 163

CHAPTER XIII.

FIRST NEBRASKA CONFERENCE.

Members—Statistics—"Crowned Ones"—Martyr Spirit
Still in the Church—Nebraska City District in 1861—
A Fearful Ride in the Cold—Popgun Elder—S. P.
Majors — Bellevue Conference — Bishop Simpson—
Crossing the Platte in a Skiff—Laura Beatty—An Awful Tragedy—A Death-bed Repentance, ... 182

CHAPTER XIV.

CIVIL WAR INCIDENTS.

The Dark Cloud—The Rainbow of Promise—National
Prosperity—"Jayhawkers"—Ordered to Halt—Camp-
meeting near Falls City—Bloody Fray—Dave Stephenson, ... 206

CHAPTER XV.

LINCOLN.

Location — Salt Basins — First Settlers — Indians — First
Sermon in the County—Elder Young—Lancaster—
Visit to the New Town—Act providing for the Change
of the Capital—Lot Sales—First Legislature in the
New Capitol—First Methodist Episcopal Church—
Other Churches, ... 212

CHAPTER XVI.

ONE OF THE EARLY PIONEERS.

Rev. Z. B. Turman, the First Preacher in Lancaster
County—Salt Creek Circuit—Great Revival—Coon-
meat—Preaching to "Spotted Horse" and His Warriors—The Captive Squaw and Her Sad Fate—A Mush-

CONTENTS. 11

and-milk Tea — Indian Troubles—The "New Ulm Massacre," . . . , ... PAGE 231

CHAPTER XVII.

DISTRICT INCIDENTS.

Eleventh Nebraska Conference—Bishop Ames—Old Sermons—U. P. R. R. completed—Rapid Growth of the Church—Hastings—Overtaken in a Fearful Storm—Three Memorable Quarterly Meetings—Sad Death of a Worldling—The Dutchman's Curse—The Confused Hostess—No Desire to Dance, ... 244

CHAPTER XVIII.

FURTHER ACCOUNT OF DISTRICT WORK.

Marvelous Growth—Privations and Toils of the Preachers—The Christmas-box—Touching Incident—Conference of 1873—Bishop Andrews—Conference of 1874—Bishop Bowman—Dr. J. M. Reid—Conference of 1875—Bishop Gilbert Haven—His Triumphant●Death—Rev. George Worley, ... , . 269

CHAPTER XIX.

THE SAME SUBJECT CONTINUED.

Appointed to Omaha District—Columbus—Osceola—Rising City—David City—The Work in Omaha—Conference at Falls City—Bishop Foster—Appointed the Second Time to Nebraska City District—A Remarkable Meeting—West Nebraska Mission formed—Dr. T. B. Lemon—Division of the Conference, ... 287

CHAPTER XX.

GRASSHOPPER INCIDENTS.

Their Origin—Depredations in all Ages—An Atheist renounces His Atheism—Wonderful Answers to Prayer—

A Touching Incident—Another Atheist changed—Annie Wittenmyer — Assistance from the East—Mrs. M. E. Roberts — Reflex Influence of Work done for Others — Man's Weakness and God's Power, ... Page 298

Chapter XXI.

BEATRICE.

Location—Founded in 1857—Emigrants on a Missouri Steamer organize a Colony—Beatrice in 1661—Albert Towle — Governor Butler—First Homestead — First Methodist Preacher—First Quarterly Meeting—Indians—Terrible Massacre —The Great Change, . . 319

Chapter XXII.

YORK.

Location—First Settlers—First Grave in the County—Methodist Class organized—David Baker—Buffaloes invade the County—Friendship of the Early Settlers—W. E. Morgan—First Quarterly Meeting—Other Churches—Appointed to York Station 1883—Great Revival—The Little Girl and the Dark Cloud—Second Year—Another Great Revival—The New Church—Subscription—Third Year—Church completed—Dedication by Bishop Warren, ... 332

Chapter XXIII.

METHODIST EDUCATION IN NEBRASKA UNIFIED.

Methodist Schools in Nebraska During the Past—The Nebraska Wesleyan University, ... 352

CHAPTER XXIV.

METHODISM'S DISTINCTIVE DOCTRINE REVIVED.

What the Doctrine is—The Great Revival—History of the Bennett Camp-meeting, ... PAGE 373

CHAPTER XXV.

THE DISTINCTIVE DOCTRINE EXAMINED, ... 398

SOLITARY PLACES MADE GLAD.

CHAPTER I.

THE "GREAT AMERICAN DESERT" A MYTH.

EARLY VIEWS OF THE WEST—THE SAHARA OF THE UNITED STATES DISAPPEARS BEFORE THE MARCH OF CIVILIZATION.

THE waters of the Missouri River, on the west, were once supposed to wash a country uninhabitable by civilized men. This country was thought to be a vast sandy plain, stretching away to the Rocky Mountains, with but here and there a shrub and spire of grass, and wholly unsusceptible of cultivation.

In the earlier history of our country the "Great American Desert" was considered about the same in extent as the Sahara of Africa; and it is really amusing to read the opinions held, only a few years ago, by some of our best geographical writers touching the territory of which Nebraska is now a part.

In 1793, Jedediah Morse published his "Universal Geography," and in this work he gives the most advanced knowledge of his time touching the interior of the North American continent. An extract or two will indicate the extent and accuracy of his knowledge. Much of his information was derived from the Indians. He says: "From the best accounts that can be obtained from the Indians, we learn that the four most capital rivers of the continent of North America—namely, the St. Lawrence, the Mississippi, the River Bourbon [the Missouri], and the Oregon, or River of the West—have their sources in the same neighborhood."

Touching the nature of the country west of the Mississippi, he says: "It has been supposed that all settlers who go beyond the Mississippi will be forever lost to the United States."

When the United States proposed to purchase from France the Louisiana territory, some of our ablest statesmen seemed to know but little of its extent or topography. Mr. Jefferson said with regard to it: "The country which we wish to purchase is a barren sand, six hundred miles from east to west, and from thirty to forty and fifty miles from north to south." "In 1803 Congress attempted to extend the Indian trade into the wild northwest, and so organized the expedition that has become historic as that of Lewis and Clarke. The instructions for it were draughted in April, 1803. On the last day of the same month Louisiana was ceded to the United States;

and so the expedition, which consumed two years, four months, and nine days in the round-trip from and to St. Louis, resulted in an exploration of our own territory."

In the Geography of Morse, and the report of the Lewis and Clarke expedition, the shadows of the Great American Desert first appeared.

Lieutenant Zebulon M. Pike commanded two Government expeditions into the country in 1805–1807. He was sent out to examine the sources of the Mississippi, Missouri, Platte, and Arkansas Rivers, and he first gave prominence to the unfortunate myth in American geography. In his report to the War-office he declares the vast regions explored as repulsive to all emigrants and impossible ever to be settled, and then says: "From these immense prairies may be derived one great advantage to the United States; namely, the restriction of our population to some certain limits, and thereby a continuation of the Union. Our citizens being so prone to rambling and extending themselves on the frontier, will, through necessity, be constrained to limit their extent to the west to the borders of the Missouri and Mississippi, while they leave the prairies, incapable of cultivation, to the wandering and uncivilized Aborigines of the country. It appears to me to be only possible to introduce a limited population to the banks of the Kansas, Platte, and Arkansas." "In the year 1819-20, Major Stephen H. Long, of the Army, by order of John C. Calhoun, Secretary of War, went out to explore the Missouri and its principal branches; and then, in succession, Red River, Arkansas, and the Mississippi above the mouth of the Missouri. The expedition took winter-quarters near Council Bluffs, and then swept the eastern base and slopes of the Rocky Mountains, along and among the heads and tributaries of the Missouri and its lower valleys. A few extracts from the report of Major Long will show how the 'desert' grew in area and in terror before the American people, and how good material it furnished to Europeans who wished to disparage the United States and discourage emigration, and prepare the way to capture Oregon. 'Of the country between the Mississippi and Missouri, it is reported that the scarcity of timber, mill-seats, and springs of water—defects that are almost uniformly prevalent—must, for a long time, prove serious impediments in the way of settling the country. Large tracts are often to be met with exhibiting scarcely a trace of vegetation.' The 'Great American Desert' manifests itself thus authoritatively in an official document in this report of a United States exploring expedition. Of the mountainous country beyond, Major Long says: 'It is a region destined by the barrenness of its soil, the inhospitable character of its climate, and by other physical disadvantages, to be the abode of perpetual desolation.'"*

From the reports of the Government explorations of Lewis and Clarke, Pike and Long, the material was furnished for the school histories and geographies of that day. These reports were considered authentic.

"In 1824, Woodbridge and Willard published their 'Geography for Schools,' and they thus spoke to the generation of pupils whom a better information is now correcting." They say:

" From longitude 96°, or the meridian of Council Bluffs, to the Chippewa Mountains, is a desert region of four hundred miles in length and breadth. On approaching within one hundred miles of the Rocky Mountains, their snow-capped summits became visible. Here the hills become more frequent, and elevated rocks more abundant, and the soil more sterile, until we reach the abrupt chain of peaks which divide it from the western declivities of North America. Not a thousandth part can be said to have any timber growth, and the surface is generally naked. . . . The predominant soil of this region is a sterile sand, and large tracts are often to be met with, which exhibit scarcely a trace of vegetation. . . .

---

*"The United States of Yesterday and of To-morrow," p. 99.

Agreeable to the best intelligence we have, the country, both northward and southward of that described, commencing near the sources of the Sabine and Colorado, and extending to the northern boundary of the United States, is throughout of a similar character."

The *Edinburgh Review*, of 1843, contained the following, from the polished pen of Washington Irving: "There lies the desert, except in a few spots on the border of the rivers, incapable, probably forever, of fixed settlements. This is the great prairie wilderness, which has a general breadth of six hundred or seven hundred miles, and extends from south to north nearly fourteen hundred miles, so complete in the character of aridity that the great rivers—the Platte, Arkansas, and Rio Grande—after many hundred miles of course through the mountains, dry up altogether on the plains in summer, like the streams of Australia, leaving only standing pools of water between wide sand-bars."

In his work entitled "Astoria," Washington Irving describes the Great American Desert in the following language: "An immense tract, stretching north and south four hundred of miles along the foot of the Rocky Mountains, and drained by the tributary streams of the Missouri and the Mississippi. This region, which resembles one of the immeasurable steppes of Asia, has not inaptly been termed the 'Great American Desert.' It is a land where no man permanently abides; for in certain seasons of the year there is no food, either for the hunter or his steed. The herbage is parched and withered; the brooks and streams are dried up; the buffalo, the elk, and the deer have wandered to distant parts, keeping within the range of expiring verdure, and leaving behind them a vast, uninhabitable solitude, seamed by ravines, the former beds of torrents, but now serving only to tantalize and increase the thirst of the traveler. . . . Such is the nature of this immense wilderness of the far West, which apparently defies cultivation, and the habitation of civilized life. It is to be feared that a great part of it will form a lawless interval between the abodes of civilized man, like the wastes of the ocean or the deserts of Arabia."

Mr. Irving's knowledge of the country he describes was not obtained from personal observation, but was gained at second-hand. He depended upon others for his information, and, relying upon their representations, unwittingly made erroneous statements that became current throughout the world. The men who gave Irving much of his information, were interested in the fur-trade, and it was to their interest to keep concealed many facts touching the country. It was the policy of these men to keep the world in ignorance with regard to this region, that it might be kept as long as possible "unoccupied as a game reserve."

Mr. Irving afterwards made the following confession touching his own writings: "I have read somewhat, heard and seen more, and dreamed more than all. My brain is filled, therefore, with all kinds of odds and ends. In traveling, these heterogeneous matters have become shaken up in my mind, as the articles are apt to be in an ill-packed traveling trunk, so that, when I attempt to draw forth a fact, I can not determine whether I have heard, read, or dreamed it, and I am always at a loss to know how much to believe of my own stories."

As late as 1849, on the map of Olney's "Quarto Geography," from Northern Texas to the British Line, and from the Missouri to the Rocky Mountains, was a space in which was found, in large letters, the words, "Great American Desert."

At a still later date an English writer in the *Westminster Review* says: "From the valley of the Mississippi to the Rocky Mountains, the United States territory consists of an arid tract, extending south nearly to Texas, which has been called the 'Great American Desert.' This sterile region, covering such an immense area, contains but a few thousand miles of fertile land. . . . Nature, marching from east to west, showered her bounties on the land of the United States, until she reached the Mississippi, but there she turned aside and went northward to favor British territory."

It is related of Benjamin Franklin that, in one of those courtly halls and gatherings in Europe, when nobility and statesmanship and diplomacy were toying with the young Republic, there hung a map of the United States, with that disheartening inscription, curving from the Texan to the British Border, "The Great American Desert." Franklin took a pen and drew a broad, erasing line through the title. The prophecy uttered by Franklin's pen has been fulfilled. The desert has disappeared.

For a number of years an army of "agricultural invaders" has been crowding the "Great American Desert," and this ghostly domain has been displaced by the best grain lands and grazing lands and mineral lands of the world. To-day, a net-work of railroads covers the "Great American Desert," and hundreds of thousands of the finest farms in the world, whose fields yield from twenty to fifty bushels of wheat per acre, and from thirty to ninety bushels of corn per acre, dot the vast plains, once supposed to be uninhabitable. A few years have entirely dissipated the delusion touching the West, and the Sahara of the United States has been found to be one of the most fertile, picturesque, and inviting regions in the world.

The salubrious climate; the dry, pure air; the clear, blue sky; the hills and valleys clothed with a rich, green sward, and decorated with ten thousand beautiful flowers; the beautiful winding streams, skirted with timber, along which herds of buffalo and antelope once grazed,—all combine to enhance the beauty and loveliness of the rich and rolling prairies of Nebraska.

And now, where but a few years ago the wild Indian lived in his wigwam, the beautiful city stands; where the buffalo, unmolested, grazed and ruminated, is seen the beautiful farm, with fields waving with luxuriant harvests. The warwhoop of the savage had scarcely died away when the sound of the church-going bell and the voice of prayer and song were heard. Where the buffalo, the elk, the deer, the antelope, lived in peace and held undisturbed sway, are now seen the church with its beautiful spire pointing heavenward, the university, the college, the common school, and all the institutions neccessary to the culture of the head and the heart.

The forces that are at work to-day for the development of the country are tenfold greater than they were thirty years ago. Cities grow up as by magic; large farms are opened in a year; internal improvements are made with a rapidity that would stagger the faith of the most credulous who lived a generation ago.

We have seen the buffalo-path transformed into the public highway, and the Indian-trail to the railroad, with its fiery steed snuffing the breeze, and sweeping with lightning speed from the Missouri River to the gold-washed shores of the Pacific.

We have seen ignorance and barbarity melt away before the mild and genial rays of civilization and the gospel; and the air that but a little while ago resounded with the wild war-cry of the savage, now resounds with the songs of peace.

We are living in a wonderful era—the brightest and most inspiring of all the past. This is an age of wonderful advancement. And I am glad to chronicle the fact that the moral and intellectual development of the country keeps pace with its material advancement. It has been the pleasure of the writer to witness the making glad of these solitary places. He has seen, with his own eyes, the dreary and desolate plains of Nebraska transformed into gardens of beauty and glory. And it is the purpose in the following pages to delineate, to some extent, from actual observation, the progress of this work.

CHAPTER II.

DISCOVERY OF NEBRASKA.

Coronado's Expedition in 1540–41—De Soto discovers the Mississippi—Father Marquette and LaSalle—Nebraska twice owned by Spain, and twice by France—Ceded to the United States in 1803—Organized as a Territory in 1854—Admitted as a State in 1867—Prosperity.

THE discovery of Nebraska dates back to a period far more distant than many really suppose.

Judge James W. Savage has given much time and thought to the study of this subject. In an address delivered before the State Historical Society, April 16, 1880, he says: "Fourscore years before the Pilgrims landed on the venerable shores of Massachusetts; sixty-eight years before Hudson discovered the ancient and beautiful river which still bears his name; sixty-six years before John Smith, with his cockney colonists, sailed up a summer stream, which they named after James the First of England, and commenced the settlement of what was afterward to be Virginia; twenty-three years before Shakespeare was born, when Queen Elizabeth was a little girl, and

Charles the Fifth sat upon the united throne of Germany and Spain, Nebraska was discovered, the peculiarities of her soil noted, her fruits and productions described, and her inhabitants and animals depicted." Three hundred and fifty years ago Nebraska was discovered by the brilliant and adventurous Coronado. The expedition of Coronado from the City of Mexico to the plains of Nebraska, in 1540-41, was one of the most wonderful undertakings in the history of the North American continent. Leaving the home of the Montezumas with an army of eleven hundred men, scaling the mountains of Mexico, pushing across arid plains and deserts of burning sand, meeting and conquering hostile tribes, swimming rivers, and surmounting almost every conceivable obstacle, he at last reached the valley of the Great Platte, it is supposed, near where the city of Columbus now stands. He and his noble band of brave and toil-worn men were the first to traverse the beautiful prairies, climb the hills, and cross the streams of the country destined in future ages to be one of the most thrifty and wealthy States of the American Union.

Not long after the conquest of Mexico by Cortes, in 1519, Nunez de Guzman governed the northern portion of Mexico. Guzman was a bitter enemy of Cortes, and envious of his brilliant discoveries. He had a burning desire to eclipse Cortes in his marvelous discoveries and the magnitude of his conquests. Visions of vast cities of wealth, beauty, and splendor, which he was to conquer, constantly rose before him. Guzman had a slave—a Texas Indian. This slave was cunning and shrewd. He went to his master one day, and told him a strange story touching the wealth and splendor of seven cities lying away to the north. He said, when a boy he often went with his father to these cities, and that in beauty, wealth, population, and magnificence, they compared with the City of Mexico itself; "that whole streets blazed with shops of gold and silver smiths, that the most precious stones abounded, and that the inhabitants were gorgeously attired, and lived in all the ease and luxury that wealth could bestow."

This story excited the curiosity of the governor, and inflamed his lust for gold. He determined, if possible, to find these cities of wealth; but all efforts to find them failed.

In 1536, four men, half-starved, half-naked, sun-burnt, and foot-sore, from eight years' exposure to cold, heat, hunger, thirst, shipwrecks, and battles, reached the City of Mexico. They were Spaniards. Eight years before, they had landed on the shores of Florida, with four hundred companions. Reaching the New World, they started out on their mission of discovery, expecting to find vast cities of wealth and splendor; but, alas! their expectations were doomed to disappointment. They waded through swamps, swam rivers, climbed mountains, and fought battle after battle with hostile tribes. They went north and then west, and after months of weary travel gazed upon the "Father of Waters," afterwards called the Mississippi. They crossed this mighty stream, and traveled several hundred miles in a northwest, and then in a westerly, direction. In their wanderings they doubtless passed over the territory that is now Kansas and Colorado, and over the Rocky and Sierra Nevada Mountains. During the eight long years of weary travel, through drenching rains and blinding snows, pelting hail-storms and savage tribes, suffering from intense cold in the winter and heat in the summer, one after another of these brave men fell, either from thirst or hunger or exposure, or from the hand of the bloody savage, and only four of all the four hundred reached the City of Mexico to tell the sad story of their sufferings. In their travels west of the Mississippi River, they heard of vast cities of wealth lying away to the north. They related what they had heard from the aborigines they had met at different points in their long and lonely journey. The story of these four men kindled anew the desire in the hearts of the Spaniards to discover the rich cities of which they had so often heard and dreamed.

In 1540 the viceroy of Mexico nominated Coronado to head a powerful expedition for the discovery of the Northwest. Coronado was a Spanish cavalier. He came to Mexico in the bloom of manhood. He was a brilliant man, of pleasing manners, and skilled in all the arts of war. He soon won the affections of the daughter of a wealthy Spanish nobleman, and they were married. His marriage to this beautiful and accomplished lady, as well as his own superior talents, soon brought him into note among the Spanish nobility, and he was chosen to take the responsible position of leading the new expedition of discovery.

Early in the spring, at the head of eleven hundred men, Coronado left the City of Mexico, scaled the rough mountains, passed over the plains, crossed the Rio Grande, and late in the fall reached a number of cities lying, it is supposed, not far south of where the city of Sante Fe now stands. The natives of these cities received Coronado and his men with the utmost kindness; their kindness, however, was returned by Coronado with the greatest cruelty and the most inhuman treatment. He burned their cities, put to death many prisoners of war, while he made slaves of many others. Having completely subjugated them, he remained during the winter. In May, 1541, he and his men left the beautiful valleys where they had remained during the winter, and proceeded on their way to the north. Day after day this little band pressed their way northward, traveling over treeless prairies, with the blazing sun above them, and burning sands beneath them. They measured the distance they traveled by each man's counting the steps he took during the day.

Late in July, 1541, Coronado reached the southern boundary of the State of Nebraska, and soon after explored the valley of the Great Platte. His description of the soil, the Indians, the buffalo and antelope, the wild grapes and plums, and the terrible hail-storms were exactly as we saw them with our own eyes more than three hundred years afterwards.

The next spring Coronado was thrown from his horse, and received an injury from which he suffered great pain for a long time; and as he had been told when a boy, by one who professed to foretell future events, that he would die from the effects of an injury caused by the fall from a horse, he imagined that the end of his life was near, and returned with his wife to the City of Mexico.

The viceroy received him with great coolness, looking upon his expedition as a comparative failure. While he had discovered a vast, rich, and beautiful territory, the cities of wealth and splendor, such as Pizarro had found in South America, and which floated in visions before the mind of the governor, had not been realized. Here the history of Coronado ends. The curtain of oblivion drops, and he is seen no more; but the country discovered by him gladdens the hearts of millions.

So the territory of Nebraska first belonged to Spain by the right of discovery. Relics that belonged, it is thought, to the soldiers in Coronado's expedition, have been found at different places. "Near the margin of the Pecos River, New Mexico, in a little crevice between the rocks, and among bones gnawed by the wolves, there were found, some years ago, the helmet, gorget, and breast-plate of a Spanish soldier. Straying perhaps from his companions, perhaps wounded in a skirmish, perhaps sick and forsaken, he had crawled to this rude refuge, and, far from the fragrant gardens of Seville and the gay vineyards of Malaga, had died alone. The camp-fires of Quivera were consumed more than three centuries ago; the bones of the profane Moor and the self-devoted Turk have bleached in the sunshine and decayed; the seven cities of Cibola have vanished; the cross of Coronado has moldered into dust, and these rusted relics are all that remain of that march through the desert and the discovery of Nebraska." Not many years ago an antique stirrup, of the exact shape and character of those used for centuries by the Moors and Spaniards, was found near the Republican, at a spot seven miles north of Riverton, in Franklin County, Nebraska. It was buried very deep in the ground, and was supposed to have belonged to one of Coronado's soldiers. Touching the above statements, I leave the reader to draw his own conclusions.

While Coronado was slowly pushing his way through unknown regions to the prairies of Nebraska, another brilliant expedition under the folds of the Spanish flag was going forward away to the southeast. De Soto, at the head of six hundred men, was pressing his way through the swamps of Florida to the north, and in the same year (1541) that Coronado discovered Nebraska, De Soto discovered the Mississippi River. While this mighty river had been crossed by a company of men a few years previous, their transient sight of it can never rob the name of De Soto of the honor which justly belongs to him as its discoverer. Descending the stream in 1542, De Soto died, and to conceal the knowledge of his death from hostile Indians, his body was sunk in the middle of the stream at the hour of midnight, and the rolling tide of the mighty river still sings his requiem.

But little was known of the Mississippi for the next hundred and thirty-one years. Matters of greater importance than its exploration engaged the attention of Spain and France, and the New World was almost entirely lost sight of.

In 1673, Father Marquette, a Jesuit missionary, with Louis Joliet and five Frenchmen, launched their birch-bark canoes on the Wisconsin River, determined to explore the "Father of Waters." Descending the stream, they soon reached its mouth, and sailed out into the broad and majestic Mississippi. They passed down the stream until satisfied it flowed into the Gulf of Mexico; then they returned, and made their report accordingly. Nine years later—in 1682— La Salle left the mouth of the Illinois River, and sailed down the Mississippi to its mouth, thus completing the work begun by Father Marquette and Louis Joliet. La Salle gave the name of the whole country drained by the Mississippi, Louisiana, in honor of Louis XIV, and took possession of the same in the name of the French king. The province of Louisiana included the vast country between the Rocky Mountains on the west, and the Alleghanies on the east. In this vast territory was the present State of Nebraska. In 1762, France ceded the province of Louisiana to Spain, and Nebraska was again the territory of Spain. In 1800 it was re-ceded to France, and Nebraska was again French territory. In 1803, France ceded Louisiana to the United States, and Nebraska becomes the territory of the United States.

DISCOVERY OF NEBRASKA.

In 1805 the district of Louisiana, by an act of Congress, was changed to the "Territory of Louisiana." In 1812, the Territory of Louisiana became the Territory of Missouri, and Nebraska was within its bounds. In 1834, by an act of Congress, all that part of the United States west of the Mississippi, and not within the States of Missouri and Louisiana or the Territory of Arkansas, was called the "Indian Country." In this territory was the present State of Nebraska. On May 30, 1854, Congress passed an act organizing the Territory of Nebraska, and President Pierce appointed Francis Burt, of South Carolina, Governor. Governor Burt reached Bellevue, October 7, 1854, and became the guest of Rev. William Hamilton, who had charge of the Presbyterian mission located at that place. Shortly after reaching Bellevue, the governor was taken sick, and, on the 18th day of October, died, having taken the oath of office only two days before his death. The vacancy in the executive office was filled by Secretary T. B. Cuming. The first official act performed in the Territory by an executive officer was the issuance of the proclamation of the death of Governor Burt. That official act bears date October 18, 1854.

On the first day of March, 1867, Nebraska was admitted as a State into the Union. The Honorable David Butler was the first governor of the

State, and under his able administration the State witnessed the most marked prosperity.

The first reunion of the old settlers of Lancaster County was held at Cushman Park, June 19, 1889. In his address to the Association on that occasion, Hon. C. H. Gere made the following reference to the first Legislature of the State, and to Governor David Butler: "Every law passed by that memorable Legislature of '69 weighed a ton. Its work was original and creative, and it did it well. Its moving spirit was the governor, David Butler. Some of its members came down to Lincoln from hostile localities, and had it in their hearts to destroy him and his works; but before the session was a fortnight old, his genial though homely ways, his kindness of heart, his sturdy common sense, the originality of his genius, and the boldness of his conceptions, captured them, and when the forty days were done, no man in the two houses avowed himself the enemy of David Butler. The history of Nebraska can not be written without giving large space to what Governor Butler did." No man has done more for the State than Governor Butler.

The beginning of the rapid development of the State dates back to the period of her admission as a State into the Union. From the time of her admission her growth has been a marvel.

An unbroken tide of emigration has been

flowing in ever since. All over her beautiful prairies, towns have sprung up, and grown, as by magic, into cities. Moral growth has kept pace with the material development of the State. School-houses and churches are seen everywhere. They dot the prairies, crown the hills, nestle in the valleys, and crowd the cities. The once dreary and desolate plains of Nebraska rejoice and blossom as the rose. What a marked difference between Nebraska now, and when the wild and half-nude savage threaded her trackless wilds! Following in the wake of civilization and the gospel come the railroad, the telegraph, the telephone, and all the valuable improvements of the age.

CHAPTER III.

TOPOGRAPHY AND RESOURCES OF NEBRASKA.

Position—Area—Elevation—Climate—Soil—Resources—Intelligence of the People.

GEOGRAPHICALLY, Nebraska is situated near the center of the United States. It lies midway between the two oceans, and between latitude 40° and 43° N. The extreme width of the State from north to south is about two hundred and ten miles, and its extreme length about four hundred and fifteen miles. It has an area of seventy-six thousand eight hundred and ninety-five square miles, or forty-nine millions two hundred and twelve thousand acres, almost every acre of which may be cultivated. It is almost twice as large as the State of Ohio. If England and Wales were placed on top of Nebraska, they would not carpet it by sixteen thousand eight hundred square miles. It has eight thousand four hundred and thirty-one square miles more than all the New England States combined. If the great State of New York were set down in the center of Nebraska, there would be twenty-nine thousand eight hundred and ninety-five square miles untouched. It has been said, " Nebraska

TOPOGRAPHY AND RESOURCES. 39

is an empire in itself." Its soil is fertile, its scenery beautiful, and its climate as healthful as its area is large and its scenery charming.

A Boston minister once went to Europe to rest and recuperate. While in London he was called on to make a speech. He rose before the assembly and said: "My home is on the third planet from the sun. The Western Hemisphere is the center of the planet; the United States is the center of the hemisphere; Massachusetts is the center of the United States; Boston is the center of Massachusetts; my Church is the center of Boston, and I am the center of my Church." I might not claim for Nebraska all that the Boston preacher claimed; and yet the rich soil, balmy atmosphere, undulating prairies, thrifty towns and cities, cultured, live men and women, make it one of the most desirable of places in which to live. The atmosphere is clear and pure. The average elevation is 2,312 feet above the sea. The almost constant motion of the air, the perfect natural drainage, and consequent freedom from all low, marshy lands, combine to give the State the purest, the most healthy and exhilarating atmosphere. It has been said, "The atmosphere of Nebraska is as clear and much purer than the far-famed skies of Italy and Greece."

The winds are very strong, and sometimes blow for three days in succession with such tremendous force that the pedestrian must struggle hard to keep his feet. While tornadoes are rare, gentle zephyrs and winds are almost constant. A gentleman after visiting the State said to a friend: "The air of Nebraska is purer, and there is more of it, than in any other country I was ever in."

Samuel Aughey, late professor of natural sciences in the University of Nebraska, gives the temperature of the State as follows: "The mean temperature of the summer months in Eastern Nebraska is between 72° and 74°, or, more accurately, close to 73°, Fahrenheit. During the winter months it averages 20°; during the spring months 47. 8°; during the autumn months $49\frac{5}{8}°$."

The soil is a black, sandy loam, very rich, and producing grains, vegetables, and fruits in great abundance.

An estimate has been made by competent and thoroughly posted men, and the conclusion has been reached that the two Dakotas are capable of supporting a population of 50,000,000. Nebraska is more than half as large as these two States, and her soil equally as good, hence she is capable of supporting a population of 25,000,000 souls. And the time comes on apace when that number will be within her borders. The average annual growth of the population of Nebraska for the last nineteen years has been sixty-one thousand. . During the past few years, one hundred thousand people have come into the State annually.

Nebraska is one of the best corn-producing States in the Union. The rate of progress in Nebraska from 1880 to 1888, in the production of corn, was more rapid than in any of the adjoining States, as the following statistics show: "In 1880 Illinois produced 326,000,000 bushels of corn. (Round numbers are used in all these illustrations.) Iowa produced 275,000,000 the same year; Kansas, 105,000,000; Nebraska, 65,000,000. In 1888 Illinois harvested 278,000,000 bushels of corn; Iowa, 278,000,000 bushels; Kansas, 158,000,000; and Nebraska, 144,000,000. Here it will be seen that Illinois did not maintain her record. Iowa gained a very small percentage, Kansas improved her record by a little over fifty per cent, and Nebraska leaped forward at the rate of one hundred and twenty-one per cent. Here Nebraska soil meets and overmatches the giants in her rate of progress."

Nebraska soil is well adapted to wheat-growing. The striking superiority of Nebraska soil and climate is shown in the subjoined table comparing the wheat-crops of 1880 and 1888 in Illinois, Iowa, Kansas, and Nebraska. Nebraska was the only one of these cereal-producing States that made progress on the record of 1880. Here is the exhibit of that fact, taken from the tenth census and report of the Washington Bureau of Agriculture for 1888:

STATES.	1880. Bushels.	1888. Bushels.	Per cent of Gain or Loss.
Illinois	51,000,000	34,000,000	Loss, 33⅓
Iowa	31,000,000	24,000,000	Loss, 22½
Kansas	17,325,000	16,000,000	Loss, 7½
Nebraska	13,850,000	14,500,000	Gain, 4⅘

In a similar way it can be shown that Nebraska is in the front rank of the world's most progressive States in the production of oats, hay, potatoes, and other farm grains and vegetables. Being one of the best corn and hay producing States in the Union, she is also one of the best stock-producing States. At her age, Nebraska has had no superior as a stock-growing State. Then, the dairy resources of Nebraska are unsurpassed.

Look at the following figures of the "Nebraska Dairymen's Association" for 1889:

Nebraska has 300,000 milch-cows, valued at, $7,200,000
Nebraska's butter product in 1888, ... 45,000,000 lbs.
Product of Nebraska creameries in 1888, . 4,000,000 "
Value of Nebraska dairy products in 1888, $10,500,000

"In no state in the Union can milk, butter, and cheese be produced at less cost per pound than in Nebraska."

At the American Dairy Show, at Chicago, in

TOPOGRAPHY AND RESOURCES. 43

1889, Nebraska took the first and second premium on creamery butter, first on granulated, and the diploma for the best and largest collection on exhibition.

As a fruit-growing State, Nebraska is abreast with other States. The flavor of her fruits is unsurpassed. Nebraska carried off the first premium on fruit at the meeting of the American Pomological Society, Richmond, Virginia, in 1870; again, at Boston, in 1873. At Chicago, in 1876, and at the Exposition in New Orleans, in 1884, she presented the largest collection of fruits, and would, without doubt, have taken the premium; but none was offered.

In popular intelligence Nebraska is at the front. By the census of 1880 Nebraska had the lowest percentage of illiteracy of any State in the Union, and Wyoming Territory alone had a better record in all the United States. A few years ago one of our most intelligent ministers had an appointment in a sparsely settled neighborhood on the prairies northwest of Omaha. The meeting was in a private house, and it was made of sod. The congregation consisted of about twelve persons. The minister was very much discouraged when he looked upon his audience. The men looked rough and hard. They were sunburnt and shabbily dressed, and, from their general appearance, he felt that he had an illiterate congregation before him, and greatly feared his sermon would not be at all appreciated. He preached, and the most profound attention prevailed throughout the entire discourse. At the close of the service, all remained to greet the preacher, and he learned that seven out of the twelve who had listened to him were graduates from Eastern universities. According to the number, this was one of the most, if not *the* most, intelligent congregations he had ever preached to in his life. The wonderful possibilities of the rich soil and charming climate of Nebraska brought into the Territory the most intelligent class of settlers at the very commencement. From the organization of the Territory, in 1854, to the present time, not only in the cities and villages, but in the rural districts, all over our broad prairies, in sod-houses and dug-outs, might be found the most highly educated men and women. To the push and energy of these cultured, live men and women are we indebted, to an extent at least, for the wonderful development and rapid growth of the State.

The soil of Nebraska is peculiar. It retains its moisture with wonderful tenacity, so that long periods of dry weather do not materially affect the crops. On the other hand, the heaviest rains retard the farmer but little in his work. In a few hours after the heaviest rain-storms the farmer may be seen in the field with his plow, cultivating his crops with as much ease as if no rain had fallen. This peculiarity of the soil guarantees to the faithful husbandman a good crop every year. A failure in crops is rarely ever known in Nebraska.

The autumns are remarkably lovely. They are usually long, mild, and dry. The "Indian summers" are delightful, even beyond description. To understand and rightly appreciate them, one must be present and enjoy them. I have lived in Ohio, Indiana, California, and Nebraska, and have traveled quite extensively through other States, and it seems to me that Nebraska combines more natural advantages than any other one State of which I have any knowledge.

CHAPTER IV.

CALIFORNIA GOLD EXCITEMENT IN 1848-50.

Gold discovered—Anxious to go—"Outfit" obtained—Farewell to Friends—Trip from South Bend to Old Fort Kearney—Perilous Passage over the "Big Muddy"—First Night in Nebraska—Terrible Storm—Beautiful Scene.

IN the year 1848 rich gold-mines were discovered in California. During that year, and in 1849, the most intense excitement on the subject prevailed throughout all the States. Flushed with the glowing reports from the mines that came by every mail, and with high expectations of becoming independently rich in a few months, tens of thousands rushed to the land of gold. The gold-fever, like a tidal wave, rolled from ocean to ocean. Many went "over the Plains," crossing the Missouri River, passing up the Great Platte Valley, thence over the Rocky and Sierra Nevada Mountains. To make this trip, from three to four months were required. Others went by water, doubling Cape Horn, a voyage requiring five or six months; while many others went by way of the isthmus, crossing from Aspinwall to Panama, and from there on the Pacific to San Francisco.

In South Bend, Indiana, my home, the "California fever" raged fearfully, carrying hundreds of the people to the Pacific Coast. Several companies were organized, and set out for the far distant West. Just before bidding their friends farewell, as their teams stood hitched to their wagons in the street, the Hon. Schuyler Colfax was called on for a speech. He was in the second story of a large store-building on Washington Street. He stepped forward to an open window, and looking down into a sea of upturned faces, spoke to the emigrants. He assured them that they would have the sympathy and prayers of the friends they left behind, and that during their absence the citizens of South Bend would never allow any of their families to suffer want. His few felicitous remarks touched the hearts of all. The faces of the emigrants, and the hundreds who crowded the streets to witness their departure, were bathed in tears. The scene was a most touching one. I shall never forget it. I shall never forget how I envied the young men that were among the emigrants, and how ardently I longed to be one of their number. The desire already kindled in my young heart for the new El Dorado, was fanned to a flame, and burned with a white heat. I said to myself, "I will go some day." During all that year the excitement continued, becoming, if anything, more intense. The mail from the

Pacific Coast came only once a month. When it arrived, hundreds gathered in and around the post-office, eager to learn the latest news from the mines. Nearly all the letters from friends were read aloud to the citizens. When a letter was received, after glancing over it himself, the person receiving it was called on to read it aloud for the benefit of all present. He would climb upon a chair or a dry-goods box, and read, while the hundreds around him stood in breathless silence, bending forward, eager to catch every word that fell from his lips. I have seen a large crowd standing in front of the post-office in the midst of a drenching rain, and while one held an umbrella over the person reading the letter, the crowd listened, seemingly unconscious of the terrible storm that was raging. And I do not suppose there was one in the vast crowd more oblivious to the storm, more anxious to hear, and more intensely interested than myself. We talked of California by day, and dreamed of it by night. Visions of the far-famed gold-regions often rose before us. In the spring of 1850 the long-wished-for time came. Judge E. Egbert, a brother-in-law, offered an "outfit" to my brother Albert and myself, with the understanding that we were to give him one-third of all the profits arising from any business we might engage in while in California.

I was then seventeen years old. With buoyant spirits, bright hopes, and visions of immense treasures of wealth before us, we bade adieu to a weeping mother, brothers and sisters, and friends, and started for the far West. Little did we know, or even dream, of the privations, sufferings, and disappointments that awaited us in the future. And well is it that a kind Providence keeps all these things hid from us! Well is it that the future, so far as these things are concerned, is all unknown. Little did we know of the dangers that would beset us on every hand, of the many imminent perils to which we should be exposed. Even now, when I think of the many narrow, hair-breadth escapes of life, I feel a peculiar chilly sensation creeping over me. I often ask: "How was it we escaped?" The answer comes in an instant: "God's guardian angel watched over us."

There is truth, as well as poetry, in Shakespeare's words:

> "There's a divinity that shapes our ends,
> Rough-hew them how we will."

Thomson, too, utters a great truth when he says:

> "There is a Power
> Unseen, that rules the illimitable world,
> That guides its motions, from the brightest star
> To the least dust of this sin-tainted mold."

I verily believe that that "unseen Power" which guides the motion of all worlds, all systems, and all atoms, guided and guarded us.

The patriotic Roman cried out: "If I had a thousand lives, I would give them all for my country."

With greater emphasis, and greater love for God than the Roman had for his country, I have often said: "If I had a thousand lives, they should all be given to God."

We were just four weeks going from South Bend, Indiana, to Saint Joseph, Missouri. The roads through Illinois and Missouri were very bad. We had never seen anything like them. There was snow and rain and mud. We had black, sticky mud in Illinois, and yellow, sticky clay in Missouri. In that early day there were but few bridges, and but very little work had been done on the roads. It is hard for any one now, in these days of improved roads and easy travel, to imagine the difficulties that were in the way of travel at that time. Illinois was full of sloughs. These have since been bridged, and no longer impede the traveler. We would cross several of these daily, and often our horses would go down to their sides in mud. We came to one of these one day; it looked ominous; we hesitated about attempting to cross. A team was just in front of us, and the driver said to the man on the other side:

"Is the bottom good?"

"Yes," was the reply. So he cracked his whip and started in. His horses began to flounder and soon went down to their sides in mud, and the whole wagon was buried except the box. The driver cried out in a rage to the man on the other side:

"I thought you said the bottom was good here?"

"It is," said the man, coolly, "but you are not half-way down to it." It was a common remark among the emigrants that the bottoms had dropped out of all the roads in Illinois.

Twenty miles east of St. Joseph, Mo., we stopped four weeks to rest our horses, lay in provisions, and prepare for the long journey over the plains. At that time St. Joseph was the extreme western border of civilization, and the outfitting point for emigrants starting for California. Beyond this, all was a wide, desolate waste. There were no white settlements west of this. The whole territory belonged to the Indians. St. Joseph was a small, unsightly, filthy town, of a few hundred inhabitants, and in looks the people compared very favorably with the dingy houses, filthy streets, and general repulsiveness of the place. Here we saw what we had never seen before. Many of the men we met wore about them leather belts, in which were large bowie-knives and revolvers. These they carried openly, and no attempt whatever was made to conceal their deadly weapons. Robberies were of almost daily occurrence, and it was unsafe for a man to walk the streets alone at night. We felt peculiar. We realized, for the first time, that we were in a "strange land," among thieves and robbers and cut-throats, and that life was none too safe. The impression made upon one, unaccustomed to such scenes, was very strong. I sometimes felt my heart creeping up into my throat, and a certain unpleasant choking sensation. But this little, unsightly, unattractive village has grown to be one of the beautiful, flourishing, and inviting cities of the West.

From this place we passed up the east side of the Missouri River into Iowa, to a point just opposite old Fort Kearney. Old Fort Kearney stood right where Nebraska City now stands. Here we crossed the "Big Muddy" in an old, dilapidated ferry-boat. The river was high, the current swift, and to undertake to cross the turbulent stream in such a rickety craft was indeed a hazardous task. The ferrymen managed the boat with oars and long poles. Only the day before the current got away with them, carried them some distance below the landing, capsized the

CALIFORNIA GOLD-FEVER.   53

boat, and a span of horses and a loaded wagon went down and were lost. The ferryman said, while there was danger, still he thought he could land us safely on the other side. We were restless, anxious to proceed on our journey, and unwilling to wait for the water to fall. We said, "We will risk it," and drove our team on board; and, with bated breath and trembling limbs, held the horses and watched the oarsmen with the most intense anxiety. When the dangerous current was passed and the pilot cried out, "Safe," the heavy strain was gone; relief came, and we breathed easy. A few moments afterwards the boat struck the shore, and on the 2d day of May, 1850, our feet pressed Nebraska soil for the first time. We pitched our tent on the western slope of "Kearney Hill;" and as it was raining and the ground wet, we cut hazel-brush, on which we placed our blankets and made a comfortable bed. That night the rain fell in torrents, and the thunder-peals were deafening. Lightning-flash vied with lightning flash, and thunder-peal with thunder-peal, and the elements seemed holding a grand carnival. In the morning we found the water running like a perfect mill-tail through our tent and under our bed. The brush, however, kept the bed from the water, and we were perfectly dry. Early that day the clouds cleared away, the sun came forth, pouring his mellow rays of light upon all around, and the scene that swept before us from the west was beautiful, even beyond all description. The lovely prairies, stretching away in every direction as far as vision could extend, with swell rising above swell, carpeted with living green, and beautified with flowers of almost every hue, made a scene which caused us involuntarily to exclaim, "Grand!"

Our first meeting with Nebraska was like the first meeting of many a young man and woman— it was "love at first sight." And that love, kindled when we first gazed upon Nebraska's beauty, has been growing in intensity for forty years.

As we stood upon Kearney Hill, it never once occurred to us that, in a very few years hence, on this very spot, would rise a great and beautiful and flourishing city. And still more remote was the thought that, in eleven short years, I should be a minister of the gospel and presiding elder of a district embracing near half the Territory of Nebraska. If such a thought had entered my mind at that time, I should have banished it in an instant as one of the wild visions of the young.

I was then an uneducated, unconverted boy of seventeen years. My heart was on this world. Bright visions of the future rose before me. Vast treasures of wealth were soon to be mine. A life of unalloyed pleasure, with everything earth can give to make man happy, was within my grasp. These were the dreams of my young heart. Little did I imagine that all my worldly plans and hopes, in a few brief years, would be dashed to atoms.

Momentous events and wonderful scenes were crowded into the next ten years. When I think of the stupendous events and wonderful changes that took place during that short period, a sensation I have no language to describe thrills my whole being.

CHAPTER V.

ACROSS THE PLAINS.

OLD FORT KEARNEY—NEBRASKA CITY—PLATTE RIVER—INDIANS—NEW FORT KEARNEY—WOLVES—MIDNIGHT ALARM—CHIMNEY ROCK—COURT-HOUSE ROCK—BUFFALOES—SWEET WATER—SUMMIT OF THE ROCKY MOUNTAINS—GREEN RIVER—BEAR RIVER—HUMBOLDT—DESERT—CARSON RIVER—SUMMIT OF THE SIERRA NEVADAS—JOURNEY ENDED.

KEARNEY HILL, where we spent our first night in Nebraska, is now a part of Nebraska City. Table Creek winds along the foot of Kearney Hill. Just across this creek, and a few hundred yards to the northwest, stood Old Fort Kearney. On the 5th day of May we left the Old Fort. We were then beyond the bounds of civilization. There were no white persons residing in all the Territory of Nebraska, save a few traders and United States troops, garrisoned at different points for the defense of the emigrants. The garrison here consisted of a block-house, made of logs, with port-holes for cannon and muskets, and two rows of barracks in the shape of an angle. In 1848 this military post was abandoned by the Government, and the troops moved to New Fort Kearney, on the Platte River, about two hundred miles west. In 1850, when we first saw the fort, the Government property was in the care of H. P. Downs. Eleven years later, when presiding elder of Nebraska City District, we became well acquainted with Mr. Downs and his family. They were then active members of the Methodist Episcopal Church in Nebraska City. When the war broke out in 1861, Colonel Hiram P. Downs assisted in raising the "Nebraska Regiment," and in August of that year he was promoted to the rank of brigadier-general.

When Nebraska City was founded and platted in 1854, the old block-house stood on Main Street, near the center of the city. Here it remained until 1886, when it was removed. Many of the old citizens strongly protested against the removal of this "old landmark." If I could have had my voice and my way in the matter, it never would have been removed, if it did stand in the center of a beautiful city of fifteen thousand inhabitants. We first saw it in 1850. We next saw it in 1860; and in 1861 we moved to Nebraska City, and for seven years, almost daily, looked upon the old garrison. And for many years afterwards, whenever we visited the city, we expected to see the "block-house"—the people's old defender. It was like looking into the face of an old familiar friend. We were sorry, and ready to drop a tear over its departure. Lay not rude hands upon the old landmarks. Let them stand as monuments of the good they have done in the past!

What a change has taken place since 1850! The old log garrison has given way to a large and beautiful city; the grass-covered prairies to the most lovely farms, whose fields wave with luxuriant grain, and whose orchards bend under the weight of rich and luscious fruits.

From Old Fort Kearney we started west, traveling over undulating prairies and across winding streams, skirted with timber, as beautiful, it seemed to us, as any on which the eye of man ever rested. After several days' travel we struck the valley of the Great Platte River. The Platte is the largest river in Nebraska. Its head-waters rise in the mountains of Colorado and Montana, some of them being fed by the "everlasting snows." It flows east, through the central portion of the State, and empties its waters into the Missouri just above where the city of Plattsmouth now stands. It is a wide, rapid, and very shallow stream; and its valley—eight to fifteen miles wide—approximates, in fertility, the valley of the Nile. This stream has been known by two different names—"Nebraska" and "Great Platte." Nebraska is an Indian name; Great Platte is a French name. They are both of the same import, signifying "broad water." It is a dangerous stream to ford, on account of the rapidity of its current and its quicksand bottom.

Descending an abrupt bluff, we struck the valley of this great stream. Here, for the first time, we met Indians. Several hundred Pawnee warriors gathered around us. They were painted, feathered, and dressed in almost every conceivable fantastic style, and armed with muskets, knives, spears, and bows and arrows. They were on the war-path against the Sioux. Being armed to the very teeth, they seemed anxious for the bloody fray. We came upon them very suddenly. Just as we descended the steep bluff into the valley, before we were aware of it, we were completely surrounded with these savages. I do not know how the other members of our company felt. I know very well how I felt, and I shall never forget the feelings I then had. At the first sight of these savage looking "red-skins," my heart, it seemed, leaped right up into my throat, and as hard as I tried, I could not possibly keep it down, and it really seemed to me I should choke, and a most strange sensation crept all over me, such as I had never felt before. It was a time that tried a man's nerve, but I did not care to have such a test repeated. There was but a handful of us compared with them, and we were wholly in their power. We knew very well they could, if they wished, kill and scalp every one of us, or take us prisoners, and put us to death by inches, with the most inhuman tortures, as they had done to many others; and we well knew that torture was their favorite amusement. And as they were on the war-path, and needed munitions of war, we knew that our provisions and teams and weapons and ammunition were a temptation to them to put us out of the way. I confess, I felt a peculiar weakness about the knees, and a strange, trembling sensation all over. However, after giving them a few articles of food, they left, passing on to the south, and we went our way rejoicing, feeling wonderfully relieved, and breathing with ease again.

Two days after this we reached New Fort Kearney, which we found situated on a lovely spot in the valley of the Great Platte. Here we found a number of United States troops quartered. The commander of the post ordered every emigrant to pass into one of the offices, where a clerk registered each name, his former residence, and destination.

From here we traveled up the Platte for days and days, with the same monotonous scenes before us, the same turbid stream, the same low range of bluffs in the distance, the same wide valley, with but here and there a lone tree or shrub to greet the eye.

The emigration was so large that year, that the grass was eaten off close to the ground, by the cattle and horses, for a great distance on both sides of the road, and we frequently had to go from one to five miles to obtain grass for our horses.

One afternoon, about three oclock, we camped on the bank of the Platte River, where we could get plenty of wood and water. There was no grass, however, so brother Albert and myself took the horses back to the bluffs, some five miles away, into a deep canyon, where we found an abundance of good grass. Here we watched the horses, until it began to grow dark, when we caught them, and were about to get on and ride back to camp. While in the act of bridling them, a strange and startling sound broke, all at once, upon our ears. It came from every direction. It was the cry of a thousand hungry wolves that broke the stillness of the evening air. In an instant, and simultaneously, they seemed to leap from their hiding-places in the caves and crags and glens, and came rushing down towards us with a hideous howl that thrilled us through and through, making our hair stand on end. The noise seemed to make the very hills shake and tremble around us. My brother succeeded in getting on his horse first, and looking back and seeing me still on the ground, he cried out:

"Henry, get on quick, or you will be overtaken." I tried again and again to mount, but was so excited and frightened I failed every time. It seemed to me I never could get on my horse. After repeated trials, I at length succeeded, and we rode down the canyon as fast as horse-flesh could carry us. When we got out of the hills, and reached the open valley, it was so dark we could not even see the horses' heads before us. Egyptian darkness could not have been more dense. We looked for the camp-fire, which we expected to see; but in vain, not a single ray of light, nor a single object, could be seen in any direction. The thought then flashed upon our minds that we might not be able to find our way back to camp again, and that we should be overtaken, and fall a prey to the hungry and ferocious wolves. We rode on for some time under the deepest suspense, goading our horses forward as fast as possible, and straining our eyes to catch a glimpse of light from the camp-fire. At length we saw away in the distance a flickering light; it seemed the most perfectly beautiful of anything we had ever seen; it came to us in that dark and dangerous hour as an inspiration. We were encouraged, and urged on our horses, and were soon seated by our own camp-fire, partaking of a hearty supper, which had been prepared for us; after which we lay down to dream over our new adventure.

When we reached the forks of the Platte River, our route was then up the South Fork of this stream. One night, about dusk, after traveling hard all day, we reached a point where the high bluffs came within a few rods of the river, at the mouth of a deep ravine. Here, at the mouth of this ravine, with high, abrupt, and rocky bluffs upon either side, we pitched our tents and stopped for the night. It was a gloomy, dismal-looking place. On our right was the river; on our left the deep ravine; in front and in our rear rose, almost perpendicular, the frowning bluffs. It was just the right place to be overtaken and cut to pieces by Indians. We prepared supper, put out our guards, and retired to our tents to rest. Foot-sore and weary, we soon fell into a deep sleep. About midnight we were aroused from our sweet slumbers and dreams of home and loved ones by the guards, who rushed to the tents, and in a low voice said: "Indians! Indians! Get up, and get your guns, quick, quick! We hear them crossing the river on their ponies. They will be here in five minutes." Startled, frightened, and trembling like an aspen-leaf, we tried to find our arms; but every thing seemed out of place. Guns, powder, balls, caps, everything was gone. The Indians, as we supposed, were just upon us, and we were without anything with which to defend ourselves. It was a time of intense excitement. In a few moments, however, we recovered our presence of mind, found our guns and ammunition, and with everything ready, we went out to meet the foe. We could distinctly hear them slowly crossing the river. Plash! plash! plash! we heard their feet in the water. The river was near a mile wide, and it took some time for them to cross. Nearer and nearer they came. At length they reached the shore, rose upon the bank, when, lo and behold! we saw, not Indians, but a large herd of buffaloes. We laughed heartily at our scare, returned to our tents, and slept soundly till morning. The next day we crossed the South Platte where Julesburg now stands.

It may not be amiss here to give a bit of history touching the founding of this city. Julesburg derives its name from a tragic and bloodcurdling incident, such as abound in the early history of Nebraska and Kansas, as well as other Western States and Territories. Julesburg derives its name from a Frenchman named Jules Beni. In 1855 Jules Beni kept a ranch at this point. At that time the mail was carried overland from the States to California, and this was one of the stations where horses for the company were kept. A noted desperado, by the name of Alf Slade, was superintendent of the stage company, and Jules Beni had charge of the stock.

Slade was said to be the most cruel and desperate character that ever frequented the frontier, and woe betide the man who ever had an altercation with him. He could kill a man in cold blood, and with as much composure as he would sit down and take his meal. One day he got into a quarrel with Jules, and told him he would cut off his ears and wear them as a charm on his watch-chain. Slade started across the yard for his arms, and Jules, knowing the desperate character of the man he had to deal with, shot and wounded him, and then, fearing vengeance from Slade's associates, he fled to a deep canyon in the vicinity. Here he remained concealed until he prevailed on one of his associates to take charge of his cattle. He then left the frontier and went to Saint Louis. In 1860 he returned to Cottonwood Springs. Shortly afterwards, with a company of men, he started westward for his cattle, which were then near Fort Laramie. He had only got a short distance on his way back, when he was overtaken by Slade, with a number of his men. "Slade immediately shot Jules and wounded him, then cut off the poor Frenchman's ears, and finally put him to death by slow and cruel tortures of the knife. After drying the ears of poor Jules, the monster attached them to his watch-chain, where he wore them as a fulfillment of his terrible threat, and as a warning to all who dared oppose him." Some years afterwards Slade came to a violent death. "His cold-blooded murders and desperate deeds became too terrible to be borne, even by men whose lives had long become inured to scenes of bloodshed, and he was hanged, as he deserved to be, by a vigilance committee."* Whenever we think of Julesburg, we think of the terrible tragedy connected with its early history.

From where Julesburg now stands, we crossed over to the North Platte. Shortly after reaching the valley of this stream, we came in sight of Chimney Rock. The atmosphere is so pure and clear that objects seem much nearer than they really are, and on this account we were often greatly deceived in the distance between us and certain objects in full view. Chimney Rock seemed at first sight not more than ten miles away, when in reality it was more than fifty miles away. When we first came in sight of it, we were traveling almost due west, and this lone column seemed to rise up out of the prairie away to the southwest. We traveled a whole day before we came directly opposite to it, and then traveled nearly two days before it faded entirely from our view. Chimney Rock is a pillar, resting on a solid rock foundation, and rising to so great a height in the air, that it may be seen for nearly a

---

*History of Nebraska (Western Historical Company), p. 533.

hundred miles away. It reminds one of Cleopatra's needle and the obelisks of Egypt. For ages around it the wild storms have swept; for generations it has looked upon the buffalo ranging with delight over the grassy prairies. Within its view many a bloody Indian battle has doubtless been fought, and many an Indian town has arisen, flourished, and passed away. It has watched the centuries come and go, and many wonderful scenes have transpired under its gaze, and still it stands in all its solitary loneliness.

Shortly after Chimney Rock faded from sight, Court-house Rock rose in view. Court-house Rock was about the same distance as Chimney Rock from the road, although it seemed very much nearer. It is several acres square, rising to an immense height, and looking very much like a massive court-house, standing alone on the dreary prairie, hence the name. The stone of both Chimney and Court-house Rock is soft, and they are rapidly yielding to the gnawing tooth of time.

The valley of the Platte, in the spring and early part of the summer, was the grazing ground for the buffaloes. The grass came earlier in this valley than on the bluffs and uplands, hence immense droves of buffalo congregated along this stream. It is hard for any one now to imagine the vast numbers that gathered along this great valley. We have seen the valley literally black with them for miles and miles in almost every direction. I am perfectly safe in saying I have seen in one herd many millions. And this scene was repeated day after day as we traveled up this river. A buffalo stampede was a most terrible and dangerous thing. A frightened drove of these wild animals running at full speed swept everything before them; and woe betide the horses and cattle of the emigrants that happened to be in their path; they were swallowed up in the herd, carried away, and perhaps never seen or heard from again. Many emigrants lost their teams in this way. The noise of a drove of buffaloes on a stampede was like the continuous roll of distant thunder. The only safety for a train of emigrants, on the approach of a drove of buffaloes coming at full speed, was to drive the wagons into a circle, make a strong corral, putting all the cattle and horses on the inside. The buffaloes, however, much more rapidly than the Indians, are becoming extinct. When we crossed the plains, forty years ago, it was not known how many buffaloes there were. There were many, many millions. The Great Platte Valley was alive with them, and the bluffs and prairies, north and south, for hundreds of miles, were covered with these shaggy cattle of the Plains.

Twenty years ago, according to the authority of the Smithsonian Institute of Washington, there were only eight millions of buffaloes roaming over the plains and mountains of the Far West. To-day there are but a few hundred. There never has been such an extermination of any large quadruped; it could not have been more successful if especially planned. Had the buffalo been a wild animal, doing immense damage to person and property, he could not have been hunted down and uselessly and wantonly slaughtered with more avidity. Only eighty-five head of wild buffaloes now remain; three hundred and four are alive in captivity, and about two hundred are under the protection of the Government in Yellowstone Park. It is said that there are about five hundred and fifty head in the British possessions, north of Montana. There is a remote possibility that the stock may be perpetuated, and a small number kept alive in the Yellowstone Park and different zoological gardens. But the wild buffalo has lost his place, and has become a rarity in the animal kingdom. The work of extermination has been carried on principally for the hides. Regular buffalo-killing parties were organized, and the animals hunted down and shot. Their hides would be taken off, and sold at the nearest post-trader's for seventy-five cents or a dollar. The war of extermination was waged vigorously and most effectively, and it was thought for a long time that it was impossible ever to extinguish the stock. It has only been a few years since the danger of the species becoming extinct forced itself upon those who are interested in natural history, and since then there has been a scramble to obtain specimens for zoological parks and menageries. The Government has also recognized the importance of perpetuating the species, and it has secured a number and placed them in the Yellowstone Park for safe keeping and the perpetuation of the stock. It is deplorable that the Government did not take steps long ago to stop the wholesale slaughter of these noble animals.

We followed the North Platte until we reached Fort Laramie. Here we found a number of United States troops stationed. From this point we crossed over the "Black Hills," and, after several days' travel over a very rough and rugged road, struck the Sweet Water. This we found to be a most beautiful stream, and its waters as delightful as its name indicates. The Sweet Water winds its way down a most beautiful valley, which we found covered with heavy, tender, and most nutritious grass. This thrifty and tender grass our horses ate with a relish, which did us good to behold. Soon after reaching this stream we came to Independence Rock, which stands near the bank of the river, overlooking the whole surrounding country. Independence Rock is a great bowlder, if my memory serves me right, covering thirteen acres, and over one hundred feet high. At one place, on the west side, this rock could, with some difficulty, be scaled. The ascent was quite steep, yet by dint of effort a man could climb to the top. We clambered up to the summit of this wonderful bowlder, and gazed with delight upon the romantic scenery which spread in every direction before us. After remaining for a short time, having taken in the magnificent view, we saw a large snake crawling up out of one of the crevices of the rock; in a little while another one made his appearance. As we had no desire whatever to see any more, never having had any peculiar love for the serpentine race, we made our descent much quicker than we had made our ascent, and left the snakes in full possession.

Just beyond this and in full view was Devil's Gap. This is an opening about thirty feet wide, through a mountain of solid rock. Through this opening the Sweet Water rushes at the rate of some fifty miles an hour. The walls on both sides are perpendicular, and two hundred feet high. This opening looks very much like a work of art, as though it had been made by human hands to form a channel for the beautiful river. This marvelous channel was cut through this mountain of solid rock not by human but divine hands. In this gap, on one side of the stream, near the surface of the water, is a shelf of rock, and over this mountain, near the precipice, was a precipitious foot-path. Up this path, and over this rough mountain, many emigrants traveled on foot. We preferred to go with our teams some distance to the south-east, where there was a good wagon-road, rather than to attempt to scale the dangerous mountain on foot. The year previous a man passed up this path to the summit, and, looking down into the stream two hundred feet below him, became dizzy and fell into the awful chasm, his body striking the rocky shelf below. His friends could not possibly recover his body, for the waters rush through the narrow and rocky channel like the dashing waters of a raging cataract. I did not see them; but others who did, said the skull and bones of the poor man were distinctly visible from the top of the precipice.

Up this stream we traveled until we reached the summit of the Rocky Mountains; but so gradual was the ascent that we were not aware we were on the summit until we saw a small rivulet flowing to the west. We reached this point Saturday afternoon, July 3, 1850. Here, in this bleak and desolate place, some twelve thousand feet above the level of the sea, we camped and remained over Sabbath, celebrating the Fourth of July, at an altitude far above any on which we had ever been before. The wind blew a stiff gale; the weather was cold, and it snowed at intervals during the whole day. We found some very good bunch-grass for our horses, and to keep ourselves warm, and while away the time, we cut sage-brush, and kept a good fire going by the side of a great rock, which served as a shelter from the fierce wind. To the right and left of us, as far as the eye could extend, rose mountain-peak above mountain-peak in solitary grandeur, crowned with eternal snow. The scene, though sublime, was at the same time a dreary and desolate one. While one enjoys such scenes for a little while, they soon become monotonous, and one longs for a more genial clime and more pleasant objects on which to gaze. From the summit of these everlasting hills we began to descend slowly to the west. We soon reached Green River, a deep and rapid stream, but not very wide. There was neither bridge nor ferry, and the water was too deep to ford; so we made a ferry-boat of a wagon-box, took our wagons to pieces, ferried them over one after another with our plunder, and swam with our horses across the river. Then we put together our wagons, reloaded our traps, and after a hard day's work in getting across, started again on our way rejoicing.

The next river of importance was Bear River. From here our journey was uneventful until we reached the Humboldt River. And of all the streams we ever saw or read of, this is the most loathsome. From its head-waters to its mouth— a distance of three hundred miles—where it sinks away in the sand, there is not a single redeeming trait. It is repulsive, and only repulsive, from one end to the other. The Humboldt River runs through a valley of alkali, and the waters of this stream, as well as the springs and rivulets that flow into it, are all strongly impregnated with this poison. And yet, for two weeks, we had to wash in these waters, cook with them, and even drink them. They had a peculiarly sickening and slippery taste that we remember distinctly, though forty years have passed since we drank them. The dust in the roads was like light-colored ashes and as fine as flour, and from one to six inches deep. The great clouds of this dust and the sweltering heat, at times, almost completely overcame us. We breathed the alkali, and ate the alkali, and drank the alkali, and lay down in the alkali, until our whole systems were completely saturated with the loathsome minerals.

Twice a day we had to swim this stream, cut grass and float it over for our horses, as there was no grass on the side of the river we traveled.

The Humboldt is a rapid stream and full of dangerous whirlpools. In these, many a poor traveler has lost his life. A man might be ever so good a swimmer, yet, if he got in one of these, he was sure to be drawn under and drowned. We saw new-made graves all along this river; and on the head-board of almost every grave was the sad word, "Drowned." Along the pathway of life the whirlpools of sin are numerous, and many a man, who thought himself strong to resist evil of every kind, in an unguarded moment has been drawn in and lost. "Let him that thinketh he standeth, take heed lest he fall."

After a number of days of weary and painful travel, we reached the mouth of this river, which we found to be an anomaly. This stream does not empty its waters into any other body of water, as other streams do, but sinks away in the sand, at the edge of a sandy desert, seventy-five miles in width. The waters of this river at its mouth spread out over a spongy marsh, some fifteen miles wide and thirty miles long. Through this spongy, sandy soil, the waters of the Humboldt sink away.

At this point we camped, rested twenty-four hours, and made preparation for crossing the desert. At five o'clock in the afternoon we broke camp, left the valley, and ascending a low range of hills, realized we were on the desolate, dangerous, and sandy desert. We did not stop from the time we broke camp until we reached the other side. We traveled all night, and the next day, at three o'clock, reached Carson River.

This sandy desert, from the mouth of the Humboldt to the Carson River—a distance of seventy-five miles—was literally strewn with wagons, goods, and the bodies of horses, mules, and oxen. Horses and mules would lie down and die in their harness while hitched to their wagons, and whole teams of oxen, from two to six yoke, would lie down and die in their yokes. Others would wander away a short distance from the road, as if in search of water, but overcome with heat, would soon give up in despair, and sink down to die at the hands of this most terrible of all tyrants—thirst.

If these carcasses had been placed together in a row, we could have walked on dead animals from one side of the desert to the other. But not only did we see scattered upon the burning sands of this desert, wagons, goods, clothing, and plunder of almost every kind, and the carcasses of horses, mules, and oxen; but, ever and anon, a sandy mound marked the resting-place of some poor emigrant, who had fallen a victim to the ravages of thirst or disease. On this desert our last horse gave out, and my brother and I had to leave him to die. Tears unbidden stole down our cheeks as we said good-bye to faithful Dick. He had done all he could for us. He could go no further. He was worn out. The last, sad look of the faithful horse we remember still. Mr.

Wesley thinks all animals will be resurrected. We think they ought to be, and rewarded for their works and sufferings here. If they are, faithful Dick will have a rich reward.

Our provisions, too, were gone; so we each took a couple of blankets, rolled them up, put them on our shoulders—as the soldier carries his knapsack—and trudged away on foot. After traveling all night, the next morning the sun rose clear and bright, and as he climbed the heavens, the heat became more and more intense, and the sands beneath our feet hotter and hotter. Stretching away in every direction, as far as the eye could extend, was a vast, sandy plain, and the heat arising from this sandy plain was like the heat from a burning furnace. About noon our water gave out. We quickened our steps, knowing well that no time could be lost without endangering our lives. On and on, we pressed our weary way, growing more and more fatigued, and our thirst becoming more and more severe. I never shall forget that day. How every nerve was taxed to its utmost! How our eager eyes were strained, time and again, to catch a glimpse of the trees skirting the river whose waters were to slake our thirst, and whose green banks were to furnish rest for our weary bodies! I never shall forget the fear and anxiety we felt as the hours passed slowly away. Many of our comrades sank by the wayside, and we knew not how soon we must succumb to the heat, sink down, and die upon the burning sands. About three o'clock in the afternoon, the waving trees along the desired stream rose in view. What a thrill of joy went coursing through every avenue of the soul as the beautiful scene rose before us! A few moments more and we sat down by that limpid stream, and drank and drank and drank of its clear, cold waters, until we were perfectly satisfied; then we threw our weary bodies on the green grass, beneath the shade of a large tree, and never was rest more sweet! After having slaked our thirst with these cooling waters, and rested for a little while, we went to a ranch near by, kept by a Californian, and bought some food—a few small, hard biscuits, made of flour and water—paying one dollar and a half each. These we ate with a relish; then resumed our journey. We were then three hundred miles from the mines; and from this on there were stations every few miles, where provisions could be had *by paying for them*. The next station we reached we bought a little flour, paying two dollars per pound, and a little bacon at the same price. With the flour and some water and salt we made pancakes, and, frying the meat, used the gravy on the cakes, and they tasted most delicious. While on the Plains and in California, however, we ate enough pancakes to last a life-time. I have never had any desire for pancakes since, and do not think I ever shall. Being short of money, we only ate about one-half as much as our appetites craved. We lived on half rations from this on, until we reached the end of our journey, which we did in six days, walking fifty miles a day from the time we left the desert until we reached the mines. Having walked for the past three months we were hardened to it, and could march from daylight until dark without being much wearied. We walked faster than any of the teams on the road, passing horse, mule, and ox teams, and leaving everything behind us. Many were worse off than we. They were not only without provisions, but without money. Many ate the flesh of mules and horses that had died of overwork and starvation, and were glad to get that in order to keep them alive. Eternity alone will reveal the sufferings of many while traveling over those plains in quest of gold.

If men would do and suffer as much for God and humanity as they do for money, it would not be long until the millennial glory would break over the world.

Near the head of Carson River we struck what was called the "Big Canyon." Up this canyon the road leads toward the summit of the Sierra Nevada Mountains. This canyon we found to be very narrow, barely wide enough for one wagon to pass. The road was very rough and rocky, and part of the way we had to travel in a little brook that came leaping and dashing down the mountain gorge. On either side rose, almost perpendicular, the rocky cliffs from one hundred to a thousand feet, with here and there a tree growing out from some crevice, and reaching up its arms as if anxious to climb up to where it could behold the rays of the beautiful sun.

On and up this gloomy defile we continued to press our way, until at length we passed out into an open space, and supposed we saw just before us the summit. A few moments afterwards, however, we reached the supposed summit; but, alas! were disappointed, for far above and beyond us rose another mountain. "That," we said, "surely must be the summit." In a few hours we reached its peak, and were again disappointed; for far away and above us rose another mountain-peak, and away beyond and above that still another. Mountains were piled on mountains until they passed up above the clouds, and bathed their snowy summits in the vaulted blue. Onward and upward we continued to climb, until we, too, passed the clouds, and at last stood upon the white crest of the most majestic mountain range on the American Continent, while the broad and beautiful California Valley for hundreds of miles swept before us, and still further on the blue waters of the Pacific rolled in endless succession their mighty billows.

In ascending the Sierra Nevada Mountains, mountain-peak rises above mountain-peak. The sweep of vision widens, the sublimity and beauty of the scene deepens, the grandeur becomes more and more impressive; and when you have reached the highest peak, and everything earthly is below, you are awed and almost overwhelmed with the splendor of the scene. I never shall forget how I felt when I stood upon Sierra Nevada's snow-capped summit. To the west was the Sacramento Valley; to the east was the beautiful Nevada; to the north and to the south, as far as the eye could extend, were the rock-ribbed and snow-crowned mountains, glittering and flashing in eternal sunshine. The unfading impression of that scene has been with me for forty years.

As we stood upon this mountain-top, with the most of our journey behind us, and the end in full view, I have thought we felt a little as the ten thousand Greeks under Xenophon did, when, after traveling for twenty-three hundred miles through the midst of their enemies, suffering for food, water, and raiment, they at length ascended a mountain from which they could behold the Black Sea, on the shores of which stood a large number of Greek cities. In raptures of joy they shouted, "The sea! the sea!" and the very heavens resounded with their joyful acclamations. From this lofty summit we descended, and in a short time struck Weaverville, a mining town, and the end of our long journey was reached.

CHAPTER VI.

CALIFORNIA IN 1850-52.

Disappointed Gold-seekers — Long Illness — Doctor Bill — Wickedness Rampant — Lynch Law — Summary Punishment the Palladium of the People — Vigilance Committees — Bold Robbery — The Victim Captured and Hanged.

WHEN we reached Weaverville we were disappointed. Things were not as we expected to find them. Our expectations had been entirely too high; gold could by no means be picked up by the handful. Others were much worse disappointed than we. On every hand we saw the sad countenance and the dejected spirit. From many hope seemed to have taken its flight, and despair settled down upon them. The prospect of a fortune ahead had nerved the drooping spirit, and kept up the suffering emigrant during his long and weary journey until he reached the goal where the supposed fortune lay. But when the journey's end was reached, instead of stumbling over nuggets of gold and picking up the yellow dust by the handful, many were found working for their board, and many more were unable to find employment even for that. Not a few were discouraged, and gave up in despair; others went to San Francisco, worked their way home on sail-vessels, going round Cape Horn, a trip which took them six months to make. Had they not been so hasty in their conclusions, and so easily discouraged, they might have saved this long and painful journey. Almost anywhere away from Weaverville ordinary wages commanded one hundred dollars per month. In two months they could have earned enough to take them home by the way of the Isthmus, and thus saved themselves three months of slavish toil.

By the roadside, a few miles west of Weaverville, sat a middle-aged man, crying. A traveler said to him: "What's the matter?" "O," said the man, "I am three thousand miles from my wife and children. I have no money, can get nothing to do. I shall never see my loved ones again." And he boo-hooed right out, and cried as though his heart would break. He was only one of hundreds. Of the many thousands who reached the "New El Dorado," only a few were successful. The great majority were bitterly disappointed.

My brother and I went some twenty miles southwest of Weaverville, where we worked at mining until October, making enough during that time to purchase our winter supplies. Then we

went to Logtown, bought a cabin, and took up a
miner's claim. Here we worked until the next
summer, when we went up on the south fork of
the American River. The next day after reaching this point I was taken very violently with
erysipelas in its most malignant form, and for six
weeks was confined to my cot, for two weeks being delirious and entirely blind. My face and
head were swollen twice their usual size. When
I began to recover, my hair all came out, leaving
my scalp as bare as the palm of my hand. For
several days the doctor said I could not live, declaring me beyond the power of medical skill.
Providence ordered it otherwise, however, and I
was restored. I have always thought my recovery from that terrible disease was owing, under
God, to the kind care and attention of the faithful brother, who watched over me night and day
with the tenderness and anxious solicitude of a
mother.

I was then irreligious, and felt that if I died
I should be lost forever. O, the terrible feeling
of a soul dying "without God and without hope!"
No language can possibly describe such feelings.
"The way of the transgressor is hard," but the
way of the Christian is delightful. It is a lovely,
smooth, sunny pathway. I know it from heartfelt experience. "His ways are ways of pleasantness, and all his paths are peace."

As soon as I began to recover, my brother Albert was taken down with the same dreadful disease, accompanied with typhoid fever, and for six weeks was confined to his cot, during which time he passed as near death's door as I had done. Providence, however, raised him up also. Our doctor's bill amounted to the small sum of fourteen hundred dollars! But the doctor, being a very kind-hearted man, was willing to *take all the money we had*, and give us a receipt in full. We paid him three hundred dollars, took his receipt, and squared accounts.

We then returned to Logtown, where we remained until we left the State. California was then new, and wickedness of every kind was rampant. The Sabbath was a day of festivity and hilarity. It was the great day of business for the gambler, the saloon-keeper, the auctioneer, the merchant, and the miner. The merchant made his greatest sales on the Sabbath; the gambler made his largest hauls from the crude and unsuspecting miner on the Sabbath; the houses whose "doors take hold on hell" were thronged with the largest number of visitors on the Sabbath; the miner washed his clothes, prepared wood, and purchased provisions for the coming week on the Sabbath; and each seemed to vie with the other in acts of crime and debauchery on the day belonging to God alone. What a record was made for eternity on the Sabbath-day in the early history of California!

In the mining districts pretty good order prevailed. The people were generally law-abiding; for citizens took the law into their own hands. The penalty for petit larceny was horsewhipping; the penalty for horse-stealing was death.

A man was tried and convicted in Logtown by the citizens for stealing a pair of boots. He was sentenced to thirty-nine lashes. He was stripped to the waist, his hands tied together around a small tree, and as he thus hugged the tree a man plied the lash. Every stroke of the whip brought the blood, from the neck to the waist. After a few lashes had been given, the agony of the poor man was so great that in endeavoring to get away he tore the flesh from his breast on the rough bark of the tree; and the blood streaming from his bleeding back and lacerated breast, and his deep groans of agony, made me sick at heart, and I turned away from the dreadful scene. Horsewhipping was a terrible penalty for crime. A horse-thief was hanged to the limb of the nearest tree, and his dangling body struck terror to the would-be perpetrators of crime.

This summary punishment of crime in the early settlement of California brought to the miner and his property almost perfect safety. We never felt more secure in our lives than when we slept under a large pine-tree by the roadside near our claim, with the gold that we had washed out the day previous in the pan, standing where every passer-by could see it. We made no effort to hide anything, for we felt that everything was safe. The thief knew what a dangerous thing it was to steal from the miner.

Some may seem surprised that a horse-thief should be hanged, when his crime is merely a question of property. "The term horse-thief," as one has justly remarked, "is really generic, or a synonym for a great variety of criminals. He is the thief of any movable property, a highwayman, a bandit, a murderer, at his convenience, defiant of government, an outlaw, and the enemy, specific and in general, of society. The execution of a horse-thief, therefore, is ordinarily the administration of justice in gross, and not in severalty of crimes."

The Vigilance Committees of San Francisco and Sacramento struck terror to the roughs, and saved those cities from the complete control of thieves, gamblers, and cut-throats.

The Vigilance Committee of San Francisco was organized in 1851. The city had at that time about fifty thousand inhabitants. While there were many of the very best class of citizens in the city, the majority were among the vilest. The roughs had their way in everything. The fame of the gold-mines had brought all sorts of people from all parts of the world. San Francisco was the rendezvous of the worst class of people that ever infested any city. The gamblers of the world seemed congregated here, and they plied their vocation without molestation from municipal authorities. A small tent on one of the principal streets rented, it was said, for forty thousand dollars a year for gambling purposes.

Nearly the whole business part of the city was swept away by several great conflagrations. These conflagrations were the work of incendiaries, who had in view plunder alone. The best class of citizens felt that neither life nor property was safe. The administrators of law afforded them no protection whatever. The police officers, the judges, and prosecuting attorneys, when they were not the tools of gamblers and thugs, were weak and inefficient. Every means of preventing crime and bringing criminals to direct punishment had failed. The better class felt that something must be done, hence the Vigilance Committee was organized. This committee executed but few men. Its main work was to banish desperadoes, outlaws, and rascals. Its work was summary, and had a most happy and desirable effect, and soon restored law and order.

At a later date, the old Vigilance Committee of 1851 was again called into requisition. James

King was shot by James P. Casey, and died in a few days afterwards. On the same evening of the shooting, the Vigilance Committee of 1851 convened, and in less that two days, twenty-five hundred names were enrolled on the books of the Vigilance Committee, who pledged themselves to work together for the purging of the city of gamblers, foreign convicts, swindlers, thieves, high and low, and of villains generally.

The Vigilance Committee selected as its headquarters one of the most prominent places of the city, cleared the streets for two blocks, mounted six brass pieces, placed swivels loaded with grape on the roof, and put the streets under control of three hundred rifles and muskets.

The excitement everywhere was at white heat. On the roof of the building used by the Committee, a massive triangle was swung, and its sounds could call thousands instantly, on an emergency. " Draymen stopped in the street, freed their horses, mounted, and went clattering to the rendezvous; store-keepers locked up hastily, and ran; clerks leaped over their counters; carpenters left the shaving in the plane; blacksmiths dropped the hammer by the red-hot iron on the anvil. All the city hurried to head-quarters for any sudden work."

At one of the meetings, one of the speakers said "that probably more than five hundred murders had been committed in California during the preceding year, yet not more than five of the perpetrators had been punished according to the forms of the law."

The newspapers, the clergy, the people generally, approved the formation of the committee. William Taylor, our bishop, now in Africa, was in San Francisco at the time, and witnessed the proceedings of the committee. He says: "In the administration of Lynch-law, so far as I have known or heard, the thunderbolt of public fury has always fallen only on the head of the guilty man, who, by the enormity and palpable character of his crimes, excited it; and then not till after his guilt was proved to the satisfaction of the masses composing the court. In proportion as the law acquires power in California for the protection of the citizens, in that proportion Lynch-law is dispensed with."

Lynching in the Territories and new States comes in, and often works admirably, where the law is crude and feeble. But where the court-house appears in due dignity and power, Lynch-law disappears in the shadow. It will come to the front on any well-grounded call.

Summary punishment for crime, when guilt is proved beyond a doubt, is one of the safeguards of the people. It is the palladium of the individual, the city, the State, the Nation.

We were present and witnessed the trial, by citizens, of two men charged with horse-stealing. One was a young man about twenty years old. The stolen horses were found in his possession. He pleaded "not guilty," and proved that he had been hired to take care of the horses, not knowing they were stolen property. He was acquitted. The other one pleaded "guilty." He was a large, burly Englishman, about forty-five years old. While the people were trying to decide what they should do with him, he made his escape from the second story of a large log house, where he had been placed and guarded. The lower room, and the yard all around the house, was full of people. How he made his escape no one could tell. It was a mystery to all. The only solution to the mystery was, that through the influence of money, he had been spirited away. He had been banished from England to New South Wales many years previous for crime. New South Wales was used by the English Government as a penal settlement from 1788 to 1840. During this time, about fifty-five thousand convicts had been sent to that land, and among them was this horse-thief. He came from there to California.

About six months after he had made his escape from the citizens near Logtown, he went on board a steamer at San Francisco, went into the clerk's office, picked up a United States express-box containing a large amount of money, and walked off with it on his shoulder in the presence of officers of the ship and a large number of passengers. When the theft was discovered, the thief was pursued, and a short distance from the ship he was discovered in a small boat in the bay, the valuable box by his side, and he was rowing away for his life. Three officers got into another boat, and, after an exciting race of four or five miles, captured and brought him back. A scaffold was at once erected. He was led to the top of the scaffold in the presence of hundreds of excited people. A noose was made in the rope, slipped over his head, and adjusted to his neck, and then he was asked if he had anything to say or any requests to make. He called for a glass of brandy and a cigar. They were brought. He drank the brandy, then calmly smoked the cigar, and having finished, he said: "I am now at your service." The trap was sprung, and his unprepared soul went into the presence of the Almighty. Such was life in the early settlement of California.

CHAPTER VII.

RETURN HOME BY WAY OF THE ISTHMUS.

SAN FRANCISCO—SAN DIEGO—"WONDERS OF THE DEEP"—ACAPULCO—TERRIBLE STORM—PANAMA—CROSSING THE ISTHMUS—FROM ASPINWALL TO NEW YORK—HOME.

AFTER remaining on the coast for two years, we left for our home in the States. We took passage on a steamboat at Sacramento City, passed down the Sacramento River to San Francisco, reaching this city late at night. At that time San Francisco was a gay and lively city. Extensive eating-houses, immense saloons and gambling-houses, splendidly illuminated, gorgeously decorated and furnished with bands of the finest music, regaled the visitor at all hours of the day and night. Some of these gambling-halls were one hundred and fifty feet long and fifty feet wide. On one side was a bar, where liquors of all kinds were dealt out to suit the tastes of the various customers. On the other side, and down through the center of the room, were rows of small tables. Each table was a "monte," or "faro-bank," on which gold and silver were piled, in some instances to the amount of many thousand dollars.

Around each table men were gathered, betting

against the banker or proprietor of the table, the proprietor always coming out ahead; the miner from the mountains almost invariably being fleeced of his hard-earned "dust." At one end of the hall was a platform, on which sat a band of well-skilled musicians. The doors of these attractive buildings were wide open, night and day, and everybody was made welcome. The "click, click," of the glasses at the bar, the "chink, chink, chink," of the gold and silver on the tables; the music by the band on the rostrum, furnished a strange medley, the effect of which was very exciting.

In these places fortunes were won and fortunes lost in a few hours. Here many rejoiced over their spoils, while others wept over the loss of all they had. Here, too, many a bloody encounter ensued. The gamblers generally went armed to the teeth, and if a dishonest trick was discovered, bowie-knives and revolvers were the arbiters. One or the other fell from the deadly weapon, and was borne away a lifeless corpse; but the music and drinking and gambling went on, as though nothing unusual had transpired.

At that time a large portion of the city was built on piles in the bay, and there was no filling under the streets or houses. In many places holes were found in the street large enough to let a man through, and I have no doubt that many a poor man went down through these openings, never again to be seen alive. Many who went to the Pacific Coast in quest of gold, and were never again heard from by their friends, without doubt found watery graves under the houses and streets of San Francisco. I shall always believe that my brother and I came very near losing our lives while there. I shudder when I think of the night we spent in that wicked city nearly forty years ago. No finer place in the world was ever afforded murderers for their victims than beneath the streets and houses of San Francisco at that time.

The next day after reaching the city, we took passage on the steamship *Northerner*. We left the harbor, passed out through the "Golden Gate," and, with our vessel headed to the south, rejoiced at the prospect of soon meeting loved ones at home. We had not been out very long until it seemed to me that "Pacific" was a misnomer. The sea was tremendously rough. I said to myself that it ought to have been named "Terrific" and not "Pacific."

The first port we entered after leaving San Francisco was San Diego, a small Mexican town some four hundred miles southeast of San Francisco, and about fifteen miles north of the Mexican border. No sooner had our ship dropped anchor in the beautiful bay than swarms of Mexican men and boys gathered around the vessel in the water, ready to perform the most wonderful feats of diving for a consideration. The passengers threw dimes and quarters into the water, to see the natives dive and bring them up. A dime or a quarter of a dollar thrown into the water was never lost, but was invariably brought to the surface by the expert diver. The boys seemed as much at home in the water as any fish ever was in its native element. It was really amazing to see how deep one would go down, and how long he would remain under the water, in order to obtain the coveted silver prize. And then when he came to the surface, with a grin of triumph on his face, he would shake his head and rattle the silver against his teeth in his mouth. North San Diego, a small hamlet four miles north of this, was the first place settled by white men in California. The Jesuits first settled here, and founded a mission, in 1768. The climate of this region has always been remarkably salubrious, and many for years have visited it as a health resort. This little, insignificant Mexican town has grown to be one of the lovely cities of the Pacific Coast. Our ship remained here only long enough to take in a supply of coal, when she weighed anchor and made for the open sea.

David speaks of "God's wonders in the deep." We had not been out on the ocean very long when we were permitted to see some of these wonders. Soon after leaving San Diego, we ran into a school of porpoises. To one unaccustomed to the sea, a school of porpoises is a great curiosity. The porpoise is about six feet long, bluish-black color on the back, similar to the color of a cat-fish, and white beneath. They are very active, and live in schools or flocks, and are frequently seen swimming and playing about vessels, running races with them, and leaping many feet out of the water. The porpoise has been called by some the "sea-fish;" by others the "sea-hog." It looks like a hog, and roots in the sand like a hog, hence the name. It seems to me that "sea-swine" is the most appropriate name that could possibly be given to the porpoise. Nothing I ever saw in my life reminded me more of a drove of swine than the school of porpoises we first saw at sea. They were swimming in front of the ship, and were leaping out of the water from one to six feet high as they scud before the vessel like a drove of frightened swine. Ever and anon we struck a shoal of these "wonders of the deep," both on the Pacific and Atlantic Oceans.

We saw, too, a number of whales. Mighty monsters they are; the largest of all living animals.

The next port we entered was Acapulco. This

also was a small Mexican town, of only a few inhabitants. Here, as at San Diego, swarms of Mexican men and boys gathered around our vessel, anxious to exhibit their aquatic skill. Acapulco is one hundred and eighty miles southwest of the city of Mexico, and at one time was a port of considerable importance, as it was the focus of the trade from China and the East Indies. After taking in a supply of coal, our vessel again headed for Panama. Soon after leaving this port we encountered the most terrible storm we ever witnessed; it was awful, beyond all description. Late in the afternoon it was evident that a storm was coming. The waves of the ocean continued to rise higher and higher. They were perfectly smooth, but appeared more and more fearful as they increased. On and on they came—mighty mountains of water. Each one rising higher than the one preceding it. At one moment we were on the crest of one of these billows, the next we were in the trough far below, and in front and rear rose mountains of water, seemingly hundreds of feet high. The old ship creaked and groaned and labored as she climbed up and down these stupendous waves. The scene was grand but awful. Such a scene one does not care to witness more than once in a life-time. The officers knew well that danger was ahead. The deck was cleared, the sails reefed, and everything put in order. As the darkness of the night settled down upon us, the storm in all its fury broke upon the ship. Wave after wave rolled over the vessel. One of the wheel-houses was washed away, all the cattle on board were swept into the sea, and in twenty-four hours afterwards the ship came out of the storm badly disabled. During the raging of the storm children cried, women shrieked, and men turned pale and trembled with fear. One man said: "I have seven thousand dollars. I will give it to any one who will save my life." Another man, frantic with fear, cried out: "I would gladly give every dollar I have if I were only on land again." Satan once said to God with regard to Job: "All that a man hath will he give for his life." Once, if never before, Satan told the truth. This truth we saw illustrated on shipboard in this terrible storm.

I have often thought it strange that men are willing to give so much for the body and so little for the soul. If a man is willing to give all he has for the body, what should he not be willing to give for perfect happiness here and eternal glory hereafter?

After twenty days' sail, our steamer dropped anchor in the gulf, about two miles from Panama. In a few moments a hundred small boats or more surrounded the ship, ready to take passengers and baggage ashore. We hired one of these boats, and in an hour afterwards stepped on the rocky peninsula on which stands the city of Panama. This city was founded by Davila, in 1518, six miles northeast of its present location. After its destruction by the buccaneers, in 1670, it was rebuilt upon its present site. The houses were mostly of stone; the streets very narrow and irregular. The porches and roofs of many of the buildings were moss-covered, and looked as though they had been standing for ages. Many of them were more than a hundred and fifty years old. From here we crossed to Aspinwall, a distance of some sixty miles. The first twenty miles we traveled on foot, leaving Panama early in the morning, and reaching Chagres River near sundown. It was the hardest day's work we ever did. We were compelled to walk, because we could not hire a mule for love or money. All had been engaged before we were aware of their scarcity. The rain fell in torrents nearly all day. The road was narrow, barely wide enough for two mules to pass each other. More than a hundred years previous to the time we crossed, this road had been paved by the Spaniards for military purposes, and at one time it was smooth, beautiful, and easily traveled. But the pavement of this once beautiful road was broken to pieces, and it was in a much worse condition than if the pavement had never been there. That day we stood upon the same mountain summit that Balboa's feet pressed when he discovered the Pacific Ocean. Three hundred and thirty-nine years before, Balboa gazed with delight for the first time upon the beautiful Western Ocean.

We reached the Chagres River about sundown, and found a good hotel, kept by an American. Our clothes were drenched through and through, and there was not a dry thread about us. We ate a hearty supper, went to bed in our wet and clay-besmeared clothes, and slept soundly till morning. The next day we took a small boat, descended the river until we struck the railroad, which was then building across the Isthmus.

The people of the Isthmus were a mongrel race. They were a mixture of the white, the red, and the black. In the same family might be found persons of almost every color. Some almost white, some of a dark hue, and some as black as tar. All smoked. The use of tobacco was as common among them as the use of bread is with us. Almost every one you met had a cigar in the mouth; little boys and girls not more than two years old were running around, puffing away like little steam-engines. The women while engaged in culinary work, smoked their cigars, and the men, no matter what their employment, did the same. The children were all stark naked;

many of the men and women were only half clad, and all were repulsive in the extreme.

Having reached the railroad, we bought our tickets, and took seats in one of the coaches. This was the first engine and train of cars we had ever seen. We said as we took our seats: "This is splendid; perfectly lovely!" The train moved off from the depot slowly and smoothly, and glided along very nicely for a few miles, when a heavy grade was reached; up this grade the train went slower and slower, and finally came to a dead halt. Then the engineer backed the train for a mile, and, putting on all the steam possible, started; but as soon as the train struck the grade she slackened her speed, and at length stood stock still again. Again the engineer backed the train, and, putting on all steam he could, once more started, and stuck fast a third time. Then the passengers all got out, put their shoulders to the coaches, and boosted the train over the grade. Our impression of a railroad was not so favorable as when we started. We were paying fifty cents a mile and working our passage. It was a little like sailing before the mast after having paid full fare. The engine was small, the grade heavy, and the engineer green. The summit passed, we got in, and in a little while reached Colon, then called Aspinwall. This town was then two years old, and had about two hundred inhabitants. It was founded by the railroad company in 1850. Here we took the steamship *Illinois*, and, after ten days' sail, reached the city of New York. From here we took the cars, and in three days reached South Bend, our old home, and greeted mother and other loved ones from whom we had been separated for two and a half years.

CHAPTER VIII.

PERSONAL RECOLLECTIONS.

A MEMORABLE CITY AND CHURCH—JOHN BROWNFIELD—
DAVID STOVER — CONVERSION — PARENTAL INFLU-
ENCE—CALL TO PREACH—ATTEND ASBURY UNIVER-
SITY—LICENSED TO PREACH—JOIN CONFERENCE—FIRST
CIRCUIT—SECOND CIRCUIT—TWO GRACIOUS REVIVALS—
FIRST CONVERT'S TRIUMPHANT DEATH — ORDAINED
DEACON—BISHOP WAUGH.

ON the banks of the Saint Joseph River, in the northern part of the State of Indiana, stands the beautiful city of South Bend. Near the center of this city stands a beautiful church. Around this church cluster many sacred and most hallowed associations.

I can not remember when I was first convicted of sin. I always felt that I was a sinner, and unless converted, "born again," I should be lost forever. I attribute my early conviction of sin to the faithful instructions given me by a devoted father and mother. From my very earliest recollections, I was taught the fundamental doctrines of Christianity. The depravity of the heart, the necessity of pardon and regeneration, a general judgment-day, a hell into which all the finally impenitent will be turned, a heaven where all the pure will enter and be forever perfectly happy, were doctrines instilled into my mind from earliest childhood, all of which I found clearly taught in God's Word.

For three years previous to my conversion I was under deep conviction nearly all the time. I have always been grateful to God for the many well-defined points in my religious experience. I was clearly and powerfully convicted of sin, clearly and powerfully converted, clearly and powerfully convicted of the need of a clean heart, and just as clearly received that blessing. I was clearly and powerfully called to the work of the ministry. So clear was my call to preach the gospel, that all doubt touching the matter was entirely swept from my mind soon after receiving the call.

On Monday morning, the 4th day of March, 1853, I attended a love-feast, held in the above-named church. From that love-feast, with a sad and heavy heart, weighed down under the crushing load of sin, I wended my way to the Bible Depository, kept by John Brownfield. Here the reader will pardon me for digressing for a moment. I can not refrain from a personal reference to my first Sunday-school superintendent. John Brownfield was superintendent of the same school for forty-three years in succession. He made a wonderful record as a Sunday-school superintendent. He was deeply pious, and very greatly interested in the welfare of the young. He was eminently practical, and availed himself of passing events and the most common occurrences to impress religious truth upon the minds of his pupils. In this he was an adept. In fact, in this, I think I may safely say, he was unusually apt. Some of his simple illustrations, taken from every-day life, I remember distinctly to-day, although I was a mere boy when I heard them. His kind words and faithful teachings as a superintendent have never passed from my memory. They have been a benediction to me for more than a third of a century.

The following testimonial card, from the Sunday-school of the First Methodist Episcopal Church of South Bend, Indiana, was presented to Brother Brownfield January 1, 1882:

Testimonial,

Approved by the Sunday-school of the First Methodist Episcopal Church, South Bend, Indiana, January 1, 1882.

WHEREAS,

JOHN BROWNFIELD

HAS BEEN THE SUPERINTENDENT OF OUR

Sunday-school

FOR THE LAST

FORTY-THREE YEARS;

AND WHEREAS,

Because of the burden of seventy-three years, he now declines to serve us longer in that office; therefore, be it said to him and to the

WORLD,

First. That we deeply deplore the occasion which has led to his declinature.

Second. That we are proud of the long and faithful record of his superintendency.

Third. That we cordially indorse the action of the Sunday-school Board by which he is now entitled

Honorary Superintendent

for life.

Fourth. That we shall never cease to feel that we are honored by his presence in the school and aided by his counsels in our work. And furthermore, we must be allowed to say to any who may see this

TESTIMONIAL

that in him whom we honor to-day we have marked,

First. The manliest type of manhood.

Second. The purest Christian character.

Third. The most patient and toilsome zeal in

ALL GOD'S WORKS.

The moral and religious characters which have grown up in the school during his administration, will make for him a more enduring monument than brass or stone. The only adequate reward of his labors will come when his

DIVINE MASTER SHALL SAY TO HIM,

"Well done, thou GOOD AND FAITHFUL SERVANT; enter thou into

The Joy of Thy Lord."

Postmaster-General Wanamaker is one of the most noted Sunday-school superintendents of the age. He has been superintendent of the Bethany

Church Sunday-school for thirty-two years. John Brownfield, as superintendent of the same school, ranked Mr. Wanamaker eleven years. Mr. Brownfield was honorary superintendent for eight years; virtually he was at the head of the same school for fifty-one years. That certainly is an honor of which any man may well be proud.

General C. B. Fisk said at the close of the war, "I have been promoted from a major-general to a Sunday-school superintendent." A successful Sunday-school superintendent outranks all the officers of the army and navy. After triumphantly leading the Sunday-school of the First Methodist Episcopal Church of South Bend, Indiana, for forty-three years, Brother Brownfield had a right to rest in peace and quiet under the laurels he had so justly won. At the advanced age of eighty-two, on the 21st day of January, 1890, he passed peacefully from his earthly to his heavenly home. David Stover was my first Sunday-school teacher. His faithful teachings have never been forgotten. I love to think of my first Sunday-school superintendent, and my first Sunday-school teacher. Their names are sacred. Brother Brownfield has ceased to work. Brother Stover, though advanced in years, is still doing effective work for God.

On that ever-to-be-remembered Monday morning, I entered the Bible Depository and purchased a pocket Bible. This was my first step towards a religious life. The next step was a firm and solemn resolve made, by the grace of God, to be a Christian. That night I went to church, and after listening to a sermon from the pastor, the Rev. James C. Reid, an invitation was given for seekers of religion to come to the altar. I was the first person on my knees at the "mercy-seat." Christian friends and relatives gathered around me, all intensely interested and anxious for my salvation. Among the number was a now sainted mother. The gloom of despair settled down upon my soul. The darkness was dense; so dense it seemed to me it could almost be felt. Satan said: "You have sinned away your day of grace. There is no mercy for such a sinner as you." Not knowing the wiles of the enemy, I believed every word he said. It was a dark hour. Never will it be forgotten. But just at that moment, when all seemed lost and hell certain, my faithful mother whispered in my ears the inspiring words, "Jesus came into the world to save the chief of sinners." I turned from Satan's lying words to Jesus, the "Mighty to save," and grasping in an instant the precious promise, the cloud rifted, the sunlight of heaven came streaming down into my soul, and leaping to my feet, I shouted, "Glory to God in the highest!" I never shall forget that hour. Its precious memory lingers with me to-day. I love the hymn, and I have sometimes thought I would sing it forever:

> "There is a spot to me more dear
>   Than native vale or mountain,
> A spot for which affection's tear
>   Springs grateful from its fountain;
> 'Tis not where kindred souls abound,
>   Though that is almost heaven,
> But where I first my Saviour found,
>   And felt my sins forgiven.
>
> Sinking and panting as for breath,
>   I knew not help was near me;
> I cried, O save me, Lord, from death;
>   Immortal Jesus, save me!
> Then quick as thought I felt him mine.
>   My Saviour stood before me!
> I saw his brightness round me shine,
>   And shouted, Glory! glory!"

Mothers will have rich trophies in glory. The power of example is wonderful. It is wonderful for good or for evil. It can not be weighed, or measured, or estimated. A boy astonished his Christian mother by asking her for a dollar to buy a share in a raffle for a silver watch, that was to be raffled off in a beer-saloon. His mother was horrified, and rebuked him. "But," said he, "mother, did you not bake a cake with a ring in it to be raffled off in a Sunday-school fair?" "O, my son," said she, "that was for the Church." "But if it was wrong," said the boy, "would doing it for the Church make it right? Would it be right for me to steal money to put in the collection? And if it is right for the Church, is it not right for me to get this watch if I can?" The mother was completely dumfounded, and could not answer her son. She had set the example, and her boy was following it.

Josh Billings, a great humorist, and a wise man as well, once said: "If you wish to train up your child in the way he should go, just skirmish ahead on that line yourself."

The mother of John Quincy Adams said, in a letter to him, written when he was only ten years old: "I would rather see you laid in your grave than grow up a profane and graceless boy." Not long before the death of Mr. Adams a gentleman said to him: "I have found out who made you." "What do you mean?" said Mr. Adams. The gentleman replied: "I have been reading the published letters of your mother." Raising himself up, his countenance all aglow, and his eyes flashing with light and fire, the venerable man, in his peculiar manner, said: "Yes, sir; all that is good in me I owe to my mother."

The hallowed influence of John Wesley's mother is felt to-day on almost every part of this planet. The benign and salutary influence of Washington's mother is molding nations and empires. No work will bring more honor to the mother, the children, the Church, and the world, than the religious training of the children. Teach them by example as well as by precept. Bishop Foss once said: "There is nothing better for children than allopathic doses of mother."

But perhaps some one is ready to ask: "What about the fathers in this work of training the children?" Well, I want to say that fathers are equally responsible with the mothers for the right training of the children. Among the many rich blessings conferred upon me by a kind Providence, not the least by any means was pious parents. Not a day passes but that I praise God for a godly father and a godly mother. Their precious memory "is as ointment poured forth." I love to think of them as they used to call us children to family prayers. They took turns in conducting family worship. One of them would take down the old family Bible, read a chapter, and then lead in prayer; the next morning the other would read and lead in prayer. I love to think of them as I used to see them wending their way to the house of God.

On quarterly meeting occasions father almost always stopped work at nine o'clock Saturday morning, and went to the eleven o'clock preaching service. That had a most wonderful effect on my young heart. I remember, just as distinctly as if it were yesterday, seeing my father start off to quarterly meeting one Saturday morning. It was at a very busy season of the year. I never shall forget just how I felt, and just what I said to myself. I said: "I know father is a good man, or he never would stop work at such a busy time to go to Church." They were just as faithful at the prayer and class meetings as they were at the public means of grace, and they were just as prompt in paying their quarterage as they were in attending all the services of the Church.

At one time quarterly meeting came when father was away from home, and mother, from some cause, could not attend. In the afternoon she gave me a two-dollar bill, and told me to take it to the class-leader. Two dollars was a good deal of money for us at that time, for we were not in the most affluent circumstances. I walked two miles and a half to the house of the class-leader, carrying in my hand the two-dollar bill. I remember distinctly the bank-bill. It was a two-dollar note on the old State Bank of Indiana. That simple incident made a deep and lasting impression on my mind. I felt that mother's religion was of some value, and that she considered it worth something. Too many, alas! place no value at all on their religion. They want it for nothing, and think it a hardship if they have to pay a small pittance quarterly to support God's messengers while they proclaim the glad tidings of salvation. When Araunah offered to give David the threshing-floor and the oxen that he might offer a sacrifice to God, David declined the liberal and kindly offer, saying: "Nay; but I will surely buy it of thee at a price; neither will I offer burnt-offerings unto the Lord my God of that which doth cost me nothing. So David bought the threshing-floor and the oxen for fifty shekels of silver. And David built there an altar unto the Lord, and offered burnt-offerings and peace-offerings." (2 Sam. xxiv, 24.) David bought the oxen, then offered them to God as a sacrifice, and they were acceptable in the sight of the Almighty. Heavenly fire descended and consumed the offering, and a great and rich blessing came to David and all his people. Had David accepted the magnanimous offer of Araunah, it would have been Araunah's sacrifice, and not David's, and the result would have been, no blessing would have come to David or his people, but the plague would have gone on as before. A religion that costs nothing is a religion that is worth nothing. No one will highly esteem the ordinances of God if they do not cost him anything.

My precious parents would sooner go without their tea and coffee, or any of the necessaries of life, than not to pay their quarterage. That fact impressed my young heart as deeply as their regularity in attending the house of God. The delightful remembrance of my devoted parents is far more precious to me than any thing this world could possibly give. Their hallowed influence has been a benediction to me for more than fifty years. The fragrance of their lives is with me to-day, and will remain with me forever. If I am ever rewarded for any good done here on earth, my sainted parents will share with me in that reward.

Only a few days after conversion the impression came, "You must preach." Many times before, often when far away on the Pacific Coast, the thought would flit through my mind, "You will preach some day." It was never entertained, however, for a moment, but was instantly banished as one of the visionary and silly thoughts that often enter the mind of the young. But when I was converted the impression came to stay. It fastened itself to my heart so strongly I never could rid myself of it. Shortly after conversion, while thinking over the matter, the pastor, Brother James C. Reid, said to me: "Henry, do you not think God has a work for you to do?" I was astonished, and looked at him with amazement. I frankly told him my feelings, and opened to him my heart. He said: "I will get you a scholarship in the Asbury University." A few months later I received the scholarship, and went to Asbury—now DePauw University—at Greencastle, Indiana, to prepare for my life-work.

I had been in Greencastle only a little while—my probation had not yet expired—when Brother G. C. Beeks, the pastor, appointed me class-leader. The class was composed mostly of old members of the Church—fathers and mothers in Israel—with only a few younger members. It met on Sunday morning at nine o'clock at the residence of Brother Dunams. With much trembling and great fear I took the class. The first meeting was owned of God. The room was filled with the Divine glory, and all seemed to enjoy a rich feast. I led this class while I remained in Greencastle, and I never shall forget the many Pentecosts we enjoyed in Brother Dunams's parlor with the members of that spirit-baptized class. I expect to hail with delight the members of that class on the plains of glory.

On the 23d of June, 1855, I was examined before the Greencastle Quarterly Conference on "Doctrines and Discipline." Several other candidates for the ministry were examined with me. The examination was rigid, and lasted several hours, but it was conducted with great kindness by Aaron Wood, the presiding elder. All the great doctrines of the Church were thoroughly canvassed, and on each one we were closely questioned. Then there was a vein of piety running through the whole examination, which made it wonderfully solemn. Every member of the Conference seemed deeply interested in it. All felt the presence of God. To me the examination was a solemn hour. The next morning the presiding elder handed me the following paper:

"June 23, 1855.

"License is hereby granted to Henry T. Davis, to preach in the Methodist Episcopal Church, by order of the Quarterly Conference of Greencastle Station.

"Aaron Wood, President.

"Hugh S. Mark, Secretary."

The following October I was received on trial in the Northwest Indiana Conference, held at Delphi, Indiana, and was appointed junior preacher of Russellville Circuit. H. S. Shaw was preacher in charge. That year I learned lessons in the administration of discipline which have been of very great value to me ever since.

Dr. T. M. Eddy was then agent of the American Bible Society. We had traveled together from South Bend, and had become quite intimately acquainted. Saturday afternoon he took me by the arm, and, looking very solemn, said: "Well, Brother Davis, it took the whole Conference to get you in." At first blush I did not catch his meaning, and I looked at him with surprise. He smiled. I understood him. The vote was unanimous.

The next year I was appointed to the Sanford Circuit. This circuit was composed of five appointments, lying just west of Terre Haute.

During this year God gave us two gracious revivals of religion, one at "Pisgah" appointment, and the other at "Bethesda." Some who were converted at these meetings are now upon the walls of Zion doing effective work for the Master. The first meeting was held at Pisgah. At the close we began one at Bethesda, and continued it two weeks, during which time seventy souls were clearly converted. God's saving power was manifested from the beginning to the close. The converts ranged from little children to gray-haired fathers and mothers. Whole families were wonderfully saved. Ten months after this meeting we saw the first convert pass triumphant to her home in glory. The scene, though solemn, was at the same time glorious.

At this meeting, Martha Romine, her father, mother, and brothers, were all converted. Ten months afterwards, Martha was stricken down with that fell destroyer, typhoid fever, from which she never recovered. Her sickness was characterized by patience, resignation, and great joy. The last visit we made, we found her very near death's door. She had not spoken for twenty-four hours, and the power of speech seemed forever gone. For some time she had been delirious. We knelt down by her bedside and prayed, and as we prayed,

> "Heaven came down our souls to greet,
> And glory crowned the mercy-seat."

When we arose, she broke forth in a clear, sweet, heavenly voice, and sung,

> "When I can read my title clear
> To mansions in the skies,
> I'll bid farewell to every fear,
> And wipe my weeping eyes."

She sung the hymn through, and in a few minutes afterwards her pure spirit went up to join the angelic throng.

I love to think of the results of that victorious meeting. It was my first great victory in the ministry. It has been an inspiration to me ever since. I expect to meet and live forever with many who were saved at that meeting, and many who stood side by side with me on that spiritual battle-field. We shall not be among strangers when we reach heaven. I have sometimes thought I could almost see the battlements of glory lined with friends and loved ones, waiting and watching our approach, intensely anxious to hail us welcome when we reach the "shining shore."

> "What a meeting, what a meeting that will be!"

On the 17th day of September, 1857, I was married to Miss Emily McCulloch, of Vigo County, Indiana, and for thirty-three years she has shared with me the joys and sorrows, lights and shadows, conflicts and triumphs of the itinerancy. Had we our lives to live over again, and were we permitted to choose our life-work, we would unhesitatingly say, "Give us the Methodist itinerancy."

This year the Conference met at Lafayette. The venerable Bishop Waugh presided. On Sunday, October 4, 1857, I was ordained deacon by this holy man. I remember well the sermon the bishop preached on the occasion. His text was Rev. ii, 10: "Be thou faithful unto death, and I will give thee a crown of life." It was a remarkable sermon, not for its eloquence or profundity, but because of its strange and mysterious power. It was delivered with an unction that thrilled and electrified every one in the vast audience. It was plain and simple; the smallest child could understand every sentence, but it was attended with overwhelming power. In his peroration the bishop seemed transported to the third heaven, and he carried the congregation up with him into the very presence of God and angels. The congregation was bathed in tears, and shouts of "Glory! Glory!" were heard all over the house. It was a memorable occasion.

CHAPTER IX.

ATTENTION TURNED TO THE WEST.

FASCINATIONS OF THE WEST—BELLEVUE MISSION OFFERED US — ACCEPTANCE — ADIEU TO FRIENDS — WE REACH SAINT LOUIS — UP THE "BIG MUDDY" — ARRIVAL IN OMAHA.

A YOUNG man who has been born and raised in one of the Eastern or Middle States, and then leaves and spends a year or two in the far West, is rarely ever satisfied, when he returns, to remain permanently in his old home. There is a strange fascination about the West that is really wonderful, and that can hardly be accounted for; and when it once gets hold of a man, it is next to an impossibility for him ever to get rid of it.

We had passed overland from South Bend, Indiana, to the Pacific Coast. We had seen the grand prairies of Illinois and Iowa, the woods and clay hills of Missouri; we had traversed "The Great American Desert," crossed the Black Hills, climbed the Rockies, scaled the rugged Sierra Nevadas, and had lived for two years and more on the gold-washed shores of the lovely Pacific. And having breathed the pure and balmy atmosphere of the West, we were not only intoxicated with the pure and exhilarating atmosphere, but delighted with the bewitching scenery, the push, and the wonderful activity so characteristic of the people in the western part of the New World. Time and again we turned our anxious eyes to the romantic scenery of the Great West, which had previously charmed us. We were not satisfied to remain in Indiana. Every thing there seemed so old and staid. We wanted a wider sphere for action, and I can assure the reader that, when we reached the plains of Nebraska we had a wide berth and a sphere of almost unlimited bounds for action.

At that time much was being said in the papers about the new Territories of Kansas and Nebraska. The eyes of thousands were turned thither. For some time we had been watching the movements of the Church along the border. Rev. W. H. Goode, an old Indiana man, was leading the hosts of Zion in Nebraska. We had read with interest his letters in the *Advocate*. We were restless and not at all satisfied where we were. We were serving our second year on the Sanford Circuit; and although we had a good work, and many souls had been saved, still there was no attraction there. There was an unaccountable drawing towards the frontier.

In the spring of 1858 we saw, in the *Western Christian Advocate*, the appointments of the Kansas and Nebraska Conference. A number of charges in Nebraska were left to be supplied. I wrote to William M. Smith, a brother of mine, who was then pastor at Omaha, telling him our desire to go to the West, and to spend our lives in laying the foundations and building up the Church along the border. He saw the presiding elder, W. H. Goode, and immediately wrote us, saying that Brother Goode would like to have us come at once and supply Bellevue Mission until conference. No sooner did we receive this word than we set about preparing to move. In a few weeks we had everything arranged, and were ready to bid a final adieu to friends and relatives and the old home Conference. As strong as was the drawing towards the West, and as earnestly as we desired to go, the severing of tender ties and cherished friends was not an easy task.

We have never had a doubt but that God led us to adopt Nebraska as our permanent home. In all we see most unmistakably the hand of God. June 23, 1858, all things being ready, we bade adieu to weeping friends, and started for our future distant home on the frontier. If we had known just what was before us, the trials, the sacrifices, the hardships, we doubtless would have shrank from the undertaking. It was well we did not know. It is well no one can see his future pathway. God wisely conceals from us the future.

We took the cars at Terre Haute, reaching

St. Louis early the next morning. This was Thursday. Here we remained until the next Monday before we could get a through boat to Omaha. Monday morning we paid our fare, and went on board the steamer *Sioux City*. The captain said we would be off in a short time. The fireman was shoveling coal in the furnace, the smoke was pouring out of the smoke-stack, and it seemed from the stir on board that we would be on our way in a very little while. We looked every moment the whole live-long day for the boat to start, but looked in vain. Tuesday morning came. The firemen were busy at work, and every thing indicated that we would start in a very little while; but the day closed, and we were still lying at anchor. Wednesday came, and went as Tuesday had. Thursday came, Friday came, Saturday came, and we were still lying at the wharf. At five o'clock in the afternoon the steamer weighed anchor, floated out into the middle of the Mississippi, and slowly started up the stream. It was a wonderful relief, and we began to breathe easy, for we had been for ten days in the deepest suspense.

The weather was hot, the water warm and muddy, and the mosquitoes were just fearful. The heat and mosquitoes tormented us without by night and by day, and the warm, muddy water made us sick within; and, all in all, the trip was most unpleasant. The mosquitoes were gallinippers, and as numerous, it seemed, as the swarms of flies that tormented Pharaoh and his servants, and corrupted all the land of Egypt.

The second day after leaving St. Louis our steamer stuck fast on a sand-bar, and remained some six hours before she got off. In less than a half a day afterwards she stuck fast again, and remained for several hours. How many times we were aground on sand-bars during the trip, I am unable to say, but not a day passed but what we struck one or more. Sometimes our steamer would back and get off at once; at other times she would work for hours before getting away. The only thing we could do was to wait and be patient, and while away the weary hours the best way we possibly could. The first two or three days out we had good ice-water to drink, and nice cream for our tea and coffee. After that, however, we were compelled to drink the warm and muddy water of the Missouri, and instead of cream we had chalk-water for our coffee and tea, while almost everything else on board seemed in keeping with the filthy water and the sham cream.

Aside from the fare, we were treated with great kindness. The captain was a perfect gentleman, and his wife a most estimable Christian lady and a member of the Methodist Episcopal Church. Their two daughters were on board also. The whole family was one of the most pleasant it has ever been our privilege to meet, and their kind, social, and genial manner made the trip much more pleasant than it otherwise would have been.

After ten days' weary travel on the "Big Muddy," in the afternoon of July 13th our steamer struck the Omaha landing, threw out her cable, and we stepped ashore, glad to bid a final adieu to the *Sioux City*. That night we took tea with the kind family of Colonel John Ritchie. My brother and family were visiting at the colonel's. From all we received a warm welcome and the most kindly greeting. Brother Ritchie was one of the leading members, and one of the stewards of the Omaha Station, and afterwards, while pastor of our Church in Omaha, he was one of the most active members we had.

We were just three weeks coming from Terre Haute to Omaha. The same distance can now be traveled in less than two days.

CHAPTER X.

THE PIONEER EVANGEL.

METHODISM COSMOPOLITAN—MISSIONARIES SENT TO OREGON IN 1834—PLANNING TO CAPTURE KANSAS AND NEBRASKA FOR CHRIST—THE TERRITORIES ORGANIZED—THE BISHOPS SEND OUT WILLIAM H. GOODE AS A SCOUT—OUR SUPERINTENDENCY AN ELEMENT OF POWER—KANSAS AND NEBRASKA CONFERENCE ORGANIZED—QUANTRELL BURNS THE CITY OF LAWRENCE—SECOND CONFERENCE—BISHOP AMES AND DR. POE ON THE MISSIOURI RIVER—A HEROINE—A SERMON INSTEAD OF A DANCE—THE THIRD CONFERENCE.

BEFORE proceeding further with my narrative, I wish to go back with the reader to the first evangelistic work in the Territory. The Methodist Episcopal Church from her organization has been a pioneer Church. She has always been in the vanguard of the advancing tide of emigration.

When the doors of the Established Church of England were closed against Mr. Wesley, and he was not allowed to preach in the churches, he felt that, while these buildings belonged to the "Establishment, the out-of-doors belonged to the Lord." He went out on the commons, and on the streets, and on the public highways, he proclaimed to the people the glad tidings of salvation. When questioned as to his good faith in holding out-of-door services without the consent of the local clergy, his reply was: "The world is my parish." These famous words which fell from the lips of John Wesley when driven from the churches, have been more quoted, perhaps, than any other of his sayings. For more than a hundred years these inspiring words have been the rallying cry of the ministers of the Methodist Episcopal Church. I am glad that Methodism has never lost the spirit of her founder. To-day, as a hundred years ago, the rallying cry of our noble leaders is: "The world is my parish." The fire that burned in the hearts of the fathers, burns in the hearts of the children. The zeal that inspired Wesley, inspires his worthy sons.

The authorities of the Church have their eyes open, and they see every new field, and are ready to enter every open door. By the side of the emigrant, whether blazing his way through dense forests, or pushing his way over pathless and treeless prairies, the faithful Methodist preacher has always been found. While the hardy pioneer has opened and developed the material resources of the new Territories, the Methodist itinerant has looked after the spiritual wants of the people. So that, under the self-sacrificing devotion of the toiling missionary of the cross, the spiritual has kept pace with the material development of the country.

In 1832 four Indians belonging to the Flathead tribe came to St. Louis from the western slope of the Rocky Mountains, asking for a knowledge of the Bible. Notice of this was published in 1833, which came to the eyes of the authorities of the Church. Here was an open door, which they felt must at once be entered. The Missionary Board sent out Jason Lee and Daniel Lee as missionaries, that they might give to these inquiring Red-men of the Pacific Slope the desire of their hearts. The Lees crossed the continent in 1834, and preached and opened a school at Wallawalla.

This was fourteen years before Oregon was organized as a Territory, for it was not until 1848 that the Territory of Oregon was organized. In 1847 the eyes of many were turned to Oregon. The Church saw this, and, taking time by the forelock, missionaries were sent out by our Board to look after the spiritual needs of the emigrants soon to pour into this new country.

William Roberts and James H. Wilbur were sent to do this work. While on their way they entered the Golden Gate on a sailing vessel which cast anchor in the Bay of San Francisco.

A small Mexican village, made of adobe bricks and covered with earthern tiles, had been built among the sand-hills. "This was San Francisco in embryo." California at that period was a portion of Mexico, but the same year was ceded to the United States by the Mexican Government. As the ship would not proceed on her voyage up the coast for some weeks, Mr. Roberts and his colleague deemed it proper to get all the information possible touching the country. They made journeys on horseback during the week to the various villages in the valleys, and returned and spent their Sundays in San Francisco. Six persons were found who had been Methodists in other lands. They were formed into a class, and Aquila Glover was appointed class-leader. A Sunday-school was also organized. This was the first Methodist society in California, and the first Protestant organization on the Pacific Coast south of the Oregon Mission. Having spent forty days in explorations around San Francisco, they proceeded northward to the field of labor assigned them by the Church.

When I reached California in 1850, three years afterwards, I found Methodist ministers almost everywhere. In every little village and mining camp was found the ubiquitous Methodist itinerant. The Methodist evangel is graphically symbolized by St. John in his apocalyptic vision of the "angel flying in the midst of heaven, having the everlasting gospel to preach to them that dwell on the earth." Wherever the people go to plant a city or a State, there Methodism goes to plant the Church and the school, and to direct the people to that city "which hath foundation, whose builder and maker is God." Methodism is truly cosmopolitan.

Long before Kansas and Nebraska were organized into Territories our Church authorities were planning to capture them for Christ. The organization of these two Territories caused a long and bitter controversy in Congress. During all this controversy the Church had an eye upon the spiritual interests of the people soon to flow into this new land.

In 1820 an act had been passed by Congress prohibiting slavery from the Territories north of 36° 30'. This was known as the "Missouri Compromise." In 1854 a bill was passed by Congress to organize two Territories, to be called Kansas and Nebraska, with a provision that the act of 1820 should not apply to these Territories. The question created the most intense excitement throughout the Nation. In almost every city, village, and neighborhood the matter was discussed. The people of the North were indignant, the people of the South generally rejoiced.

No sooner had the bill passed than population

from the North and the South flowed rapidly into the new Territories, each desirous of getting control. The great battle-field of the pro-slavery men and anti-slavery men was Kansas, and here for some time the storm raged fearfully. What was known as "border ruffianism" for awhile reigned triumphant. The scenes that were acted and the outrages committed upon the innocent and helpless during these troubles, beggar all description. A Methodist minister, an eye-witness of some of these outrages and atrocious crimes, related them to the writer in 1861. They are too shameful and harrowing, however, to place upon record. To shoot down, in cold blood, helpless women and children, is an awful crime. But to torture to death by slow and the most infamous and cruel processes that human ingenuity can invent, is a thing too monstrous to be described. I prefer to let the curtain of oblivion fall and hide forever these awful scenes and crimes from the gaze of men.

The first election resulted in the triumph of the pro-slavery interest. But in 1859 the free party triumphed, and Kansas was finally admitted as a free State. In Nebraska the slavery question did not disturb the people as in Kansas.

Shortly after the passage of the organizing act, in the spring of 1854, three of the bishops met in Baltimore. Their attention was turned to the new field providentially opened. They unanimously agreed to enter at once the open door, feeling assured that a mighty tide of emigration would soon roll into the new empire. Thousands of immortal souls would soon be there, all purchased by the blood of Christ. These thousands would need the bread of life, and they determined to give it to them. They knew but little of the country and its needs. They determined therefore to send out a scout to reconnoiter this extensive field. The Rev. William H. Goode, of the North Indiana Conference, was the man selected for this important and responsible work, receiving his appointment from Bishop Ames, June 3, 1854. He was authorized to explore the country thoroughly, to collect all the information possible, to ascertain the wants of the people, and how many men would be needed to take up the work, and at what points they should be placed.

Five days after receiving his formal appointment from the bishop he was on his way to the frontier.

One great element of our success as a Church has been in her superintendency,—the general superintendency of the bishops, and the special superintendency of the presiding elders. If a preacher falls at the post of duty, or for any cause whatever leaves his work, the presiding elder is on the ground, and is prepared in a few days to supply the place; and the work goes on as smoothly and harmoniously as if no change had occurred. If a new field opens in some far-away territory, or on some distant island or continent, the bishops at once set about having this field occupied. They generally know of well-qualified men who are ready to go anywhere with the message of salvation; and they say "go," and they go with alacrity and delight. On the 5th day of July, 1854, Brother Goode entered Kansas Territory, and first visited the Wyandotte Mission, then in charge of Rev. John M. Chivington. Then he passed up through the Territory, entered Nebraska, and pushed his way as far north as there were any settlements. After a personal survey of the field, which took several months, he returned to Indiana, and in his report to the bishops said there were in the two Territories some five hundred families, and recommended that four mission circuits be established, two in Nebraska and two in Kansas; and that the two Territories should be included in one district, with a presiding elder or superintendent of missions, who should travel at large, make further discoveries, organize new fields of labor, and employ preachers as occasion required. His suggestions were approved by the appointing power, and carried into effect that fall. Brother Goode was transferred to the Missouri Conference and appointed presiding elder of the Kansas and Nebraska District. He traveled through the district comprising the two Territories for one year. During the year many new charges were made and supplies obtained. Among the men employed by Brother Goode that year was Hiram Burch, whose name is familiar throughout Nebraska Methodism. Brother Burch was sent to take charge of the Wolf River Mission. At the next Conference he was admitted on trial, and appointed to Nebraska City, and has been a faithful and devoted worker in Nebraska for thirty-six years.

In the fall of 1855, Brother Goode visited the Iowa Conference, which met at Keokuk, and reported to it the work in the two Territories. The Conference passed resolutions requesting the General Conference to form a new Conference comprising the Territories of Kansas and Nebraska. From the Iowa Conference Brother Goode went to Saint Louis, and reported his work to the Missouri Conference, which concurred with the action of the Iowa Conference requesting the organization of the Kansas and Nebraska Conference. Three districts were made in the two Territories, two in Kansas and one in Nebraska. Brother Goode was temporarily transferred to the Iowa Conference, and appointed presiding elder of the Nebraska District, and the two districts in Kansas were supplied from the Missouri Conference.

The winter of 1855-6 was one of intense severity. The cold weather was wide-spread, extending from the Dominion of Canada on the north to the Gulf of Mexico on the south, and from the Atlantic to the Pacific coast. That winter I was traveling my first circuit in Indiana— the Russellville Circuit. It was in a heavily timbered country, and we rarely ever felt the winds, but the mercury often dropped to twenty degrees below zero. In Nebraska, however, it was different. In addition to the intense cold, the winds, unbroken by a single forest from the snow-crowned summits of the Rocky Mountains, sweeping for hundreds of miles over fields of ice and snow, reached the unprotected settlers. Cattle in large numbers were frozen to death, travel was almost entirely suspended, and many human lives were sacrificed. Brother Goode in his book, "Outposts of Zion," gives the following: "A man and his son, who had forced their way with a load of provisions, for thirty miles through cold and snow, perished within one mile of home. I often visited the bereaved and helpless widow and orphans. I personally knew another case not less sad: A father and son, named Poe, set out on foot from the neighborhood of Nebraska City in search of claims: the father aged but robust, the son a lad of fifteen. Some days were spent in searching, when they were caught in a snow-storm. They spent days and nights without fire, taking refuge in a vacant cabin, where they found some abandoned bedding. They cut their boots from their frozen limbs, and applied bandages of strips torn from the bed-clothing. Unable to walk, they made an attempt to crawl away; but their strength failed, and they returned to the cabin. The father folded his son in his arms, and lay down to die. At that moment a man appeared, attracted by the noise; help was obtained, and they were removed. The son soon died. I saw the father in extreme agony; some of his limbs were amputated, and he expected further dismemberment. But death came to his relief. The morning following my visit I was sent for to preach at his funeral. In all his sufferings he expressed Christian peace and confidence in God." Eternity alone will reveal the terrible suffering endured by the settlers during that and the following winter. They are memorable in history as winters of intense cold.

At the ensuing General Conference the request of the Iowa and Missouri Conferences was carried into effect, and the Kansas and Nebraska Conference was formed.

The first session of the Kansas and Nebraska Conference was held in the city of Lawrence, Kansas Territory, October 23–25, 1856, Bishop Osmon C. Baker presiding. At this time "border ruffianism" was rampant. Great excitement prevailed throughout the Territory, and grave fears were entertained by the preachers from the pro-slavery element. Lawrence was founded in 1854, and became the head-quarters of the anti-slavery settlers of Kansas. The pro-slavery party never had any peculiar love for the place. On August 21, 1863, it was surprised by a band of three hundred Confederate guerrillas, led by Quantrell, who killed one hundred and forty-five of the inhabitants, and burned the city. The history of that bloody massacre is before the world.

When the Conference assembled, the city presented a warlike appearance. Strong fortifications had been made. United States troops in large numbers were quartered there, and a strong body of the Territorial militia.

Some of the preachers attending this Conference had not only spiritual weapons, but carnal weapons as well. From occurrences that were constantly taking place, these preachers felt that it was absolutely necessary for them to be ready for any emergency; not to be ready would be culpable negligence on their part. The Conference was held in a large tent, and was pleasant and harmonious throughout. Eleven hundred and thirty-eight members, including probationers, were reported; of these, three hundred and two were in Nebraska. The bishops were requested to change the time of the annual session from fall to spring, which request was complied with, and the time fixed for the next Conference was April 16, 1857. This change reduced the first Conference year to six months. Nebraska City was the place fixed for the next session.

The following is a list of the appointments of the Nebraska District of the first session of the Kansas and Nebraska Conference:

NEBRASKA DISTRICT.

WM. H. GOODE,	Presiding Elder.
Omaha City,	J. M. Chivington.
Florence,	Isaac F. Collins.
Fontanelle,	To be supplied.
Omadi,	To be supplied.
Rock Bluffs,	J. T. Cannon.
Nebraska City,	Hiram Burch.
Brownville,	J. W. Taylor.
Nemaha,	To be supplied.

The winter of 1856–7, like the previous one, was memorable for its severity. Many during the winter were frozen to death, and in various parts of the Territory stock in large numbers perished.

Bishop Ames was to preside at the second session of the Conference. But on the morning of the opening of the session the bishop was on board a Missouri steamer, hundreds of miles below, endeavoring to make his way up against the mighty current. Mr. Goode was elected president, and presided with dignity and satisfaction to the Conference. He was a good officer, and business was transacted with dispatch. He would have made an excellent bishop, and at one time he lacked but a few votes of reaching that honorable place. The bishop arrived late, reviewed, approved, and read the appointments. Two districts were made in Nebraska; Omaha District, including the territory north of the Great Platte River; and Nebraska City District, including the territory south of the Great Platte.

J. M. Chivington was appointed presiding elder of the Nebraska City District, and W. H. Goode presiding elder of the Omaha District. Three districts were made in Kansas; so the Conference had five districts in all.

Doctor Adam Poe, Agent of the Methodist Book Concern, accompanied Bishop Ames to this Conference. At a subsequent Conference, the Doctor gave an account of that memorable trip. Their journey up the turbid and dangerous stream was slow, and was made under very great difficulties. One dark night the boat tied up, as was the custom on dark nights. During the night she broke loose from her moorings, drifted down the stream, and for a long time was at the mercy of the fearful and dangerous current. The engineer at length succeeded in getting up steam, and again she began to stem the mighty tide.

On Sunday, as the steamer was slowly making her way up the river, an incident occurred which shows the wonderful influence and power of the family altar and the Sunday-school.

Dr. Poe said: "There was a young man on board who was very officious and pert. He was exceedingly anxious to have a dance. The cabin was cleared, a fiddler employed, and everything was made ready for the hop, when the young man stepped up to a young lady who sat at my side, and, after a very polite bow, said: 'Will you dance with me?'

"'No, sir; I was better raised,' was the prompt reply.

"'And where were you raised?' said the young man, somewhat abashed.

"'In the Sunday-school and at the family altar?' calmly replied the lady. Involuntarily I clapped my hand on her shoulder and said, 'Good!' [Dr. Poe was a tall man, standing six feet in his stockings, and proportionately large in body.]

"The young man squared himself up, thinking he saw something in my proportions that would do to fight, and then said, 'Well, if we can't have a dance, perhaps we can have a sermon.' 'Yes, sir;' said I. Knowing the bishop could preach much better than I, we put him up, and Bishop Ames gave us one of his best."

The young lady and her parents left the boat at Nebraska City, intending to make their home somewhere in the interior of the State. Dr. Poe was anxious to learn something of the future history of that noble young lady. He thought Nebraska had nothing to fear, composed of settlers with the courage and mettle manifested in that graceful heroine.

The third session of the Conference was held in Topeka, Kansas, beginning April 15, 1858, Bishop E. S. Janes presiding. Early in the month the preachers in Nebraska left their fields of labor, and started on horseback, with their saddle-bags, in the old-fashioned way, for their Annual Conference. On the 10th of April, some fifteen of these hardy, toil-worn pioneers concentrated at Falls City, where Brother Goode was holding a quarterly meeting. They spent a delightful day together, and, with the good people of the infant town, enjoyed "seasons of refreshing from the presence of the Lord." As the country over which they were to travel was new and strange to the most of them, they determined to select competent guides; accordingly, they elected two of their number who were best acquainted with the country, and put themselves under their guidance, all agreeing to follow faithfully their instructions.

They were ordered to meet at a certain place on Monday morning. Monday morning came, cold, snowy, dreary, and forbidding in the extreme, but all were on hand at the appointed hour and place. The weather, no matter what it may be, rarely stops a Methodist preacher on his way to an appointment. Through drenching rains, blinding snow-storms, and fearful blizzards, he is found pushing his way to meet the promised engagement. And by this heroic, self-sacrificing spirit, Methodism is planted almost everywhere.

From Falls City they passed down to near the mouth of the Nemaha River, where they crossed the stream in a ferry-boat. The ferry was an old-fashioned flat-boat, not very inviting, and withal not the safest in appearance. They dismounted, led their horses onto the boat, and held them by their bridles until they reached the other side. While crossing, when near the middle of the river, Brother Turman's horse jumped overboard into the stream. Brother Turman held onto the bridle, and the animal, by the side of the boat, swam to shore, then remounting his horse, dripping with water, and riding up by the side of Brother Burch, said in a whisper: "Brother Burch, I have just found out the sentiment of my horse. He is a Campbellite. I will sell him. I won't have such a horse." Only those knowing his great aversion to the doctrine of Campbellism can appreciate the above remarks. Campbellism and Calvinism were both extremely obnoxious to him.

After a weary ride through rain and mud and snow, the seat of the Annual Conference was reached. The year had been one of exposure, of toil, and of sacrifice. It had been a year of great spiritual victories as well. The toils, the sacrifices, the victories and triumphs of that year are fittingly described by Charles Wesley:

> "What troubles have we seen,
>   What conflicts have we passed,—
> Fightings without, and fears within,
>   Since we assembled last!
> But out of all the Lord
>   Hath brought us by his love;
> And still he doth his help afford,
>   And hides our life above."

At this Conference another district was formed in Kansas, making in all six districts.

A wild and reckless spirit of speculation had prevailed among many of the people. Towns all over the Territories were laid out, wild-cat banks were established, and the country was flooded with worthless bank-notes. The result of all this was disastrous, both to the Church and the country. Confidence in the people was to a great extent destroyed. But, notwithstanding all these demoralizing influences, the year had been one of great prosperity to the Church. The membership had more than doubled; the population had increased greatly; peace had prevailed; the future outlook was hopeful, and preachers and people were of good cheer.

In four years the Church had grown, in the

two Territories, from nothing to an Annual Conference with six districts, fifty-seven appointments, and two thousand six hundred and sixty-nine members. This growth was phenomenal. True, the area was large. It was an empire within itself. It was the "Great American Desert." But this desert, true to prophecy, was beginning to "rejoice and blossom as the rose."

The wonderful growth of the work in the new Territories is most aptly described in another of Charles Wesley's beautiful hymns:

> "When he first the work began,
>   Small and feeble was his day;
> Now the word doth swiftly run,
>   Now it wins its widening way.
> More and more it spreads and grows,
>   Ever mighty to prevail;
> Sin's strongholds it now o'erthrows,
>   Shakes the trembling gates of hell."

CHAPTER XI.

FIRST WORK IN NEBRASKA.

CRUDE IDEAS OF NEBRASKA—BELLEVUE—STORY OF A DIAMOND—HOW THE PEOPLE VIEWED US—HUNTING FOR A TOWN WITHOUT HOUSES—FIRST SERMON IN NEBRASKA—WILD SPECULATION — ITS DEMORALIZING EFFECTS—FIRST QUARTERAGE RECEIVED—GLAD OF GREEN PUMPKINS—THANKFUL FOR POTATOES AND SALT—HOSPITALITY OF FRIENDS.

THE people of Massachusetts at one time decided that the country would not be settled west of Newton, a suburb of Boston. And the inhabitants of Lynn, having surveyed the country fifteen miles west, determined that it never would be densely populated beyond that point.

When we first reached Nebraska, we believed, and so did everybody else, that Nebraska never would be settled west of the first tier of counties lying along the Missouri River. Coming from a densely-timbered country, Nebraska had a very dreary and desolate look. We almost feared there would not be wood enough to keep us from freezing to death during the first winter. In 1858 Nebraska had a population of about sixteen thousand souls, and during the few following years the population decreased rather than increased.

Many became discouraged, and declared they would not stay in such a "God-forsaken country." They felt that God had intended this country for the Indians, and that in remaining they were trespassing on Indian rights.

Bellevue was our first appointment in Nebraska. It is ten miles south of Omaha, situated on a beautiful plateau, overlooking for miles the Missouri River. It is said that in 1805 a Spanish adventurer came to Bellevue, and, in climbing the bluff to the plateau, was so struck with the natural beauty of the spot that he exclaimed, "Bellevue"—"beautiful place;" hence the name.

Something more is necessary, however, to make a city than a beautiful location. If a beautiful location could make a city, Bellevue would have been the finest and largest city in the State. A more exquisite spot for a city I never saw.

Bellevue at that time was the county-seat of Sarpy County, the county being named in honor of Colonel Peter A. Sarpy. From 1823 to 1855 Colonel Sarpy was agent of the American Fur Company at Bellevue. He was raised in St. Louis, and brought up in refinement. But when he grew to manhood he preferred the freedom of the Western prairies to the gayety and refinement of civilized life.

I remember reading a story published in the *Omaha Herald* about Colonel Sarpy. It was told by the Hon. J. Sterling Morton, and was called

"THE STORY OF THE DIAMOND.

"The beautiful bluffs that rise so majestically from the mission at Bellevue, shimmering in the morning sunlight, and the deep verdure that covered them that summer day, made them look like a string of gigantic emeralds just fallen from the clouds. Colonel Peter A. Sarpy met me that morning, up back of the old mission-house, by the grave of Big Elk. He was buoyant, and his eye glistened, and he was in the best of health and spirits. He was dressed neatly, and upon his breast I noticed for the first time a diamond, which gleamed and flashed with striking brilliancy. 'Colonel,' said I, 'you have been adding to your jewels;' and, looking steadily at the gem, 'is that something new?' 'O no, my friend,' said he, 'that is old, very old; and I will tell you all about it, if you will listen, and what is to come of it in the hereafter, if you will.' He continued: 'Many, many years ago, when St. Louis was a village, my good Catholic mother died—may God rest her soul in peace!—in that town. We children followed her remains to the cemetery, and laid them quietly in the grave, and wept until our eyes could weep no more. And then, shortly after, I came up here to Nebraska among the Indians to trade, and my brother John remained in Saint Louis. But a few years ago I went down to that city to purchase goods; and one afternoon, after I had been there several days, my brother said, "Peter I want to see you privately in the counting-room, to talk about the dead;" and so I went in, and John said: "Peter, this city is growing very rapidly. It is stretching out to the south and the west and the north. It needs more room, and the old graveyard where our mother is buried must be given up. We must remove her remains to another resting-place, and we will do it together while you are here; we will do it to-morrow." And so the very next day we went to our mother's grave, and carefully we brought the coffin to the light, and lifted it up tenderly on to a bier. It was badly decayed. The top was moved a little to one side, and I could not resist a desire to look in. As I did, the sunlight streamed in, and I saw something gleaming there. At once I remembered the diamond which my mother had worn always, and which had been buried on her breast, and I reached in and took it out, and this is it which you now see.

"'It is mine now; and when these bright days come, I feel young again, and remembering my mother, I put it on and wear it; for it makes me a better man.

"'It is a charm, sir; and the memories which it brings to me are brighter and richer and more precious than all the gems in the world; for they are the sacred recollections of a Christian mother, a holy woman, whose teachings were purer than any diamond that ever glowed. And now, while men think I am only an old Indian trader, who sees nothing in the future, who believes in no destiny for this beautiful Nebraska of ours, I know, sir, that not many years will come and go before I, too, will be called to another life in another world. And then these vast plains will be settled up; somewhere in this Missouri Valley, perhaps in sight of where we now stand, a great city shall have been builded. Then I may have been in my grave many years. And some day, very likely, they will come to you, as they did to brother John about our mother, and say: "Here, sir, your old friend, Peter A. Sarpy, is in the way; the city needs more room, and, sir, you must take his old bones away."

"'And if so, do it; do it decently and kindly; but remember this diamond. Peep into my old coffin. It is a pure gem, sir—first water—and will surely flash whenever your eye can see. Then you reach in—I'll be still—and snatch the diamond out, and put it on and wear it.

"'The years will roll on, and you will have grown old; then death will rap at your door, and you, too, will have come into another life in that other world. Tell your boys to bury this stone with you. But not many years more will have followed the trail of those who have gone into the shadowy hunting-lands, before your boys will be called upon by the authorities to move your bones also.

"'Tell the boys, when that time comes, to reach into your coffin again, and take this glittering jewel out from the grave.

"'Tell the oldest to put it on and wear it, and be buried with it too, leaving instructions for its re-resurrection again.

"'And so, sir, we'll keep this diamond glittering among the generations to come. It shall be buried and raised, and worn and buried again, until finally it shall be buried for the last time, away off in some of the islands of the Pacific, when the West shall have been found and settled in full, and finally perfected.

"'I tell you, sir, this cry for room, more room, will never cease.

"'And let this diamond go on from grave to grave, from generation to generation, gleaming and flashing forever like a star, in the shield of one who shall always be a pioneer in the vanguard of progress and civilization.

"He stopped his speech, and in silence we walked to the trading-post. But there was an element of prophecy in that summer morning talk of Colonel Sarpy, which makes it ring in my ears and thrill in my veins even unto this day. He looked into the future as into a mirror, and saw the face of to-day and to-morrow as clearly and plainly as a child sees trees and flowers shadowed in a pure brook."

In the grave-yard, near where Colonel Sarpy stood when the above remarkable speech was made, sleep the remains of our first-born child.

When Colonel Sarpy uttered this prophecy, Omaha was a little village with only a few houses. Lincoln was an untrodden prairie, save by the Indians, the buffalo, and the wild beasts that roamed the plains. But Omaha has become a mighty city, stretching away to the north, the west, and the south, and the cry has been heard for years, "More room." Lincoln, the magic city of the plains, in the heart of the "Great American Desert," has arisen, and grown, and to-day has a teeming population of near sixty thousand souls. Addition after addition has been made, and still the cry rings out over the prairies from her authorities, "More room."

The "Great American Desert," where is it? Echo answers, Where? Driven from the plains of Nebraska to the western slopes of the Rocky

Mountains, then on toward the setting sun, the "Great American Desert" "has become a vagabond on the face of the earth."

When we reached Bellevue, we found no church or organization. The outlook was not encouraging by any means, but gloomy in the extreme. A class had been organized, but had gone down. The acts of some, we learned, had not been in harmony with their profession. Methodism had no standing in the community, and the people looked at us with curious eyes. To get hold of the hearts of the people, and give Methodism a respectable standing required time, patience, and labor. The foundation of the church had to be laid, and the superstructure reared, and we were there for that purpose; so we went to work with a will, though discouragements met us at every step, and in almost every form.

We had been on the ground only a short time, when Mrs. Davis was taken ill and remained so for several weeks. For a long time we had but little hope of her recovery. The people were very kind, and rendered every possible assistance; night and day they stood by us in the dark hours of our trial. We shall never forget them. The remembrance of their kindness and many tokens of love, is indelibly written upon our memories, and will never be erased.

The summer of 1858 was a very sickly one. Nearly everybody in the community was prostrated. To hire help was an impossibility, and we had to do all our own work, save what was done by our kind neighbors. I kept house, cooked, washed and ironed, waited on Mrs. Davis, prepared for the pulpit, and preached on the Sabbath. It was a new experience—a bitter but useful one. I shall never forget the first trip I made to Fairview. I was told it was a town eight miles west of Bellevue. I sent out an appointment, and on Sunday morning started on horseback. We had been told it was beautifully located on an elevation, overlooking the whole surrounding country. I rode on until I thought I must be getting near, and began to look for the new town. I strained my eager eyes in vain to get a glimpse of the expected beautiful village. On and on I urged my horse, thinking every moment that the village would rise in view. At length, away to the right of the road, I saw a little shanty. I reined up my horse, rode out toward the shanty, but before reaching it was met by the man of the house. I said to him: " Will you be so kind as to tell me the way to Fairview?"

"O, yes," said he. "Which way did you come?"

"From Bellevue."

"You came the main traveled road from the east, I suppose?"

"Yes, sir."

"Well, sir, you passed through Fairview two miles east of this."

"How is that?" said I; "I have not seen a house for miles until I saw yours."

"O," said the gentleman, "there are no houses in Fairview yet. It was only laid out a few months ago."

I told him that I had sent out an appointment to preach there that day.

"Well," said he, "I think I heard there was to be a meeting there to-day, and I guess some of the neighbors have gone there for that purpose. If you will go back two miles and look very carefully in the grass, you will see some white stakes; then if you will look to the south, you will see, at the head of a little ravine, a log cabin with some trees near by. Robert Lang lives there, and I expect the meeting is to be at his house." I rode back, found the stakes, saw the log cabin, and on reaching it found a number of persons waiting for the preacher. In a little grove near by I preached my first sermon in Nebraska to about a dozen hearers. I took dinner with Brother Lang, a jolly, whole-souled, deeply pious Scotchman. Some years after this Brother

FIRST WORK IN NEBRASKA. 157

Lang entered the evangelistic work, and has been instrumental, in the hands of God, in leading hundreds of souls to Christ. He has been a faithful worker in Christ's vineyard, and will have many stars in his crown of rejoicing.

After dinner I rode twelve miles to Plattford, where I had sent out an appointment for evening service. Here I expected, from what had been told me, to find a good town, a good society of Methodists, and a large congregation. But, alas! I was again doomed to disappointment. I found no town, no members of our Church, no congregation. Plattford, like Fairview, was only a paper town, and its location was marked alone by a few stakes seen here and there in the grass. Just at dark I rode up to a small house some distance north of the town site, where I was hospitably entertained by a kind family belonging to the Congregational Church.

This was my first Sabbath's work in our new field of labor, on the frontier, in the territory of Nebraska. It was anything but pleasant, and the future outlook was not a very flattering one.

In 1856-7 the wildest excitement prevailed. Speculation was rife. New towns were spread upon all the county records. Town companies were formed, towns laid out, and agents sent East to sell the lots. Many innocent and unsuspecting parties were taken in by these unscrupulous agents. It is said that the recorder of one of the northern counties laid out a town, then went East and sold lots at fabulous prices. In addition to the money received from them, he made large sums for recording the deeds of these worthless lots. Soon after reaching Bellevue I received a letter from a Methodist minister in Ohio, asking for a description and the location of the town of Platonia. He had sent three hundred dollars, the little savings of years, to a friend, who had purchased for him several lots in this new town. He had written again and again, but could hear nothing from his old friend. I began to make inquiry about the new town, and finally met a man who told me where it was located. A few days afterwards I went down and took in the new village. I found a half-finished, dilapidated frame building, standing in the midst of a large field of corn. The town, to this day, is used as a farm for raising corn and hogs. Many professing Christians were carried away by the mighty tide of speculation that swept over the country. It was not strange, when professing Christians engaged in such dishonorable transactions, that the Church should fall into disrepute and lose its power for good. When we learned the history of the past, we were not at all disposed to censure any for scanning us with curious and suspicious eyes.

The prospect for a support from the people was not very flattering. An appropriation of one hundred dollars from the Missionary Society had been made to the mission. Our house-rent was at the rate of one hundred dollars per year. This would take all our missionary money, and we must depend on the people for a living. We had no assurance whatever that the people would pay us any thing. In fact, the intimations were that the people had all they could possibly do to provide for themselves.

After we had been there a few weeks, a good Baptist brother by the name of Simpkins brought us a few new potatoes and some green pumpkins. Mrs. Davis thanked him very kindly for the potatoes and green pumpkins. The next time he came he brought a splendid lot of vegetables of all kinds, then kept us in vegetables during the season, and in the fall filled our cellar for the winter. He afterwards often laughed and said: "I first tried you with green pumpkins, for I thought if you were thankful for green pumpkins you would do for Nebraska." Brother Simpkins and family afterwards became useful and faithful members of the Methodist Episcopal Church.

Soon after Mrs. Davis began to recover from her long illness, her appetite became ravenous, while my own was not a whit behind hers. It seemed almost impossible for us to get enough to eat. We were ready to devour everything we could get in the way of edibles, and almost everything was palatable. We had a wonderful relish for food. We began to get into straitened circumstances. Our money was almost gone, and our larder about empty. All we had left was a little bread, potatoes, and salt. We sat down one morning to our meager breakfast—bread, potatoes, and salt. After the blessing was asked my wife said: "Well, I am thankful for potatoes and salt." No queen in her palace, with a table before her groaning with the richest and most delicious viands, ever breakfasted with a greater relish or more thankful heart than ours as we ate our humble meal that morning.

God gave us access to the hearts of the people. They rallied around us. In many ways they convinced us they were our friends indeed. At the end of three months a brother offered us a house free of rent if we would move, and we accepted his kindly offer. The rooms were on the second floor of a two-story building; the lower room had been used as a store, but was empty. Not long after moving into our new quarters we had our first blizzard. The day before was beautiful. The sun was bright, the sky clear, the atmosphere soft and balmy. It was almost like a summer day. Mrs. Davis washed and hung out her clothes, and as there was no indication whatever of a storm, she left them on the line. We retired to rest; the soft wind, like a gentle zephyr, blowing from the south. About ten o'clock the wind shifted to the north. It began to snow, and the wind blew a perfect gale. The building rocked like a cradle, and we thought it certainly would go to pieces. In the morning the weather was freezing cold, and the snow was piled in drifts many feet high around the house. We looked out and saw the line, but no clothes, save one or two pieces. We tried to find them, but in vain. They were gone. Not a shred was left. And we never saw or heard of them again. Our neighbors, who were acquainted with Nebraska blizzards, said: "Your clothes were in Kansas long before morning." Our wardrobe was not the most extensive, and we felt keenly the loss.

Some two months before Conference our landlord told us he wanted to repair the house, and we must move. We were arranging to move into another building when Mrs. Rogers, a neighbor, a member of the Baptist Church, and one of the best friends we ever had, heard of it. She came at once to see us, and said: "You are not going to move into another building, but you are coming to our house. Mr. Rogers and I have talked over the matter, and you are to take our front parlor and bedroom." We told her that would be an imposition, and we did not feel as though we could take advantage of her good nature in that way. She said: "No; it will be a pleasure, not an imposition." So we had to yield to her kind offer, and she and her noble boys helped us move into their nice and comfortable parlor and bedroom. Here we remained until Conference. Mrs. Rogers never had anything nice that we did not have a share. Such hospitality we have never seen surpassed. How often we have prayed for God's blessing on that noble family!

Our first work in Nebraska, which opened so unpropitiously, closed under bright and most promising circumstances.

Just before leaving for Conference, the good people made us a donation amounting to seventy dollars, and we never saw people enjoy themselves better than on that occasion.

CHAPTER XII.

OMAHA.

When Founded—Indian Tradition of the Name—Amusing and Thrilling Incidents—George Francis Train—Moving in an Ox-wagon—Indians—First Methodist Episcopal Church—Ride on Horseback Two Hundred Miles to Conference—Falls City in 1860—John Brown—The Conference divided.

OMAHA was founded in 1854. The first dwelling-house in the city was erected by Mr. A. D. Jones, who, in the spring of 1854, received the appointment of postmaster, and immediately erected a cabin of logs, which he completed in the latter part of May, only a few days before Congress passed the bill creating the Territory of Nebraska. On this rude cabin a sign was placed, consisting of a wide shingle with the words, written with a lead-pencil, "Post-office, by A. D. Jones." The style of this quaint sign attracted as much attention as the information it communicated. This was the beginning of the present marvelous city of Omaha, a city whose fame is world-wide.

For some time Mr. Jones carried the mail in his hat. The first letter ever received in Omaha by mail was from Mr. Henn to Mr. Jones relating to an independent mail-route between Council Bluffs and Omaha. This letter was dated Washington, May 6, 1854. During my pastorate in the city in 1859-60, Mr. Jones and his family were regular attendants at our Church, his wife being a member.

The name Omaha was derived from an Indian tradition. The tradition is, that ages ago two tribes met on the Missouri River and engaged in a bloody battle, in which all on one side were killed but one, who was thrown into the river. Rising suddenly above the surface he exclaimed, "Omaha!" meaning that he was on top of the water, and not under it as his enemies supposed, and those who heard it took that word as the name of their tribe. "Omaha," "On top." A significant name, not only of the renowned Indian tribe, but the city as well.

Mr. Jones, who was a surveyor, was employed by the Council Bluffs and Nebraska Steam-ferry Company to survey the site, and he spent the greater part of the month of June and a part of July in this work. The city was laid out in 322 blocks, each 264 feet square. This was the original city of Omaha, as first founded, and the founders had but little, if any, idea at all that an addition to the original plat would ever be needed.

In the *Omaha Illustrated* we are told that

Omaha had a newspaper very early in her history. This paper was called the *Arrow*. There were only twelve issues of the *Arrow*, covering the period from July 28 to November 10, 1854. In the first issue of the *Arrow*, which was the first newspaper ever published in Nebraska, the editor wrote a fanciful sketch containing a prediction of Omaha's future. It was entitled "A Night in Our Sanctum." It was such a remarkable prediction, and has been so literally fulfilled, that I give a large portion of it to the reader. Here it is:

"Last night we slept in our sanctum—the starry-decked heaven for a ceiling, and mother earth for a flooring. . . . To dream-land we went. The busy hum of business from factories and the varied branches of mechanism from Omaha reached our ears. The incessant rattle of innumerable drays over the paved streets, the steady tramp of ten thousand of an animated, enterprising population, the hoarse orders fast issued from the crowd of steamers upon the levee loading with the rich products of the State of Nebraska, and unloading the fruits, spices, and products of other climes and soils, greeted our ears. Far away toward the setting sun came telegraph dispatches of improvements, progress, and moral advancement upon the Pacific Coast. Cars, full-freighted with teas, silks, etc., were arriving from thence, and passing across the stationary channel of the Missouri River with lightning speed, hurrying on to the Atlantic sea-board. The third express train on the Council Bluffs and Galveston Railroad came thundering close by us with a shrill whistle that brought us to our feet, knife in hand, looking into the darkness beyond at the flying trains. They had vanished. The hum of business, in and around the city, had also vanished, and the same rude camp-fires were before us. We slept again, and daylight stole upon us, refreshed and ready for another day's labor."

That dream, written thirty-six years ago, and which was considered at the time visionary in the extreme, and which no one ever expected to see fulfilled, has been more than realized. Had that dream been told us when we first visited Omaha in 1858, we should have said, "It is the dream of a madman."

The city grew rapidly from the time it was laid out, flourishing on all lines until the panic of 1857 struck the country. Then Omaha came to a dead halt, and no advance whatever was made for several years. In 1860 a slight change for the better was manifested. In 1862 Congress passed the act authorizing the construction of the Union Pacific Railroad from the Missouri River to San Francisco, and in 1863 President Lincoln designated its eastern terminal "at a point on the western boundary of Iowa, opposite section ten, in township fifteen, north of range thirteen, east of the sixth principal meridian in the Territory of Nebraska."

This decision gave to Omaha a new and wonderful impetus, and soon after Omaha became the metropolitan city of the West.

Some amusing incidents occurred in the early history of the city. Omaha was the capital of the Territory. Mark W. Izard, afterwards appointed successor to Governor Burt, was United States marshal. It is recorded that "Izard was a stately character physically, though mentally rather weak, and felt a lively sense of the dignity with which the appointment clothed him. He had never known such an honor before, and it bore upon him heavily." When the time came for him to deliver his inaugural message, he arranged for a Negro to announce his approach to the legislative chamber in the following words: "Mr. Speaker, the governor is now approaching." The poor Negro forgot his text, and electrified the assembled wisdom with the sentence, "Mr. Speaker, de gubner has done come."

In 1865, George Francis Train made large investments in Omaha property, and took a lively interest in building up the new city. He was a guest of the Herndon House. One day he sat at the table in the dining-room, opposite a broken window, through which the wind was blowing at a lively rate. He complained of the annoyance, but no attention was paid to his complaints. Then he paid a darky ten cents a minute to stand between him and the draught until he had finished his dinner. He there vowed he would build another hotel, and that very afternoon purchased two lots and employed men to commence the foundation. Within sixty days he had the Cozzens House completed at a cost of $40,000. Mr. Train was an anomaly. George D. Prentice thus describes him: "A locomotive that has run off the track, turned upside down, with its cow-catcher buried in a stump, and the wheels making a thousand revolutions a minute; a kite in the air, which has lost its tail; a human novel without a hero; a man who climbs a tree for a bird's-nest out on a limb, and, in order to get it, saws the limb off between himself and the tree; a ship without a rudder; a sermon without a text; handsome, vivacious, versatile, muscular, as neat as a cat, clean to the marrow, frugal in food, and regular only in habits; with the brains of twenty men in his head, all pulling in different ways; not bad as to heart, but a man who has shaken hands with reverence."

When the war broke out in 1861, Omaha responded to the call of Abraham Lincoln for troops. Three military companies were organized and mustered into service. Upon the departure of the troops, a lady, full of patriotism, donned soldier's attire and took passage as one of the "boys." Her sex was undiscovered during the trip to St. Joe; but when the boat left that city and went down the river, the adventure terminated suddenly; for she was discovered by her husband and sent back to Omaha, where, at a recent date, it is said, she was still living.

Some sad as well as amusing incidents occurred during the early history of the city.

The community was infested with thieves and roughs of various kinds. Many of these pests of the human race, averse to labor, and determined to obtain a living in any way save by honest work, fled from Eastern States to the frontier, where they could have a better opportunity of committing their depredations. The citizens felt that the safety of themselves and their families depended on their visiting summary punishment upon criminals; and when guilt was proved beyond all doubt, they often took the law into their own hands. This course often becomes absolutely necessary for the safety of the people in new Territories and States. It was necessary in the early history of California, and since then it has been necessary in other new Territories as well.

At a still earlier period, history tells us that in Ohio and Kentucky, and other new States, the people often had to take the law into their own hands. It has often become necessary for the citizens to organize what is known as Vigilance Committees. These are not mobs. A mob is a very different thing from a Vigilance Committee. A mob is a riotous assembly, a disorderly crowd, composed generally of the vicious and lower classes of society; and the acts of a mob are committed under great excitement, and without any regard to law or justice. A Vigilance Committee is an orderly crowd, with an eye only upon the welfare of the whole community, cool and deliberate in all its actions. A Vigilance Committee inflicts no punishment until guilt is proved beyond the shadow of a doubt. A mob often inflicts punishment upon the innocent. A mob is a dangerous element in society. A Vigilance Committee has often been the saving of the community.

A mob entered the jail in Omaha in 1859, took two men from the prison, and hanged them. The circumstances were as follows: Two men, named John Daily and Harvey Braden, were confined in the jail at Omaha for horse-stealing. On Saturday night, January 8, 1859, a party of men entered the jail. The sheriff was absent, and the keys were in charge of three women. From these the mob took the keys by force, entered the cell, took the prisoners to a point two miles north of Florence, and there hanged them. A jury was impaneled, and after an examination which lasted several days, returned a verdict in accordance with the facts, finding four men, whose names we withhold, guilty of aiding and abetting the murder. These four men were granted a change of venue, and were tried at Bellevue, and we were present and witnessed the trial. The evidence of their guilt was very strong. The impression of those who heard the testimony was that the prisoners were guilty. They were, however, acquitted. We learned afterwards that the affair ruined each of the four men both mentally and physically. Although they had previously been prosperous, after the trial they met with reverses from which they never recovered. The judgments of Almighty God follow the murderer, and from them it is vain for him to try to escape.

During the six years of territorial organization no murderer had met the punishment due his crime. Robbery and assassination triumphed over industry and virtue. The citizens became incensed at the slow and unjust process of the courts. A Vigilance Committee was organized, and at the hands of this committee many outlaws met their fate.

In March, 1861, two young men, Iler and Bovey by name, at the hour of midnight, entered the house of Mr. George Taylor, living ten miles west of the city. Mr. Taylor was absent. His wife was alone. The desperadoes demanded of Mrs. Taylor her money. And as it was death or the money, and loving life more than her money, she turned over to them all she had, and they left with one thousand dollars in cash. A few days afterwards the two men were arrested. Mrs. Taylor was sent for, and identified them. They were lodged in the county jail. The most intense excitement prevailed among the citizens. A committee was appointed to inquire into the guilt or innocence of the prisoners. The committee held a long interview with them, and they finally made a full confession of their guilt. The committee reported accordingly, and recommended that the life of Iler be spared. During the next two days further confessions were made.

On Saturday morning, March 9, 1861, Bovey was found hanged at the door of his cell, his body dead and cold. The news reached us just after breakfast. I immediately left the parsonage, and walked slowly to the jail. A stream of men and women, too, were going to and from the tragic scene. Gloom was on every face, and tears in many eyes. The conversation was in low and whispered tones. I entered the prison, and saw the body of the unfortunate man lying on a board. The blood had settled about the thickness of an inch, and left a black circle around the neck where the rope had been fastened. Such a necklace I had never seen before. The sight was frightful, and I turned instinctively away from the ghastly scene. Death under such circumstances is appalling beyond all description. For days the whole community was shrouded in gloom. The body was left for several hours where all could see it—a warning to all criminals.

The first sermon ever preached in the region of Omaha was in 1851. This was three years before the city was founded. In 1851, William Simpson was sent to Council Bluffs Mission from the Iowa Conference. He learned that there were a few settlers on the west side of the Missouri River. In harmony with the spirit of the Methodist Episcopal Church, and with the instinct so characteristic of every true Methodist minister, he crossed the river, called the handful of immigrants together, and at the base of the abrupt hills where the city of Omaha now stands, he gave to these pioneers the bread of life. This was supposed to be the first Methodist sermon ever preached on Nebraska soil.

The first sermon preached in Omaha after the city was founded, was by the Rev. Peter Cooper. In the *Arrow*, published in August, 1854, the announcement was made that Rev. Peter Cooper would preach on Sunday, August

13th, at the residence of Mr. William P. Snowden. Mr. Cooper was an Englishman, and came to the village of Omaha when it contained less than one hundred inhabitants. He opened a stone-quarry on the bank of the Missouri River, just below the present bridge of the Union Pacific Railroad. He was a local preacher of the Methodist Episcopal Church. When it was discovered that he sometimes preached, he was invited to address the people of the village, and accordingly delivered the first sermon ever preached in Omaha. The congregation numbered about fifteen, there being present, among others, Mr. and Mrs. Alexander Davis, Mr. A. J. Poppleton, and Mr. A. D. Jones.

In the spring of 1855, Rev. Isaac F. Collins was sent as a missionary to Omaha, and organized a class of six members. On the 12th of September, Rev. William H. Goode held the first quarterly meeting ever held in the city. The following persons were present and partook of the sacrament of the Lord's Supper on that first sacramental occasion: Mr. and Mrs. Amsbury, the parents of Rev. W. A. Amsbury, now presiding elder in the West Nebraska Conference; Mr and Mrs. Collins, Mrs. Crowell, Mrs. George A. McCoy, and Mrs. Harris. It is related of Mrs. Harris that she reached Omaha from Iowa City, traveling on foot until she gave out and could walk no further, then riding the rest of the way upon a cow, the only beast of burden which she possessed. These were the days of small things, but they were not despised. That little handful of devoted Christians have become "a thousand times so many as they were."

In December, 1856, the first Methodist Episcopal Church was dedicated, the Rev. Moses F. Shinn officiating. Rev. J. M. Chivington succeeded Isaac Collins as pastor at Omaha; Rev. J. W. Taylor succeeded J. M. Chivington, Rev. William M. Smith succeeded J. W. Taylor and I followed Brother Smith.

The fourth session of the Kansas and Nebraska Conference met in Omaha April 14, 1859. The minutes of the first day's proceedings contain the following record: "The transfers of Hugh D. Fisher, a traveling elder, from the Pittsburg Conference, and H. T. Davis, a traveling deacon from the Northwest Indiana Conference were announced, and they were introduced to the Conference."

We received a royal welcome from this hardy band of pioneer Methodist preachers, and at once felt at home among them. At this Conference I was ordained elder by the venerable Bishop Scott, and was appointed to Omaha City Station. We had supplied Bellevue the nine months preceding the Conference, and had, under God, made many warm friends. They confidently expected our return. When we returned from the Conference and the people learned that we had been appointed to Omaha, they manifested the deepest sorrow and the bitterest regrets. We were very glad they were sorry. It was a real comfort to us. We would not for the world, hardly, have had them feel otherwise. No minister wants the people to feel glad when he is gone.

Believing that a farm would not be a bad thing for a preacher to have when old and no longer able to preach, we availed ourselves of the privilege of the pre-emption law, took a claim, built a small house, moved in, and lived there the time prescribed by law; then "proved up," and I received a title to our land from the Government.

From our claim, eight miles west of Bellevue, we moved to our new appointment. We could not go by railroad or steamboat. We were beyond the reach of these. The whistle of the locomotive had never been heard in Nebraska, and only those living along the Missouri River had the benefit of steam navigation.

To obtain a carriage in which to ride was out of the question. We tried to hire a span of horses and wagon in which to move, but in vain. So we had to do the next best thing, take what we could get—an ox-team. In the wagon we loaded our goods, and about the twenty-fifth day of

OMAHA. 177

April the pastor of the Methodist Episcopal Church of Omaha, and his wife, might have been seen riding behind a yoke of oxen up Farnham Street and down Seventeenth to the parsonage.

At that day Omaha was five years old, and had a population of about two thousand souls.

The Indians were then very numerous in Nebraska. They frequently passed through the city, and hardly a day went by but what we met some of them. Often the window would suddenly darken, and Mrs. Davis would look up and see from one to a half dozen "red-skins" staring at her through the window. At first the sight would startle her, but she soon became accustomed to it, and when they came would cry out to them, "Pucachee! Pucachee!"—"Begone! Begone!" Sometimes they would leave at once; at other times they would hang around for a time, waiting for a present. They were great beggars, and often when they came would not leave until something in the way of food or clothing was given them.

At that time we had a small brick church, right in the center of Omaha. On this church there was a debt of $500. The panic of 1857 had left the city flat, financially. The creditors wanted their money. To raise it from the people of Omaha was an impossibility. The Quarterly Conference requested the pastor to go East and try and raise the amount needed. I went back to my old Conference in Indiana, and in a few weeks returned with money enough to liquidate the debt. The official Board was happy, and the whole Church rejoiced. The Conference year closed under favorable auspices. The society, though small, was in a healthy condition, and was entirely free from debt.

The Kansas and Nebraska Conference met that year — March 16, 1860 — in Leavenworth, Kansas. There were no railroads, and travel on the Missouri River at that season of the year was very uncertain. So we took it the old-fashioned way, and went on horseback. The distance we had to travel in order to reach the seat of the Conference was about two hundred miles. We were one week going and one week returning, and at the Conference a week, being absent just three weeks.

On our way down we stopped over night at Falls City, near the Kansas line. This city was then two years old, and had about a dozen houses. We were kindly entertained during the night at the residence of Brother and Sister Miller. Afterwards, while traveling the Nebraska City District, I was often hospitably entertained by this kind family.

During the Kansas 'troubles Falls City was one of the stations of the "underground railway" of old John Brown. The mettle of which the old hero was made was shown in an incident which took place on one of his last trips from Kansas with his "dusky train." Having reached this station with his refugees, he was overtaken by a band of South Carolina Rangers, who proposed to carry their chattels back "to the galling serfdom of the sunny South." But the proud Southerners had mistaken the strength of their foe. Brown, with his men, quietly surrounded them, and compelled them by superior force to surrender; then stepping to the front, he gave them a scathing rebuke for the profanity they had heaped upon the "colored folks." He ordered the rangers to kneel down. They obeyed, and repeated after him the Lord's Prayer. Then, taking from them their horses and arms, he sent them back on foot from whence they came, while he and his freed slaves proceeded on their way rejoicing.

At the Leavenworth Conference a resolution was passed requesting the General Conference, which met the following May, to divide the Conference. That request was acceded to, and the Conference was divided in May, 1860. The Kansas Conference included the Territory of Kansas, and the Nebraska Conference the Territory of Nebraska.

On the 19th of March, after a harmonious sitting, the Kansas and Nebraska Conference closed its fifth session. And as that beautiful and touching hymn of Charles Wesley rolled up from a crowded audience, the hearts of all present were filled with solemnity and deep emotion—

> "And let our bodies part—
> To different climes repair."

That hymn was made doubly impressive from the fact that we believed the General Conference would accede to our wishes and divide the Conference, and that in all probability we would never be permitted to meet many of our brethren again until we hailed them in the skies. With anxiety we waited to hear the appointments read.

I quote the following from a letter I wrote to the *Western Christian Advocate* at the close of this Conference:

"Having received our appointments, we took each other by the hand, gave the parting good-bye, and hurried away to our respective fields of labor. In looking over the history of the Kansas and Nebraska Conference we can but exclaim, 'What hath God wrought!' The little handful who, five years ago, raised the standard of the cross in these Territories, has swelled to a mighty army. And to-day is heard the clarion voice of the faithful itinerant, rousing the soldiers of Christ to arms, and calling for volunteers for Jesus, in almost every settlement of these Territories, and throughout the valleys and peaks of the Rocky

Mountains, from the base even to the very summit."

We returned to Omaha. Our second year was a pleasant one, even more so than the first. During the winter a gracious revival took place, and some fifty souls were converted. We closed our second year with a larger membership, and much stronger in every respect than when we took the charge. The pastoral limit was then only two years, and we knew the bishop would assign us to a new field of labor.

CHAPTER XIII.

FIRST NEBRASKA CONFERENCE.

MEMBERS—STATISTICS—" CROWNED ONES "—MARTYR SPIRIT STILL IN THE CHURCH—NEBRASKA CITY DISTRICT IN 1861—A FEARFUL RIDE IN THE COLD — POP-GUN ELDER—S. P. MAJORS—BELLEVUE CONFERENCE—BISHOP SIMPSON—CROSSING THE PLATTE IN A SKIFF—LAURA BEATTY—AN AWFUL TRAGEDY—A DEATH-BED REPENTANCE.

THE first session of the Nebraska Annual Conference was held in Nebraska City, beginning April 4, 1861. Bishop Thomas A. Morris presided.

The following persons were members: Isaac Burns, H. Burch, H. T. Davis, J. T. Cannon, Wm. M. Smith, J. W. Taylor, Martin Prichard, T. Munhall, Philo Gorton, Jerome Spillman, Z. B. Turman, and J. L. Fort. L. W. Smith and David Hart were admitted into full connection, making in all fourteen members.

The following are the statistics:

Number of districts, ... 2
Number of appointments, ... 21
Number of members, ... 948

We have seen that little Conference of fourteen members grow into three Annual Conferences, thirteen districts, three hundred and fifty-four appointments, and thirty-one thousand two hundred and twelve members. "The little handful has become a thousand, and the small one a strong nation." Of the fourteen charter members of the Nebraska Conference, four have "ceased to work and live."

Of the "crowned ones" of that noble, heroic, and God-honored band, the first was Isaac Burns. Brother Burns was a simple-minded, conscientious, sweet-spirited, deeply pious man. A very common remark of his was, "It is a nice thing to be a Christian." One always felt benefited spiritually by being in his company. He had an easy way of giving to every one a spiritual uplift. Not long before he died, while on his way to Conference he preached a sermon in Nebraska City which made a most profound impression on all who heard it. His text was taken from the 73d Psalm and 24th verse: "Thou shalt guide me with thy counsel, and afterward receive me to glory." He began by saying: "Whatever the sermon may be, one thing is certain, I have the prettiest text in the Bible." It was a sermon full of the marrow of the gospel, as all his sermons were. The fragrance of that one sermon has come down through the years, and its rich aroma still lingers in the hearts of some who heard it.

Martin Prichard was the second who received an honorable discharge from the Master. On the 24th of March, 1877, he heard the welcome words, "It is enough, come up higher." Among those who took a most active part in laying the foundations of our Zion in the eastern part of Nebraska, was Brother Prichard. In Cass, Otoe, Nemaha, Richardson, and Pawnee Counties, as pastor, and as presiding elder of the Lincoln and Nebraska City Districts, he did a work for God and the Church, the grand results of which will only be known in the great day of eternity.

Next to follow was David Hart. He was an Englishman by birth, a Methodist through and through, consecrated wholly to God; and his death, as his life had been, was a triumph. On the 14th of January, 1878, in Colorado, where he had gone for his health, the chariot came from the skies to meet him, and he passed triumphantly home.

The fourth of this true and tried band was J. T. Cannon. July 24, 1883, Brother Cannon, from his home in Cass County, went up to join his comrades in the skies. He was a Methodist preacher of the olden type, zealous, devoted and true. Many and many a time I was hospitably entertained by him and his noble wife, at their home on their farm in Cass County. Their house was the home of the Methodist itinerant.

The gap made by the death of these was filled by others who proved themselves just as true as their predecessors. "The workmen die, but the work goes on." Many of these have fallen, and they in turn have been succeeded by others.

Aside from the charter members of the Conference, others, who joined later, have also been "crowned." The following are their names: J. J. Roberts, Thomas Alexander, D. J. Ward, T. A. Hull, A. J. Combs, W. B. Slaughter, C. W. Giddings, A. L. Goss, A. G. White, H. W. Warner, Samuel Wood, W. D. Gage, W. E. Davis, T. S. Goss, S. P. Vandoozer, William Peck, and Thomas B. Lemon. Mr. Wesley said: "Our people die well." The above long list from the roll of the Nebraska Conference was not an exception. These brave men fell, all covered with glory. "Let me die the death of the righteous, and let my last end be like theirs." They fell, "as the plumed warrior on the field of battle, with the ensigns of victory waving all around him." Noble dead! Peace to their ashes.

"Servants of God, well done!
Your glorious warfare's past;
The battle's fought, the race is won,
And ye are crowned at last."

Of the ten remaining charter members of the Nebraska Conference, two have fallen away; eight remain to till the Master's vineyard. Of these eight, only two are "effective,"—Hyram Burch and the writer. Brother Burch is strong and vigorous. His name is familiar throughout the State. He has been an untiring worker for God. Modest and retiring in disposition, he has never pushed himself to the front. When the final day of reckoning comes, and every man shall stand upon his own merits, Brother Burch will occupy a higher position, and on his brow, methinks, will rest a brighter crown, than those of some who have occupied more prominent positions in the Church militant.

The other six, J. L. Fort, J. W. Taylor, L. W. Smith, Z. B. Turman, W. M. Smith, and P. Gorton, are on the superannuated list, and work as they are able. Their heads are silvered with the frosts of many winters, but the fire of youth burns in their hearts. They have, like the venerable patriarch Abraham, reached "a good, old age, full of years," and will soon be "gathered to their people."

Three were admitted on trial at the first Nebraska Conference, and four, who had been received on trial by the Kansas and Nebraska Conference the year previous, were advanced to the second class, making in all seven. Among the seven probationers of that memorable little conference was Rev. T. B. Lemon. Dr. Lemon's name is familiar in almost every household of the

State. For twenty-five years he was one of the leaders of the hosts of our Zion on the frontier. Every position that he was called to fill by the Church, whether as pastor, presiding elder, superintendent of missions, or agent of a great university, was filled with credit to himself and honor to the Church. On Wednesday, February 19, 1890, at the ripe age of seventy-one, at his home in Omaha, he was called from the Church militant to the Church triumphant in heaven. His praise is in all the Churches.

Of those seven probationers, three only remain: J. W. Alling, now of the Rock River Conference; Wm. A. Amsbury is presiding elder in the West Nebraska Conference, and is doing a grand work in laying deep and broad the foundations of our Church; and Dr. J. B. Maxfield is presiding elder in the North Nebraska Conference, and is establishing our Church in that part of the State.

We need not go back to the earlier history of the Church to find heroes and heroines. They are in the Church to-day. The days of self-sacrifice for the Master's cause have not passed. The martyr-spirit is still in the Church.

From the day when Christ said to my happy soul, "Thy sins, which are many, are forgiven," I have been very deeply interested in the cause of missions. I read years ago, with delight, of

Cox, and Judson, and Morrison, and, later, of Coan at Hawaii, and Taylor in India and Africa; and as I read of their noble deeds and daring, there came to my heart a thrill of inspiration. Often since then have I been inspired anew as I have read of the missionaries who have bid adieu to friends, loved ones, and their native land, and have gone to foreign shores to proclaim the gospel to the heathen, and spend the balance of their lives in a land of strangers. All honor to these brave men and women! A rich reward awaits them in the skies. But a nobler band of heroes and heroines never graced this planet than the men and women who are laying the foundations of our Church on the frontier in the West. Many of them have lived, and are to-day living, on a mere pittance—hardly enough to keep soul and body together. My heart has bled a thousand times for these noble men and their heaven-honored families. No brighter gems will flash from the coronets of the redeemed than will blaze forever from the crowns of many who have spent their lives on the frontier, laying the foundations of the Church. All hail, blessed workmen of the Master!

The following statistics tell their own story: In 1861 the average amount received from each preacher in the Nebraska Conference was $228. The largest salary received was $495, and the smallest $28. Think of a pastor and his wife living a whole year on a salary of $28! In 1887 there were seven preachers in Nebraska who received an average of only $44.80 each for the year's work. On this small stipend these brave men stood at the post of duty, counting not their lives dear unto themselves for the Master's cause. Talk about moral heroes! You do not have to go to the annals of the past, nor to heathen shores to find them. They are here right among us, in the bounds of our own Conferences. These persons are making a record for eternity of which they will be proud when the world is on fire.

At the first Nebraska Conference held in Nebraska City, beginning April 4, 1861, I was appointed presiding elder of the Nebraska City District. My district comprised all the territory south of the Platte River. In this territory is now the Nebraska Conference, and part of the West Nebraska Conference.

The following is a list of the appointments:

OMAHA DISTRICT.

WILLIAM M. SMITH, ... Presiding Elder.
Omaha, ... To be supplied.
Bellevue, ... Martin Prichard.
Elkhorn, ... J. Alling,
Platte Valley, ... T. Hoagland.
Calhoun, ... David Hart.
Tekamah, ... Wm. A. Amsbury.

Dakota, ... Z. B. Turman.
Fort Kearney, ... T. Munhall.

NEBRASKA CITY DISTRICT.

H. T. DAVIS, ...	Presiding Elder.
Nebraska City, ...	T. B. Lemon
Wyoming, ...	J. T. Cannon.
Rock Bluff, ...	Philo Gorton.
Plattsmouth and Oreapolis, . .	J. Spilman.
Glendale, ...	L. W. Smith.
Beatrice, ...	{ Joel Mason, J. B. Maxfield.
Tecumseh, ...	William H. Kendal.
Table Rock, ...	Isaac Burns.
Falls City, ...	J. W. Taylor.
Brownville, ...	H. Burch.
Peru, ...	J. L. Fort.

This was before the days of railroads in Nebraska, and I traveled the district with my own conveyance, which consisted of a bronco pony and a light buggy. I did not allow the weather to interfere with my work. My motto was, "Never miss an appointment." I went, rain or shine, cold or hot. Many and many a time I was drenched through and through with the rain, and many times almost frozen to death. In the winter of 1862, I left home for a two weeks' tour, went to Falls City, and held quarterly meeting, and from thence went to Table Rock, and held another. After services Sabbath evening, I said to my good host and hostess, Brother and Sister Griffin: "I should like very much to leave for home early to-morrow morning." I had fifty miles to travel, and it was necessary for me to get an early start. They were up bright and early, and had breakfast before daybreak. At dawn of day I was ready to leave for home. The weather was bitter cold; the sun rose bright and clear, and there were two sun-dogs as bright almost as the sun himself. My course was northeast. Soon after starting, a heavy wind arose and blew a stiff gale the whole, livelong day. This wind I had to face. I was dressed warmly; I had on three coats, an undercoat, a heavy overcoat, and over this an oil-cloth coat to keep the wind from penetrating the other clothing. I had not gone many miles before I was chilled through and through. A person may be ever so warmly clothed on these prairies, so that the wind can not possibly penetrate the clothing, yet in breathing the cold air he soon becomes chilled, and if he did not exercise he would freeze to death. After leaving Table Rock I had a stretch of some thirty-five miles to go over a bleak prairie without a single house. When I became chilled I got out of the buggy and walked, or rather ran, until warmed up; then I rode and ran alternately the whole day. Many times during the day I greatly feared I should not be able to make my home, and must succumb to the cold. About four o'clock in the afternoon I came to a little frame house on Spring Creek, some fifteen miles from home. Here I stopped, thinking I would remain over night if I could obtain accommodations, for I felt it was extremely hazardous to proceed further. The little shanty was not plastered. Nothing but thin clapboards protected the inmates from the fierce December winds. Around a cook-stove a mother with half a dozen children stood shivering with the cold, trying in vain to keep warm. My teeth chattered, and I shook with the cold more violently, it seemed, than any one ever did with the old-fashioned ague. Really it seemed colder in that house than on the open prairie. I said to myself: "I can't stay here. This is worse than out-doors." I went out, got into my buggy, drove on, and at eight o'clock, almost frozen and completely exhausted, reached home. I felt the effects of that fearful day's ride for many years.

I was only twenty-eight years old when appointed presiding elder of the Nebraska City District, and, of course, looked quite youthful. Accustomed to associate with the eldership gray hairs and corpulency, neither of which I possessed, my first round on the district struck the people with great surprise, and caused many quaint comments. The first quarterly meeting was held in Nemaha City, on the Brownville Circuit. When I entered the school-house with Brother Burch, the pastor, at two o'clock, Saturday afternoon, and took my seat at the desk, a sister whispered to a friend and said: "It is too bad the presiding elder did not come himself. He has sent a mere boy to take his place." Similar remarks were made by many during the first-quarter about the boy presiding elder.

On my way to this quarterly meeting I stopped over night at Peru. Here for the first time I met the Honorable S. P. Majors, and was kindly entertained at his home; and ever afterward was welcomed by him and his devoted wife to their hospitalities. After introducing me to his wife, his little son came into the room, and Brother Majors introduced him, saying: "Johnny, this is Brother Davis, our elder." Soon after, Brother Majors went out to do his evening chores; Johnny followed, and as they walked together to the barn, he said: "Pa, did you say that was the elder?"

"Yes," was the reply.

"Is that the kind of elder they make pop-guns out of?" said Johnny.

The joke was too good for Brother Majors to keep to himself. No man enjoyed a joke better than he. After supper was over, and we were all in the sitting-room together, he told us what Johnny had said. Johnny ran out of the room, ashamed and mortified, while the rest of us laughed heartily. Ever afterwards when I met Brother Majors in company, he hardly ever failed to relate the incident, and Brother Majors and his friends had many a hearty laugh at the expense of poor Johnny and myself.

Some time afterwards, on our way from the Brownville Conference, in company with Bishop Ames and a number of preachers, we all dined at Brother Majors's. In the presence of Johnny and myself, as usual, Brother Majors told the story of the "popgun elder," and the good bishop laughed until it seemed his great fat sides must certainly be sore. Johnny grew up to manhood, and on January 21, 1882, I united him in marriage to Miss Nettie J. Mutz, a most estimable Christian young lady, whom I had known from childhood.

At Johnny's home, in the northern part of the State, July 13, 1886, Brother Majors passed peacefully away to his home in the skies. His remains were brought to Peru for interment, and on the twenty-ninth day of April, 1886, I preached his funeral sermon to a large congregation of relatives and friends, from Genesis xxv, 8. He occupied prominent positions of trust, both in the State and the Church. He presided over the State Convention which framed the first constitution of Nebraska, and was a lay delegate from the Nebraska Conference to the General Conference of 1872. He honored every position he was called to occupy. His wise and safe counsels in the State, the Church, and the family still live. The fragrance of his life is with us to-day, and its rich aroma will remain through all time.

When I took the district, in 1861, the population was sparse and the people poor. They had come from the Eastern and Middle States to the West to procure for themselves homes. There were only three or four places on the district where the people had coffee, tea, or sugar. As a substitute for coffee they used burnt corn, rye, or wheat, and many used what was called "Coffee Essence"—a compound of various ingredients. The principal article for sweetening was "sorghum molasses." Many of these kind-hearted people, who at that time had hardly enough to keep soul and body together, have, to-day, large farms, elegant homes, and are among the wealthiest citizens of the State. They have passed from poverty to affluence, and the distance from the one to the other has seemed very short.

The Conference of 1862 was held at Bellevue. Bishop Simpson presided. He and his wife came by stage from St. Joe, Mo., and in consequence of the high water and the ice in the Platte River were delayed a day. They crossed the turbid, swift-flowing Platte in a skiff, and, the river being full of ice, the passage was a most dangerous one. One man, with a pole in hand, kept the rushing ice from capsizing the boat, while another rowed; and after a most perilous passage, they reached the northern bank of the stream. Stepping on shore, the party breathed easy after a half-hour's painful suspense. Then on a hay-rack the bishop and his good wife rode to Bellevue, a distance of some five miles, reaching the Conference in time for the opening services Friday morning.

In 1864 the General Conference met in Philadelphia. During the session Bishop Simpson gave the Conference a reception at his own home. I had the privilege and honor of attending that reception. In conversation with Mrs. Simpson on the occasion, she said: "Our trip from St. Joe, Missouri, to Bellevue is one of the most interesting chapters in our lives."

The bishop was just recovering from his long illness, and was quite feeble in body. We greatly feared he would not be able to preach for us on Sabbath. Saturday afternoon I said to him: "Bishop, we expect you to preach for us to-morrow morning." He gave us a significant look, and smilingly said: "Yes, I will give you a little Presbyterian sermon." As we listened to his thrilling sermon next day, we said: "If that is a little Presbyterian sermon, what must a big one be?" His graphic description of the "seven stars and the seven golden candlesticks" was wonderful. And then, as he said in his peroration, "Christ is still walking in the midst of the Churches, holding in his right hand the seven stars," the people were thrilled as with an electric shock, and shouted all over the house, "Glory! Glory!" The memory of that precious hour lingers with the writer to-day.

The bishop was entertained by Rev. Wm. Hamilton, pastor of the Presbyterian Church. Brother Hamilton was sent out in an early day by the Presbyterian Board of Missions as missionary to the Indians, and in 1855 he organized the first Presbyterian Church in Bellevue. He was greatly delighted with the bishop and the proceedings of the Conference. He had never attended a Methodist Conference before in his life, and seemed much surprised and pleased, and said to me at the close of the Conference: "Do you always have such precious seasons at your Conferences?" My reply was: "Our Conferences are always good, and often seasons of refreshing from the presence of the Lord."

In 1862, I had the great privilege of witnessing another most triumphant departure from earth. I stood for a little while in the antechamber of the skies. The poet has truthfully said:

> "The chamber where the good man meets his fate
> Is prized above the common walks of life,
> Quite on the verge of heaven."

On Saturday afternoon I went out to hold quarterly meeting at Union, an appointment on the Mount Pleasant Circuit. I reached Brother Beatty's, where the meeting was to be held, at two o'clock. Before entering the house a friend said to me: "Laura Beatty is lying very low with fever, and wishes to see you as soon as possible." She was at her sister's, about two miles away. I said to my friend: "I will go and see her as soon as the afternoon services are over." The services ended, I hurried over to where she was, and on entering the room felt, it seemed, as Jacob did at Bethel when he said: "Surely the Lord is in this place." A few weeks before death she had a remarkable dream. She dreamed that her sainted mother came to her, led her out into the grove near by, and talked with her for some time; and as the heavenly visitant was about to leave, said, "Laura, you will come to me soon," then disappeared. Laura told her dream to friends, and remarked: "I shall live but a little while." She was just blooming into womanhood when stricken down with that fatal disease, typhoid fever. I entered the room. On her face rested a sweet, heavenly smile. The room was pervaded with a most hallowed atmosphere. The fragrance of the skies had been wafted to that humble prairie home; it was good to be there. She made every one in the room promise to meet her in heaven; then she sent for neighbors and friends, that she might talk with them touching their soul's salvation. She spoke of the beauties and glories of heaven, glimpses of which she had seen. Just before her happy spirit took its upward and eternal flight, she exclaimed in an ecstasy of joy: "The angels are coming; don't you see them? O how beautiful! There is mother with them! And there is Jesus, my Savior" And shortly after, her enraptured spirit joined that heavenly throng. How these wonderful scenes speak in language that can not be misunderstood, of heaven, the eternal "home of the soul!"

In the winter of 1862, I held quarterly meeting at the house of Brother Goolsby, on "The Muddy," a small stream some five miles north of Falls City. On Sunday morning a snow-storm set in. It snowed all day and all night, and on Monday morning the snow was drifted in piles from two to twenty feet deep. The roads were completely blockaded, rendering travel impossible, and I was compelled to remain for several days.

While here I preached every night to two families. Brother Goolsby made me a "jumper," and then, twisting hemp into ropes, he made me a rope harness. On Friday morning I ventured to start to my quarterly meeting, which was to be held at Pawnee City. My pony with the hemp harness was hitched to the quaint sleigh. I got in and started, and after two days of hard travel through heavy drifts of snow and the cold, piercing wind, filled with frost, I reached my appointment late Saturday night. After conducting the quarterly meeting I traveled over the bleak prairie to Nebraska City, my home. Though the weather was fearfully cold and stormy, every engagement was met, and I have reason to believe that the meetings were seasons of great profit to all.

After serving four years on the district, I was appointed, in 1865, to the Nebraska City Station. Here we remained three years, as long as the rule of the Church allowed. These years were passed pleasantly, and we trust profitably to the Church. During my first year as pastor of this station, a most unpleasant affair took place. One of the most atrocious and cold-blooded crimes in the annals of the State was committed about five miles southwest of the city. William Hamilton, a boy eleven years old, was herding cattle for his father, some two miles from home. Failing to return as usual in the evening, diligent search was made, and his body was found in the edge of a pool of water, in a stooping posture, his feet buried in the mud. He had been shot three times,—in the corner of his right eye, once in the ear, and again under the arm. A coroner's jury decided that he came to his death by pistol-balls supposed to have been fired by a man named Cash. After committing the horrible deed, Cash (or Deiricks, as his proper name was) rode into the city and sold the cattle, claiming that he had a large herd. He received a small sum down, the balance was to be received on delivery of the cattle next day. Becoming alarmed, he immediately left the city, crossing the Missouri River into Iowa. The news of the awful tragedy reached the city, and the most intense excitement prevailed. About one hundred men started in pursuit of the murderer. He was captured the next morning at Plum Hollow, Iowa, and on the 16th of August brought back to the city. At ten o'clock, an immense crowd of citizens assembled in the public park, just in front of the parsonage. Addresses were made by several prominent citizens. A president and secretary were appointed, a jury of the oldest and best citizens impaneled, and counsel for the prisoner employed. A just trial was given the prisoner. Seven witnesses were examined, and at two o'clock in the afternoon the case was submitted to the jury. The prisoner was lodged in the county jail.

A few moments afterwards a messenger came to the parsonage and said: "The prisoner desires to see the Methodist preacher." I immediately repaired to the jail, in the basement of the courthouse, and was conducted to the door of the cell. The bolt was turned, the door opened, and I entered. The door was quickly closed and the bolt turned on us. I was left with the prisoner, and remained with him to the last. Mr. Dan Laur, the secretary of the trial, was also in the cell. Soon after entering the cell a citizen beckoned me to the window, and in a whisper said: "The jury have found Cash guilty of murder in the first degree, and recommend that he be hanged; but it will probably not be done before to-morrow." I at once communicated the fact to the poor man. He was very much afflicted, and wept freely. I did all I could to get him to confess the crime, but in vain. He persisted to the last in declaring that the witnesses had not examined thoroughly the holes in the boy's body, if they had he declared, "they would have been convinced they were made by the turtles, and not by bullets from a pistol."

I prayed with him, and he professed to feel much better. About four o'clock I was called again to the cell-window by a citizen, who said: "The people are terribly excited, and are becoming more so every moment. Many want to hang Cash immediately." I told the prisoner of the excited condition of the people on the outside, and said to him: "If you have any requests to make before death, make them at once, for you are liable to be hanged at any moment." A few moments later, Mr. Davenport whispered to me through the iron grate: "They have determined to hang Cash at six o'clock." I told the prisoner the decision of the people. He then made his will. I prayed with him a number of times, and he said he believed he was prepared to meet God. At precisely six o'clock the cell-door opened, and he was led to the place of execution. As soon as the door opened, he seized me by the arm and held on with a death-grip until we reached the top of the scaffold. It seemed as though his fingers would bury themselves in the flesh of my arm. Never did any one cling to me as that poor man did to the very last. I can almost feel the grip of his hands on my arm now, although more than twenty-five years have passed since that fearful day. Reaching the scaffold, the rope was adjusted to his neck. I offered a prayer, then shook hands with him, bade him good-bye, and descended. The drop fell, and Cash was no more of earth.

Was he converted and prepared for heaven? I hope he was. I earnestly prayed that he might be. But not for a thousand worlds would I have my salvation suspended on such a slender thread. I have been utterly disgusted, time and again, with the sensational reports, in the secular press, of the conversions of murderers just before being launched from the gallows into eternity. I do not doubt but that some may have been converted, but I greatly fear their number is very small. I would not for the world sit in judgment upon any human soul. God alone is the judge, and I know the Judge of all the earth will do right. I greatly fear Cash was not converted, and my fears are grounded on the following facts:

First. He did not manifest "godly sorrow" for sin. This is absolutely necessary in order to a genuine penitent. A man may sorrow and not repent; he may sorrow because he is found out. That is not "godly sorrow." Deep, heart-felt sorrow for having sinned against God and high heaven, is the first element in genuine repentance. Second. He did not manifest the fruit of a genuine convert. A converted man has the Spirit of God; and "the fruit of the Spirit is love, joy, and peace." These he did not show. Nor, lastly, did he confess his crime. A friend of mine, living near Ashland, related to me the following some years ago. The circumstance came under his own observation. Several men were buried in a coal-mine in Pennsylvania. All were Christians but one, and he was a very profane man. The passage-way was entirely closed, and they knew it would be many days before they could be rescued, if rescued at all. All felt prepared to die except the unconverted man, and he requested the others to pray for him. They did so, and he professed to be converted. After eighteen days they were rescued from what they all supposed was to be their living tomb. They were barely alive when taken out. By superior medical skill and kind nursing they recovered. No sooner was the man who had professed conversion in the mine restored fully to health than he was just as profane as he had ever been. Was his conversion in the mine genuine?

The late Rev. J. J. Roberts, of the Nebraska Conference, once said to the writer in substance, in a private conversation, touching death-bed repentances: "I have known a number during my ministry who, when very sick and expecting to die, sought, and professed to obtain, religion. They afterwards recovered, and in every case were, after recovery, just as wicked as ever." Was their repentance sincere and their conversion genuine? It is, to say the least, very questionable. Few, he thought, who live under the light of the gospel were ever converted on a death-bed. He who trusts his salvation to a death-bed repentance, runs a risk that no wise or sane man will run.

CHAPTER XIV.

CIVIL WAR INCIDENTS.

The Dark Cloud—The Rainbow of Promise—National Prosperity—"Jayhawkers"—Ordered to Halt—Depredations—Camp-meeting near Falls City—Bloody Fray—Dave Stephenson.

THE spring of 1861 was gloomy in the extreme. The dark storm-cloud of civil war was gathering. That portentous cloud grew darker and more dense with fearful rapidity, and soon covered the whole Nation with its sable mantle. Then the storm of fratricidal strife broke with unrelenting fury upon the land. For four long years brother fought brother, until the whole Nation was crimsoned with the best blood of the American people. In every household there was mourning; on every face rested the gloom of sadness. Of all wars, the one most to be deplored is civil war.

Many in Missouri, who sympathized with the Rebellion, fled from the State. Nebraska City was the rendezvous for these during the war. Here they congregated in great numbers. The Union men in the city were very strong and outspoken, and brave as they were strong. Many of the rebels had lost property in Missouri, and their friends were in the rebel army, and they, of course, were very sensitive on the war question. On the other hand, the Union men had friends in the Union army, and they were incensed at the insult given the Stars and Stripes; and they, too, were sensitive. They saw the best Government on which the sun ever shone menaced with destruction. They saw the mightiest Nation on this planet—a Nation whose flag was respected on every sea and in every land—in danger of being rent asunder, and blotted from existence. And as they saw all this, it was not at all strange that their hearts were stirred to their inmost depths. At times matters grew fearfully hot. We knew not what the final result would be. No one could predict with certainty the outcome. May such times never again occur! May such scenes never again be witnessed! May such a cloud never again darken our National horizon! How glad we were when the rainbow of promise arched our National firmament after the fearful storm, and how our hearts thrilled with delight when the snow-white dove was seen bearing the olive-branch of peace in her bill!

The storm passed. The moral atmosphere of the Nation was purified. The greatest evil of the age—" the sum of all villainies "—was wiped out.

Emerging from the dire conflict, the Nation entered upon a career of prosperity unparalleled in history. The wealth of America is phenomenal. Our Nation is the youngest Nation on the globe, and yet it is one of the largest and most wealthy. And what is more significant still, the most of this wealth has been accumulated since the Civil War closed. Other nations have been centuries amassing their wealth; the greater part of the wealth of the United States is the product of about twenty-five years.

During the war, there were bands of men who went under the name of "Jay-hawkers." They first made their appearance in 1862. Sometimes they claimed to be "Unionists;" at other times, "Confederates." They sailed under the flag that best suited their own convenience. They were more loyal to themselves than to either party. They took advantage of the war to fill their coffers by plunder and robbery. Some of these bands of freebooters were, however, strong in their allegiance to their party. They were quite numerous in the southeastern part of the State. In traveling through my district I often met them. They knew me, and I generally knew them. They very frequently attended my meetings. They never interfered with me but once, and that was by mistake. Midway between Peru and Nebraska City, as I rode leisurely along the road, one beautiful Monday afternoon, two of them came dashing up behind me. They were armed to the teeth with knives and revolvers, and their long, uncombed hair hung in mats over their shoulders. They were not the most prepossessing and inviting men I had ever seen, by any means. On reaching the buggy, they parted. One rode up to my right, and the other to my left. The one on my left drew a large navy revolver, and cried out, "Halt!" I reined in my horse, and stopped. The other one recognized me, and immediately said to his comrade: "Hello, Bill, this is Elder Davis!" They turned, put spurs to their horses, and were soon out of sight; while I passed on, unharmed, to my home. They entered a house near Peru. The husband and father was in the army. The mother and daughters were at home, alone. The Jay-hawkers demanded of the woman her money. She refused to tell them where it was. In the house was an old-fashioned fireplace, and, as the weather was cold, there was a good fire. The desperadoes drew out a large bed of coals, ordered the mother to take off her shoes and stockings; then, setting her in a chair, placed her bare feet on the burning coals of fire, and told her they would release her when she told them where her money was. Of course she did not remain long in that position. The robbers got what they went for—all the money the family had. This is only a sample of their mode of operations.

We were holding a camp-meeting near Falls City, in 1862. At this meeting were a number of our "boys in blue." With many of them I was intimately acquainted. Brave, noble boys they were—loyal to the core, and true to the "old flag." Saturday night a number of rebel "Jayhawkers" from Missouri came over. We knew they were present, and greatly feared the consequences. We all felt certain there would be trouble. "Our boys" were not in a mood to hear the slightest insinuation against the Government in its efforts to put down the Rebellion. They were ready at a moment to resent any word or act not perfectly loyal. Sunday evening, about sundown, as I stood near the stand, I noticed a large crowd at the upper end of the ground. A moment afterwards, a woman came rushing down towards the pulpit, intensely excited, and exclaimed: "Elder, elder, go up there quick! They are killing our boys!" I ran up; but before reaching the spot the crowd had dispersed. Poor Dave Stephenson, however, had received a fearful stab in the side from one of the rebels. We carried him down to his father's tent, arranged a bed in a wagon-box, and made him as comfortable as possible. Here he lay, suffering great agony, all night long. All thought the wound would prove fatal; but a kind Providence ordered it otherwise, and he recovered. The whole camp-ground was in a perfect ferment of excitement. Soon, however, the excitement subsided, the people assembled at the stand, the usual services were held, God owned and blessed the Word, and souls were saved. Many earnest prayers went up for "Dave's" recovery. These prayers were answered. "Dave" has since held responsible positions of trust in the State, at one time filling the position of surveyor-general. His father and mother were devoted Christians, ardently attached to the Church, and they did much for God and our Zion in that early day.

The Civil War revealed the true character of many men, and many supposed good men were found to be, when opportunity offered, as vile as the vilest.

CHAPTER XV.

LINCOLN.

Location—Salt Basins—First Settlers—Indians—First Sermon in the County—Elder Young—Lancaster—Visit to the New Town—Act Providing for the Change of the Capital—Lot-sales—First Legislature in the New Capital—First Methodist Episcopal Church—Other Churches.

IN the present chapter I wish to sketch the history of Lincoln, giving a brief outline of its rise, growth, and prosperity.

Lincoln is the county-seat of Lancaster County, and the capital of the State of Nebraska; it is fifty miles west of the Missouri River, and stands on the banks of Salt Creek. The beautiful capitol crowns the highest elevation of the plateau on which the city stands. A circle of low hills, a few miles away, surrounds the city. The scenery on every hand is the most charming. In full view, to the west of the city, are the "Salt Basins." On a bright summer day—and for these Nebraska is noted—these basins resemble large bodies of limpid water; they are, however, level surfaces of compact earth, covered with a layer of "saline crystal, and intersected with tiny rivers of brine flowing into the creek," from which the creek derives its name and character. They were discovered in 1856, and their value was at once recognized. Long before Lincoln was founded, the early settlers came for many miles to these basins, and made the salt necessary for their yearly supply. The brine from the springs and rivulets is very strong, and in a short time the farmer, by boiling the brine, could make salt sufficient to last during the year. When traveling the Nebraska City District from 1861 to 1865, I found that many of the settlers from Johnson, Pawnee, Gage, and other counties, came here, made and laid in their yearly supply of salt. In no distant day these basins will, without doubt, be a source of great revenue to the State.

In 1850, when passing over the Plains, we crossed Salt Creek, eight miles south of Lincoln, at a point now called Saltillo. Here we camped during the night, little dreaming that near where we were, in a few short years, would rise one of the greatest cities of the West, and the capital of one of the largest and richest States of our Union. Six years later, the first settlement was made in the county, a few miles further south, by Mr. John D. Prey and his sons. I first met some members of the family in 1861, at a quarterly meeting held at the residence of James Eatherton.

Mrs. Prey was a devoted Christian, and a member of the Methodist Episcopal Church. The Preys reached Salt Creek June 15, 1856. At that time the land in the county was not surveyed; the following year the land-office was established in Nebraska City. The same year the county of Lancaster was partly surveyed, and Mr. Prey and his sons located their claims. For some time they were the only people living anywhere near the salt basins.

During the first summer all the settlers could do was to break land; as they came late in the season, they were unable to raise any crops. In 1857 very little was raised; but in 1858 a large crop was harvested; prosperity dawned upon the settlers, and the future began to look bright and hopeful.

In the early history of the county, when the settlers numbered only eight or ten, the first Indian scare occurred. It was in 1857, when a man by the name of Davis settled near Saltillo. This man had a vain and wicked desire to kill an Indian, and it was not long until an opportunity of gratifying this unholy desire was given him. Without provocation he deliberately shot down an innocent Indian. The Indians were numerous, and when they found that one of their number had been killed in cold blood by a white man, they at once went upon the war-path. Who could blame them?

The white man was the aggressor. The settlers were alarmed, and fled to Weeping Water Falls. Here they remained for two weeks. The Indians, however, soon quieted down, and the settlers returned to their claims.

In 1859 another Indian scare occurred. A band of Cheyennes and Arapahoes came to the salt-basins, evidently bent on mischief. Unexpectedly they reached the homestead of Mr. Prey when the men folks were all away. Mrs. Prey, her daughter Rebecca, twelve years old, and two boys, aged eight and fifteen years, were alone. When the Indians appeared, Rebecca was some distance from the house, and the Indians were about to seize and carry her away a captive; but their plans were frustrated by the courage of the mother, and the timely arrival of the male members of the family. They did but little damage as they passed on to the north.

Five years afterwards, in 1864, another Indian scare took place. The bloodthirsty Sioux were on the war-path. They were coming from the west, killing and plundering and laying waste the country as they came, and the settlers of Lancaster County fled in terror to the east. A few of the men, however, determined to remain until they should see the Indians approach. Some days elapsed; but the murderous Sioux did not put in an appearance. Then these brave men, eight in all, determined to go west until they learned something definite with regard to the Red-skins. Mounted, and armed to the teeth with rifles and revolvers, they started in pursuit of the foe. The party was composed of Captain W. T. Donivan, John S. Gregory, E. M. Warens, Richard Wallingford, James Morgan, John P. Loder, Aaron Wood, and one other. With most of them I was personally acquainted. They pushed on to the west until they reached the valley of the Blue, near where Milford now stands; and as they were looking for the wily Sioux, they saw a single Indian, peeping over the hill, some distance to their rear. The lone Indian, looking over the hill, boded no good to the whites. They were fully convinced that he was a picket-guard, and that near by, in all probability, there was a whole tribe of warriors. They determined to ride back, but had only started, when, from the low ground, there suddenly rose up before them several hundred well-mounted and well-armed Indians. The Indians were right across their path, and the savage Red-men began to bear down upon the little band of whites. It was a critical moment, and the cheeks of the brave men for once were blanched. Death seemed inevitable. They determined to make a desperate effort to escape, and, in the attempt, to sell their lives as dear as possible. They strapped their rifles to their shoulders, and, with drawn revolvers, they started, determined to force a passage through the line of well-armed savages or die in the attempt. Just as they were starting, the Indians put up a white flag; and one of their number, throwing away his gun in token of friendship, came forward to meet them, and as he came up to them said: "How? Me no Sioux; me Pawnee. Me no fight white man." What a relief it was to the whites! It proved to be true; they were a band of Pawnee warriors, on the war-path against the Sioux; and when they first saw the white men they supposed they were a party of Sioux stragglers. The Pawnees passed on after the Sioux, and the whites returned to their homes, glad to let Indians fight Indians.

Among the first settlers who came after the Prey family were W. T. Donivan, James Eatherton, John Cadman, R. Wallingford, W. E. Keys, E. Warens, J. A. Wallingford, and John S. Gregory. John Dee came about the same time the Preys did. As late as 1860–63 a buffalo might occasionally have been seen, and over the prairies where Lincoln now stands herds of antelope gamboled; coyotes were numerous, and their shrill bark was often heard, especially during the night.

In the history of Lincoln we find the following about Mr. John S. Gregory: "During the winter of 1863 Mr. John S. Gregory, not having any other business to attend to, gave attention to destroying some of the numerous wolves which then infested this region. He would insert a few grains of strychnine into little balls of fat, and then pass around a large circuit and drop the balls into the snow. The wolves would follow the trail, and snap up every ball. Every wolf that swallowed a ball was dead in a short time. He would then skin the animals, their pelts being valuable at that time. The carcasses he piled up in cords, north of Lincoln, to prevent the poisoning of domestic animals by eating the flesh. They were frozen stiff and stark, and corded up like wood. Toward spring Mr. Gregory had a couple of cords of carcasses piled up at one place. Then a lot of Pawnee Indians came along, and stopped near the cords of wolf-carcasses. Mr. Gregory, fearing they might eat the wolves, rode over to warn them of the danger. He found the squaws and papooses lugging the wolf-carcasses into camp, and he at once expostulated with them by signs, trying to make them understand it was dangerous to eat the wolves. The old chief thought he was demanding the return of the wolves because they were his property, and, at the chief's command, the squaws and papooses lugged the carcasses back, and piled them up again. They were not well pleased at the prospect of losing a feast, and returned the wolf-meat with long faces. Finally, a member of the tribe, who could speak a little English, came along, and Mr. Gregory explained to him that he did not care for the wolf-carcasses, but did not want the Indians to be poisoned. This explanation was made to the Indians, who set up a big guffaw, and the squaws at once began to gather up the wolf-carcasses and take them to camp, laughing and indulging in expressions of great satisfaction. They cooked up the last one of the wolves, and had a great feast. Mr. Gregory learned from the interpreter that the Indians were well acquainted with the use of strychnine in killing wolves, and were in the habit of eating animals killed in this way. They had no fear of the drug, and suffered no apparent damage from eating the wolves."

In the fall of 1859 the settlers met under the shade of a large elm-tree, standing on the bank of Salt Creek, near where the B. and M. roundhouse now stands, to effect a county organization. A committee was appointed to select a site for a county-seat and lay out a town. The committee selected the present site of Lincoln, and called it "Lancaster." For some time "Lancaster" was only a paper town, without inhabitants. The same year John Cadman settled in the southern part of the county. Subsequently he was made county judge, and ever afterwards was familiarly known as "Judge Cadman." The writer first met him at a quarterly meeting, held in 1861, south of Saltillo. The meeting was held in the private house of James Eatherton, on the bank of Salt Creek, twelve miles south of the city of Lincoln. The judge was deeply interested in laying the foundations of the Church in the new Territory. He was not only an active Church member in that early day, but was an enterprising citizen as well. He took an active part in having what was known as "The Steam-wagon Road" built from Nebraska City west to Fort Kearney. A steam-wagon was invented, and the inventor brought this wagon up the Missouri River to Nebraska City. When it landed, a most profound sensation was produced. The most intense excitement prevailed among the citizens. It was thought by many that it would create a complete revolution in traveling and freight-carrying over the plains. Streams were bridged, hills graded, sloughs filled, and a good road was made for the "steam-wagon." Although the "steam-wagon" proved an utter failure, and never amounted to anything at all, a most excellent highway was built, and the people living along the road were more than compensated for their labor and expense. Judge Cadman took an active part also in having the capital of the

State changed, and located in Lancaster County. For many years he lived in the city, and aided in building up the new capital. He is now living in California, in the city of Los Angeles.

The first sermon ever preached near where the city of Lincoln now stands was by Rev. Z. B. Turman, in 1857. A detailed account of Brother Turman's work may be found in the following chapter.

In 1863, Elder J. M. Young, whose name is familiar to all the early settlers of this county, a minister of the Methodist Protestant Church, located at this point with a colony. Elder Young organized a Methodist Protestant society, and the society afterwards erected a large stone church— one of the first church edifices built in the city of Lincoln. He also organized societies at different places in the county. The design of Elder Young and his colony was to locate and build up a denominational school of high grade. A seminary was founded, and a stone building erected, which stood where the *State Journal* block now stands. The seminary, however, did not prove a success.

In 1866, I visited Lancaster, and spent a Sabbath in the new town, which had at that time half a dozen houses. I preached on Sunday morning in a little unfinished school-house to a small congregation of attentive and intelligent listeners, little dreaming that this unpretentious town was so soon to become one of the mightiest of Western cities, and the capital of one of the most thrifty and populous States in the American Union. I never was more impressed in my life with the beauty of any place than I was with Lancaster and the whole surrounding country. It seemed that nature had never been more prodigal in lavishing beauty and attractions upon any place than the country where the city of Lincoln now stands. I returned to my home in Nebraska City, and immediately located some land near the new town.

On June 20, 1867, a bill passed the Legislature providing for the removal and permanent location of the capital of Nebraska. Omaha was then the seat of government. The bill, of course, had its bitter enemies, and was fought to the very last with all the ability and energy its opponents could command. The contest was a long and heated one, full of acrimony, and no small amount of ill-feeling was engendered. The bill provided, first, "That the governor, secretary of state, and auditor be, and are hereby, appointed commissioners for the purpose of locating the seat of government and the public buildings of the State." And second, "On or before July, 1867, the commissioners, or a majority of them, shall select from the lands belonging to the State within the following limits, to-wit, the County of Seward, the south half of the County of Saunders and Butler, and that portion of the County of Lancaster lying north of the south line of Township Nine, a suitable site of not less than six hundred and forty acres lying in one body, for a town, due regard being had to its accessibility from all parts of the State, and its general fitness for a capital. They shall immediately survey, lay off, and stake out the said tract of land into lots, blocks, streets and alleys, and public squares or reservations for public buildings, which said town, when so laid out and surveyed, shall be named and known as Lincoln, and the same is hereby declared to be the permanent seat of government of the State of Nebraska, at which all of the public offices of the State shall be kept, and at which all of the sessions of the Legislature shall hereafter be held." The bill further provided that the State University and State Agricultural College should be united as one educational institution, and should be located upon a reservation selected by the commissioners in said "Lincoln," and the necessary buildings erected as soon as funds could be secured from the sale of lots donated to the State; and that the penitentiary of the State should be "located upon a reservation selected by the said commissioners in Lincoln, or upon lands adjacent to said town of Lincoln."

Immediately on the adjournment of the Legislature, the commissioners—Governor David Butler, Secretary T. P. Kennard, and Auditor John Gillespie—entered upon their duties. They traveled over the country, personally surveyed the lands from which the selection was to be made on which the new capital was to be located, and after a careful survey of all the lands, "due regard being had to its accessibility from all parts of the State," they selected as the future capital of the State of Nebraska the site on which the city of Lincoln now stands. The wisdom of that selection has been vindicated by the marvelous growth of the city, and the general prosperity of the State. Lincoln is to-day the great railroad center of the State, easy of access from every part of our commonwealth.

The city was platted into lots, blocks, and reservations according to the provisions of the act of the Legislature, and the following September the lots were offered at public sale. I had the privilege of attending this public sale, and saw the first lot in the city of Lincoln sold at auction.

There were only a few houses then in the new town. Many felt that accommodations for those attending the sales would be limited, hence they came with tents and covered wagons, bringing with them their own provisions. The public square, where the Government post-office now stands, was covered with a heavy crop of prairie-grass, and furnished a delightful camping-ground for those in attendance. Here they pitched their tents, and camped during the sales.

Judge Cadman kept the hotel in the stone house which was formerly the old stone seminary building. At this hotel the commissioners, the writer, and many friends from Nebraska City were entertained. No pains were spared by the judge and his large-hearted wife to make us all as comfortable as it was possible for us to be made under the circumstances. The three days of sale were memorable days, and will never be forgotten by those who were present. The first day was a gloomy one. During the forepart of the day there was a drizzling rain. There were not as many people present as was expected, and the commissioners felt as gloomy and sad as the weather looked dark and forbidding. In the afternoon we followed the commissioners to the northeast corner of the plat, and the first lot, in block one, was offered for sale. Governor Butler bid the minimum price. Rev. J. G. Miller overbid the governor twenty-five cents, and the first lot in the future great city of Lincoln was knocked down to him for forty dollars and twenty-five cents. The bidding in the afternoon was very slow and dull. There was no enthusiasm whatever. But few were willing to take the risk of a purchase, as the success of the scheme was a very doubtful one. Only a few lots were offered, when the governor announced the sales closed until the next day at nine o'clock. At the close of the first day's sales the success of the new project looked doubtful in the extreme. I think all the commissioners felt that the whole thing was a complete failure.

That night a syndicate was formed, mostly of men from Nebraska City, with a capital of fifteen thousand dollars. This amount the syndicate agreed to invest in lots, also to bid on every lot offered for sale. Rev. J. G. Miller agreed to invest fifteen hundred dollars in lots. Mr. James Sweet was authorized to bid for the syndicate. The sales began at nine o'clock, and the bidding at once became lively.

The people became enthusiastic, and the enthusiasm kept up during the whole day. The day closed most hopefully, eighteen thousand dollars worth of lots having been disposed of. The success of the wonderful undertaking was assured. Doubts and fears left the minds of the commissioners. Every one interested in the movement was jubilant. The dense cloud that had hung so long over the friends of the movement broke into fragments, scattered, and entirely disappeared, and the bright sun of future success poured his genial rays upon all. In a short time money enough was secured from the sale of lots to build the new State-house.

Plans and specifications for the new State-house were adopted by the commissioners. The contract for the building was at once let, and the foundation was laid before cold weather.

There is an unwritten history connected with the carrying forward of this great undertaking, known only to the commissioners and a few of the older settlers of the county. At almost every step, from the very first, the commissioners were met with difficulties. Obstacle after obstacle rose before them, barrier after barrier impeded them in their progress. These obstacles, however, were overcome; these barriers, one after another, gave way before their untiring energy, and at last victory crowned their efforts. The building was ready for occupancy the following winter. All the State offices were moved from Omaha to Lincoln, and in January, 1869, the Nebraska State Legislature was held in the new capital.

In the spring of 1868, "Lincoln" first appeared upon the Minutes of the Nebraska Annual Conference, and the writer was appointed pastor. The town contained a population of some two hundred souls. There was no parsonage, beautifully and richly furnished; no large society to greet the pastor and his family, and give them a royal welcome and a grand reception. The pastor built his own house, and furnished it as best he could. While our house was being finished, Mrs. Davis did her cooking in the largest kitchen we ever had, and never once complained for the want of room. The ceiling was high, the floor beautifully carpeted with living green, the ventilation perfect, and our appetites of the very best. Here we lived a number of days in the most roomy apartment we ever had.

We found sixteen members of the Church, including men, women, and children, and a small church on Tenth Street, inclosed only. We found another thing we did not like so well. On this shell of a house we found what the little girl called " the latest improvement "—a four-hundred-dollar mortgage.

We went to work, finished the building, and consecrated it to the worship of Almighty God, Dr. W. B. Slaughter preaching the dedicatory sermon. At the end of one year the building became too small for the congregations. The trustees authorized the pastor to dispose of the church, and the next week I sold it to the School Board of the city for a school-house. We then built a frame building on M Street, on the lots given by the State to the Church. This building was afterwards enlarged. In this the congregation worshiped for a number of years. Finally it gave way to the present elegant and massive church, known as "Saint Paul." The city grew rapidly from the beginning, and the Church kept pace with the material development of the city. Other denominations organized societies. Earnest, faithful pastors led on these societies, and soon good houses of worship were erected; and to-day the Presbyterians, Congregationalists, Baptists, Episcopalians, Christians, and Roman Catholics, all have elegant churches—churches that would be an honor and a credit to any city of the land. The membership of our Church increased very rapidly, and soon we had a large society of intelligent, live, working members.

Among the first members were Simon C. Elliott, James Kimball and wife, A. K. White and wife, John Cadman and wife, J. Schoolcraft and wife, C. N. Baird and wife, A. J. Cropsey and wife, Mrs. W. Lamb, Mrs. Metcalf, Dr. Strickland and wife, and E. G. Coldwell and wife. That little handful has multiplied until, instead of one small church, there are seven, and the city has grown from a population of two hundred to near sixty thousand souls.

Though the beginnings were not very propitious, and the outlook was anything but flattering, yet the longer we remained the better pleased we became. We left the charge at the end of three years with a membership of two hundred and two, and never had the privilege of serving a more pleasant people.

Lincoln is not only a city of commerce and of Churches, but a city of education. Here is located the State University, the Nebraska Wesleyan University, the Christian University, the Second Advent University, and other denominations are looking to Lincoln as the place to locate their universities. Here, where only thirty years ago the antelope gamboled, the buffalo roamed, the coyote barked, and the war-cry of the wild savage resounded, stands a great city—the railroad center, the educational center, and the religious center of a great and powerful State. Prophecy is fulfilled. The desert rejoices and blossoms as the rose.

CHAPTER XVI.

ONE OF THE EARLY PIONEERS.

Rev. Z. B. Turman the First Preacher in Lancaster County—Salt Creek Circuit—Great Revival—Coon-meat—Preaching to "Spotted Horse" and his Warriors—The Captive Squaw and her Sad Fate—A Mush-and-milk Tea—Indian Troubles—The New Ulm Massacre.

As Rev. Z. B. Turman was so intimately connected with the early history of Lancaster County, and not only with the county, but the early history of the Territory as well, it seems eminently fitting that I should speak more fully with regard to him and his labors. There were many thrilling events connected with the early history of Brother Turman's work in Nebraska which can but be of very great interest and profit to the reader. At the second session of the Kansas and Nebraska Conference, in 1857, the Salt Creek Mission was formed, and Zenas B. Turman was appointed preacher in charge. The first sermon ever preached in the county of Lancaster was by Brother Turman. This was in 1857, and in the private house of James Eatherton, some twelve miles south of where the city of

Lincoln now stands. The same year he preached the first sermon ever preached on the present site of Lincoln. Salt Creek Mission embraced seven counties, and Brother Turman established sixteen preaching-places. The settlements were sparse, and confined to the streams, and the distance from one to the other was often very great. Over these prairies, under the burning rays of the summer sun, and the fierce winds, blinding storms, and terrible winter blizzards, Brother Turman rode from settlement to settlement, and calling the people together in their rude dwellings, proclaimed to them the Word of life. All over this part of the State we see to-day the grand results of the sacrifices and toils of this noble man of God. The Church planted by him has arisen in beauty, grandeur, and glory, and we now enjoy its sacred privileges.

I have been intimately acquainted with Brother Turman for thirty years, and I have often heard him tell of his work in the State in an early day; but never have I heard a murmur escape from his lips. He has always been a genial, uncomplaining, happy, sunny-hearted minister of the gospel.

The winter of 1858 witnessed one of the most powerful revivals of religion under his labors, near where Louisville now stands, that was ever known in that region of the country. The singing, praying, and rejoicing could be heard for miles away. The people said, "The only reason why there were not more converted, was because there were no more people to convert." The revival swept the entire community into the Church—men, women, and children. During this revival, a young man by the name of J. B. Ford was most wonderfully saved. Brother Turman said of him: "He was the most powerful man in prayer I ever heard in my life. His appeals to the Father of all mercies were clothed in such eloquent and powerful strains, that it seemed heaven and earth were coming together." At the following quarterly meeting Brother Ford was licensed to preach, and soon after left the State and returned to the East. What the future history of that promising young man was we know not. For aught we know, he may to-day be upon the walls of Zion, preaching the "everlasting gospel." Waves of hallowed influence were started at that meeting that have been widening and rolling on ever since, and will continue to go on widening their circles and rolling on forever. "The good men do, lives after them." It never dies. It lives and moves, and its power is felt through all the ages. By our words and looks and acts, we may send out an influence that will tell upon the happiness of men forever.

During this winter there was no grain, and "Jack," Brother Turman's horse, had to eat potatoes. These he learned to eat with a relish, and he did nicely. At one time "Jack" was offered some old corn. It was so poor and musty, however, that he refused to eat it. Brother Turman ate bread made from the same lot of corn without making any complaints or asking any questions. In speaking of this, he once said to the writer: "We have reason; horses have not. We eat to satisfy hunger; horses, to suit their taste. We have souls; they have not. We ought to take the better care of their bodies." Not only did the stock fare hard during that winter in consequence of the scarcity of grain, but the people fared hard as well. Their tables did not groan under the weight of sweetmeats and delicious viands. Their fare was plain but substantial, and such as the people had they freely gave to their pastor. The good people invited him to sit with them at their tables, and often the only meat they had was raccoon. Whether he really relished the raccoon or not, I do not know. I am inclined to think he felt a little as the man did who was asked, after having taken a meal on 'coon, "Do you like it?" He replied: "I can eat it, but I do not hanker after it." Chickens were scarce. He never got any of these birds. They went to the more highly-favored ministers, who labored among more highly-favored people.

During this winter he received a request from "Spotted Horse," a chief among the Pawnee Indians, to go and preach to him and his people. Brother Turman obeyed the call, went out and met the chief, with his warriors, at their reservation on the south side of the Platte River, just opposite Fremont. He preached the gospel to these Red-men of the plains. He told them of God's infinite love in the gift of his Son. He told them the wonderful story of the incarnation; how Jesus, the Son of God, came down into this world; suffered; was crucified; died, and was buried; and on the third day rose from the grave, and ascended up into heaven! He told them of the tragedy of Calvary, and its attendant phenomena; how the rocks rent, the earth quaked, the sun veiled his face and refused to look upon the awful scene; how the graves opened, and the dead came forth! He told them that Jesus suffered all this in order that they, as well as the white men, might be saved. They listened with the greatest interest and the most rapt attention, and treated Brother Turman with the highest respect and the most profound reverence. The chief and all his warriors kneeled down during prayer, and looked upon the minister as a messenger from the skies. After the services were over, "Spotted Horse" said: "We believe every word you say. Our forefathers had the 'Great Book' [referring to the Bible], but lost it." Spotted Horse was a man of more than ordinary mind for an Indian, but remained a savage and died the same.

Brother Turman was never maltreated by the Indians, although he very frequently met them, and often preached to them. But on this occasion he was very uneasy, and not a little fearful, not that they would do him personal violence, but that they would take all his clothing from him, and that he would be compelled to return to the settlements in a nude condition. This they had done with others, and he greatly feared he would suffer the same fate. They eyed him very closely, and with the greatest curiosity examined all his clothing. He was finally greatly relieved, however, by getting away with only the loss of his black cravat.

At one time, while visiting their reservation, he saw a young squaw whom they had taken captive. She was a Sioux, and had been taken captive by the Pawnees in one of their raids. The Sioux and Pawnees were bitter enemies, and were at war with each other. It was the custom of the Pawnees, when an Indian squaw was taken prisoner, to give her to any one of their men who might desire her for his wife. If no one desired her, then their barbarous custom was to put her to death. In this case no one desired the young and handsome Sioux squaw for a wife. The poor captive was in the greatest agony. She knew very well what the terrible result would be. Brother Turman could do nothing. He did not dare interfere. A band of the Indians started to the grove near by with their victim, the poor captive weeping most bitterly as they disappeared. Soon after the Indians returned, but the girl was not with them. All was quiet. Not a word was spoken. The silence of death reigned throughout the Indian village. All knew the fate of the young and beautiful captive. She had paid the penalty of her captivity.

Such is life among the wild savages. How much they need the gospel! How long will it be ere the barbarous tribes of our world shall be lifted from their barbarity, and made the happy recipients of the refining, purifying, and elevating effects of the gospel? "How long, O Lord, how long?"

Along the valley of the Great Platte, up and down Salt Creek, the Blue, the Nemaha, Weeping Water, Walnut Creek, and Wahoo, Brother Turman first blew the gospel-trumpet. Along all these streams, and over the hills and plains of this vast region, he sowed the seed of gospel truth, and the seed sowed by him in that early day was like a "handful of corn in the earth on the top of the mountains; the fruit thereof shakes like Lebanon." He saw the stately elk, the agile antelope, the fierce coyote, the mighty buffalo, roaming over the wild prairies where the marvelous cities of Lincoln and Beatrice now stand.

The first Methodist class in Lancaster County was organized in Brother Eatherton's house in 1857. At that time Brother Eatherton said to Brother Turman: "Do you think this country will ever be settled up?" Brother Turman replied: "Not till the next comet strikes the earth." They imagined that ages would pass before this country would amount to anything at all. Many had serious doubts whether their farms were worth the Government price—one dollar and twenty-five cents per acre. But a wonderful change soon came over their dreams. This supposed worthless country has become one of the garden-spots of the earth.

In 1859, Brother Turman was appointed to the Fontenelle Circuit. Here he found three men professing to be heralds of the cross, who believed that God from all eternity had foreordained whatsoever comes to pass. When they told him their belief, he said: "The cold tremors ran over me."

Soon after reaching Fontenelle, having fully

taken in the situation, he felt deeply impressed that a revival of religion was greatly needed. He sent for Brother L. W. Smith, of Fremont, to come and assist him in a protracted effort. The meeting began with considerable interest. The Calvinists were present and took part in the services. Brother Turman was compelled, by ministerial courtesy, to treat them as co-laborers in the vineyard of the Lord. This was very hard for Brother Turman to do, and Brother Smith as well, after these Calvinists had proclaimed their belief in the "horrible decrees."

At an experience meeting one of these ministers gave in his testimony. He said: "I never was converted right out like many others; but my mother was a pious woman, and I naturally grew up into a pious state." Brother Turman thought religion was a work of grace, not of nature, and that men were converted by the power of God, and not by natural growth.

One of the ministers of the village invited them to tea. They gladly accepted the invitation, but when they sat down at the supper-table they were not a little surprised to find mush and milk instead of tea. Brother Turman was very much disappointed. He had his heart set on an excellent supper, and, as he never liked mush and milk, to be compelled to eat what he had no relish for at all, was really an affliction.

At this time there were serious troubles with the Indians. They had committed various depredations against the whites, and the settlers were constantly harassed by these marauding bands. On the south side of the Platte River, just opposite Fremont, stood a village of some four thousand Pawnees. In July, 1859, the Sioux came down in a body, attacked and completely routed them. The Pawnees fled from their foes, crossed the Platte, and passed up the Elkhorn River. Along this stream were a few settlers, and they were in the bounds of Brother Turman's circuit. As the Indians passed up the river they killed and drove away the settlers' stock, plundered their houses, killed some of the inhabitants, and committed many other depredations.

At the hour of midnight these outraged people reached Fontenelle, hungry, weary, and almost frightened to death. They told the sad story of the violence received from the Indians. The next morning the citizens of Fontenelle, sixty in number, armed themselves as best they could, and on horseback started in pursuit of the murderous savages. Brother Turman, fully believing the Savior's words, "They that take the sword shall perish with the sword," joined the company, and aided in bringing to justice the bloodthirsty criminals. They followed the In-

dians to a point some five miles north of where
West Point now stands, and here they found a
house belonging to a Mormon, in which were a
number of Indians. Whether or not the Mormon aided the savages in their dastardly work is
not known. They immediately surrounded the
house; the Indians rushed out, and firing on the
whites, wounded one of them in the arm. The
whites returned the fire, and in the skirmish
succeeded in taking one of the Indians a prisoner. With him they started back to Fontenelle.
Passing near the bank of the Elkhorn, the boys
not watching their prisoner very closely, he leaped
into the stream, and diving, swam for some distance under the water, then arose, and, reaching
the opposite bank, made his escape.

Great excitement prevailed, and it was generally believed that the Pawnees would at once
begin a war of extermination against the frontier
settlements. Governor Black was notified, and at
the head of an expedition, composed of infantry,
cavalry, and artillery, started in pursuit of the Indians. When he reached Fontenelle, Brother Turman entered the expedition as chaplain. Some
distance beyond West Point the Indians were
overtaken, and Governor Black demanded of
Spotted Horse, the chief, why he had been disturbing the settlers. His reply was: "My warriors will not obey me." A parley ensued, and he

was finally given the choice, either to give up the braves who had committed the depredations, and to pay the expenses of the expedition out of the moneys then due his people from the Government, or to fight. He chose the former, surrendered seven braves, and signed an agreement authorizing the keeping back certain moneys belonging to them from the Government. All but one of the braves surrendered made their escape. The expedition returned, and the troops were disbanded, and the Government paid the Indians all that was due them, leaving the expedition to pay its own expenses; the Indians thus faring better at the hands of the Government than the whites. This was the end of what was called the "Pawnee war."

In 1862, Brother Turman traveled the Dakota Circuit. During this year what was known as the New Ulm Massacre took place, in which nine hundred whites were wantonly and in the most cruel manner put to death. Many of them were impaled on sharp stakes by the inhuman savages, and left to die a lingering and most painful death.

While on this circuit he received into the Church Brother and Sister Wiseman, and at their home in Cedar County preached the gospel. Brother and Sister Wiseman were called to suffer what but few in this world are called to suffer. During the Indian troubles in 1863, Brother Wiseman and Brother Turman joined General Sully's command, with other citizens of the county, and while they were absent and in pursuit of the Indians, Mrs. Wiseman went to Yankton, a few miles away. While away, the Indians attacked their children, and killed them all—six in number. Four were killed outright, the older one being a boy seventeen years old. They had evidently done noble battle in defense of their sister and brothers. Nancy, fifteen years old, lived three days, but never spoke. Her body had suffered the most brutal outrages from the bloodthirsty savages. The youngest of the family, a little five-year old boy, lay on the bed disemboweled, and when his mother came in he said to her, "Indians did it," and died.

Such were some of the thrilling scenes through which Brother Turman passed during the early settlement of the State, in laying the foundations of the Church.

CHAPTER XVII.

DISTRICT INCIDENTS.

Eleventh Nebraska Conference—Bishop Ames—Old Sermons—U. P. R. R. completed—Rapid Growth of the Church—Hastings—Overtaken in a Fearful Storm—Three Memorable Quarterly Meetings—Sad Death of a Worldling—The Dutchman's Curse—The Confused Hostess—No Desire to Dance.

THE eleventh session of the Nebraska Annual Conference was held in Lincoln, beginning March 29, 1871. Bishop Ames presided. This was his fourth visit to Nebraska. Being personally acquainted with many of the preachers, he received a cordial welcome. His sermon on Sabbath morning was a masterpiece. His text was Rev. xix, 10: "The testimony of Jesus is the spirit of prophecy."

A few months afterwards he preached the same sermon in Washington. A correspondent of the *Central Christian Advocate*, in writing to that paper said in substance: "I heard Bishop Ames preach this sermon in St. Louis thirty years ago. It was delivered yesterday with the same power, the same fire, and the same wonderful effect it was thirty years previously." Age and use had done it no harm, but had rather sharpened its edge and increased its force and power. A sermon need be none the less efficient, elegant, and powerful because of age. A faithful minister may lop off, add to, and retouch an old sermon until it will sparkle and flame with beauty and power. I think it was Whitefield who said he had to preach a sermon the thirtieth time before he could preach it perfectly. A minister ought not to preach an old sermon unless he makes it better every time he delivers it; then every time it will be new.

General Sheridan made a little speech in London that electrified the world. All at the time thought it impromptu. It was published and commented upon by many of the papers of Europe and America. It was afterwards ascertained, however, that it had been carefully written and rewritten, touched and retouched, until every sentence was a polished gem. Then it was perfectly committed to memory, and at the proper time delivered with overwhelming effect.

Abraham Lincoln's famed speech at Gettysburg was thought by some to be impromptu. It is said that just before reaching Gettysburg he took a slip of paper and jotted down the notes for it. But, without doubt, previously every sentence had been carefully thought out, and every word weighed.

The speech was brief, but every sentence was a diamond of the first water. Splendid productions are the result of deep thought and hard labor. A splendid sermon, carefully and prayerfully prepared, may be repeated a hundred times, before new audiences, with increasing rather than diminishing power.

The three years preceding 1871 were years of great prosperity in the young State.

One of the great events of the nineteenth century was the completion of the Union Pacific and Central Pacific Railroads. This wonderful event took place May 10, 1869. "On that day two oceans were united, a continent was spanned with iron bands, and a revolution was accomplished in the commerce of the world. California shook hands with New York, and the mingled screams of steam-whistles upon engines constructed three thousand miles distant waked the echoes of the mountains."

No State in the Union shared more largely the grand results of that most wonderful achievement than Nebraska. This great highway of the Nation runs through the entire length of the State from east to west, a distance of over four hundred miles. Along this public highway, up the great valley of the Platte, thousands of emigrants came to settle and make their permanent homes. The admission of Nebraska as a State into the Union, and the building of the Union Pacific Railroad gave to it a new and wonderful impetus.

The Burlington and Missouri River Railroad was pushing its way to the West. Emigration was pouring in from the East. The Church was "enlarging the place of her tents, stretching forth her curtains, lengthening her cords, and strengthening her stakes." Everywhere Churches were springing up and growing most rapidly.

Bishop Ames, being a Western man, readily took in the situation, and planned the work accordingly.

In 1870 there were three districts and forty stations and circuits. This year the bishop made five districts and fifty-nine stations and circuits, an increase of two districts and nineteen stations and circuits over last year. I was appointed presiding elder of the Lincoln District, which embraced the counties of Lancaster, Cass, Polk, Hamilton, Adams, Clay, and Fillmore, the eastern half and northern part of Seward, the west half of Otoe, and all of Saunders and Butler Counties, except a few appointments in the northern part of these counties, including an area of about five thousand miles. My first district, in 1861, embraced all the territory south of the Platte River; my new district was only about one-fifth as large as my first.

In addition to the twelve appointments assigned

me at the Conference, Bishop Ames requested me to superintend the work on the line of the Burlington and Missouri River Railroad as far west as Fort Kearney, and organize and supply the work as fast as the necessities of the case might demand. The western terminus of the Burlington and Missouri River Railroad at this time was Fairmont. I immediately employed Rev. George W. Gue, transferred from the Central Illinois Conference, to go into Fillmore County and organize a circuit. He went to work, visiting the people, and preaching to them in their cabins, sod-houses, "dug-outs," and tents, and succeeded in organizing several classes, receiving into the Church ninety-nine members.

There were no towns west of Fairmont, south of the Platte River. The place where Hastings now stands was then an untrodden prairie, save by the Indians and wild animals that roamed the plains. That year Walter Micklen homesteaded the quarter-section of land on which a part of the city of Hastings now stands. It seems almost incredible, nevertheless it is true that, only twenty years ago, the land now occupied by the city of Hastings belonged to the Government, and the thought of a city being built there had never entered the mind of a living soul. Where only twenty years ago nothing was seen growing but the wild prairie-grass, and the beautiful prairie-flowers, and the only inhabitants were the savage

Red-men and the wild beasts, to-day stands a great city, which is one of the great railroad centers of the State, and which is destined to go on increasing in wealth and population for all time. Hastings has had a marvelous growth. Her future brightens every year.

Three new charges were organized during the year, and there was a net increase in the membership of eight hundred and forty-three. In my report to the Conference at the close of the year I said: "At Fairmont, nine months ago, there was not a single house; nothing but the wild, unbroken prairie, stretching away in every direction, as far as vision could extend. Now these prairies are dotted all over with houses; large farms have been opened, thousands of acres have been broken and prepared for crops this season. Fairmont was then nothing but a grassy plain; now it is a thriving village with five stores, a large hotel, a beautiful church, with a live and intelligent membership. As I have traveled over these counties, and looked upon this beautiful and most delightful country, with its broad and undulating prairies, its many winding streams, skirted with timber, meandering in every direction; with its deep black soil, unsurpassed in richness; as I have mingled with the settlers in their rude dwellings, and partaken of their hospitalities, in the cabin, the sod-house, and the 'dug-out;' as I have conversed with them upon their present and future prospects; as I have heard them tell of the many friends away back in Eastern States that were soon coming to join them in their Western homes, it has seemed that I could almost hear 'the tramp of the coming millions,' and see villages and cities rising in every direction, and farms crowning every hillside and beautifying every valley; and then, as I have thought of the great work for the Church to accomplish in this new land, I have involuntarily exclaimed, 'Who is sufficient for these things?' We tremble when we think of the responsibilities resting upon us as God's servants. Here must be laid deep and broad the foundations of our Zion. This country must be given to God. These 'coming millions' must be won to Christ. These villages and cities must be crowded with churches. God's people must breast the waves of wickedness flowing into these cities, villages, and rural districts. The religious element must keep pace with the material development of the State, or we as a Church will be culpable, and on our skirts the blood of immortal souls, at the judgment day, will be found. I have held meetings in the beautiful church, in the tented grove, in the frame and sod schoolhouse, in private dwellings built of sod, and in the 'dug-out,' and in all these places of worship—some of them rude sanctuaries indeed—and have witnessed the most signal displays of divine power in the conversion of souls. And the many happy meetings we have had in these places of worship will never be erased from memory. I have been forcibly reminded of the fact that happiness comes not from surroundings, but from within, and have changed that couplet a little, and sung,

> 'Sod-houses palaces prove,
> If Jesus dwells with us there.'"

Many interesting events took place while I was traveling this district.

On June 10, 1871, I left home and started for my quarterly meeting on the Seward Circuit. About four o'clock in the afternoon I was overtaken by the heaviest rain and hail storm of the season. I was on the open prairie and miles from any house, and wholly unprotected from the storm. The only thing for me to do was to make the best of it—"grin and bear it." I was completely drenched with the rain, and severely pelted with the hail. My poor ponies seemed to suffer more than I did myself from the violence of the storm. They held their heads down between their forelegs, doubled themselves up, turned from one side of the road to the other, and at one time stood stock-still, and my whalebone whip was powerless to make them move an inch. Providentially, the hail lasted only a few moments, or we should all have perished. At Lincoln great damage was done. Culverts were washed away, cellars flooded, houses unroofed, and goods and property damaged to the amount of many thousand dollars. The storm passed, the clouds broke away, and the sun came forth shining more brightly than ever. Just at dark we reached Seward, covered with mud, wet to the skin, sore from the pelting hail, and in miserable plight generally. I stopped over night with my old friend, Brother Davis. The next morning I went fifteen miles northwest, up Lincoln Creek, to where the Quarterly Meeting was to be held. The meeting was in a sod school-house. The walls were of sod, two feet thick; the roof was of plank laid on rafters. In the fall the planks were covered with sod, to keep out the cold. In this rude house, at the appointed hour, the people assembled, and God came with them.

In the early settlement of Ohio and Indiana, the people lived in log cabins, with floors made of puncheon. But here, on the prairies of Nebraska, the early pioneers lived and worshiped God in houses made of sod—built entirely of the turf, from foundation to roof. Along the streams, where logs could be procured, there were a few cabins.

At two o'clock I preached to a most devout and attentive congregation, held Quarterly Conference, and then, in company with the pastor, Brother Burlingame, went to Brother Reynolds's, one of the stewards, to stay over night. The house was small. It had but one room, which served as parlor, dining-room, kitchen, and bedroom. About four rods from the house I discovered a new building, made of logs, seven feet square and five feet high. In this strange building was a door three feet high and about two and a half feet wide. I wondered what it was for. I said to myself, "It must be a chicken-house." Supper over, the hour for retiring came, and after the evening prayer I was conducted to the seven by seven building. Stooping, I entered the little door and found a comfortable bed, with clean, snow-white sheets. Here the presiding elder was stowed away, and slept soundly till morning. When I awoke, the sun was pouring his mild genial rays through the wide cracks between the logs. I arose greatly refreshed and feeling strong for the day's work before me.

A large awning in front of the school-house had been made of boughs from the trees that grew along the banks of the creek near by. The space beneath the awning was seated, and would accommodate as many as the house itself. Early in the morning crowds were seen coming from various directions over the new-made roads. The house was packed, the seats under the awning were filled, and many stood at the windows, and in front of the awning. Some came in their bare feet and shirt-sleeves, some on foot, and some in ox-teams. The people were all poor, having come from Eastern States to get homes under the "Homestead Law." They were poor, so far as worldly goods are concerned, but were "rich in faith and heirs of the kingdom." This their tears, their prayers, their faith, their songs and radiant countenances well attested.

What people want to make them happy is not earthly riches, but "godliness with contentment;" not fine mansions, but Jesus in the soul.

November 24th, of this year, I held a quarterly meeting on this circuit, twelve miles north of Seward, at the private residence of Brother Crosby. Brother Crosby was a steward, and one of the leading members of the Church. The dwelling was made of sod, and covered with the same material, but within the walls were plastered beautifully white, giving it an air of neatness and comfort. Brother Crosby and his excellent and amiable wife made all feel at home. At two o'clock I preached and held Quarterly Conference. Late in the afternoon the wind changed to the north, it began to snow, and the weather became intensely cold. Brother Wilkerson and family rode four miles in an ox-team that night, facing that terrible storm, to meeting. When they reached the house they were so chilled and so near frozen they could hardly get out of the wagon, and into the house. As they entered, the people were singing,

"We're going home, we're going home."

An excellent spirit pervaded the congregation. Although almost frozen, Brother Wilkerson caught the inspiration in an instant; his eye kindled, his countenance lit up with unearthly joy, and he said to me as he stood by the stove warming: "When half-way here I came very near going back, but I bless God I came on." In two minutes after he entered the room he seemed more than rewarded for his cold and dreary ride. On Sabbath morning the wind blew a perfect gale, and the air was filled with snow and frost. The mercury was down to sixteen degrees below zero. Facing this storm, Brother Wilkerson and family rode four miles in an ox-team, and were with us at the love-feast at nine o'clock. I shall never forget the experience of Sister Wilkerson at that love-feast. Her face was radiant with joy. She stood on Pisgah's top, and the glories of heaven seemed all mapped out before her. Every word was an electric shock to the congregation. The angel of the new and everlasting covenant hovered over the assembly; God was with his people, and his saving power was wonderfully displayed. After preaching and administering the sacrament, several united with the Church. That meeting, in Brother

Crosby's private dwelling, on the wild and bleak prairies of Nebraska, will be remembered forever.

My next quarterly meeting was on the Milford Circuit. The place fixed for holding the meeting was a school-house, three miles west of Camden. My home during the meeting was at Brother William Staunton's. He was a cousin of the Hon. Edward Staunton, then Secretary of War under Abraham Lincoln's administration. Brother Staunton lived in a log house on the bank of a small creek. The weather was bitter cold. On Sabbath the mercury was down to twenty-eight degrees below zero, and the wind from the north was so strong it blew the shingles from the roof of the house. Water thrown into the air would freeze into ice, like bullets, before it reached the ground. It was dangerous for a person to undertake to travel any distance. A few rods from Brother Staunton's house, in the bank of the creek, was a "dug-out," or a cave dug in the side of a hill; the south end, and east and west sides, were partly made of logs, the roof was made of poles and brush covered with earth. This "dug-out" was very warm. In this Brother Fair and family lived, and here we held our quarterly meeting. In the forenoon we had two families at service, and at night three. After the sermon I called for "seekers;" four came forward and kneeled down for prayers. An unusual manifestation of the Divine presence was felt. We sang and prayed and talked until all four were clearly and powerfully converted. The storm raged fearfully without, but within we had calm, peace, joy, and spiritual victory. Thirteen years afterwards, when appointed to the York Station, I found two of those that were converted in that "dug-out" at that quarterly meeting, members of my choir, faithful and consistent Christians, and joyfully pursuing the path they entered thirteen years before. The good accomplished at that meeting, on that cold December day, will only be known in the great day of eternity. From that meeting went out a salutary influence that will go on forever. God is not only in the splendid church, where crowding thousands meet to worship him, but in the humble cabin as well, and in the unpretentious "dug-out," far away on the Western prairies.

That same winter, 1871, I left home for a two weeks' tour up into Butler and Polk Counties. I had two quarterly meetings to hold, one in Butler and one in Polk County. My course from Lincoln was northwest. I left Lincoln in the morning, and, after traveling some hours, found myself on the divide between Oak Creek and Seward. Although the road was new, one I had never traveled, I felt perfectly safe, because the points of the compass were clear in my mind, and I felt sure I was going in the right direction. I was facing the wind, and about two o'clock it began to snow, and the wind blew with increasing violence. The snow fell thicker and faster, and the wind rose higher and higher. I found I was losing the points of the compass. The blinding storm bewildered me. The road was filling with snow so fast it was with great difficulty I could see it at all. I knew very well that in a little while I should lose my way, and be entirely at the mercy of the awful storm. Silently I breathed a prayer to God for guidance. In a short time afterwards I discovered at my right a dim road leading down a deep ravine. I entered this road, and followed it for two miles, when I discovered, in a clump of trees beside a beautiful creek, a log cabin. The sight of this cabin brought joy to my heart. My fears in a moment were all gone, and I breathed easy once more. The man of the house was at the barn putting away his horses, and when I rode up, spoke to me very kindly. I requested the privilege of remaining with him during the night, and the request was most cheerfully granted. I entered the cabin, and found a splendid fire, which I greatly enjoyed after the cold day's ride. This man and his excellent wife were members of the Baptist Church, and devoted Christians. They had just returned from the grave of a neighbor, and I said to them:

"Was your neighbor a Christian?"

"O no," was the reply. "He was a man of the world. He was a very wicked man. He pretended to be an infidel, and worked on the Sabbath just as on any other day. He had bought a large tract of land and was working hard to improve it. He seemed determined to be a rich man."

"Well," I said, "how did he die?"

"Without any hope," was the reply. "A short time before he died, he said, 'O, I can not die, I can not die. If I only had my life to live over again, how differently would I live!' He exhorted his friends not to live as he had lived. 'If I could just live my life over, I would live a Christian life,' were among his last words."

It was the old story over again—the story that has been repeated all along the ages, and I fear will go on repeating itself until the trump of God shall call a wicked world to judgment—a life of sin and a death of despair. He had lived "as the fool liveth, and died as the fool dieth."

The next morning the storm had ceased, the weather greatly moderated, and I passed on to my appointment in Butler County, then on into Polk County, and after two weeks of hard labor and weary travel, returned to my home to rest only three or four days, then to go out again on a similar trip.

The last day of 1871, and the first day of 1872, I spent in Plattsmouth, holding quarterly meeting. I find in my diary the following: "The old year passed away amid very pleasant surroundings. The first day of the new year we had a most excellent love-feast; in the morning had great liberty preaching the word. A deep feeling pervaded the congregation."

The Methodist Episcopal Church has never given an uncertain sound on the temperance question, and on this she has a record of which she may well be proud. The wicked, unwittingly, often highly compliment the Church touching her unstained record on this subject. When the Rev. J. G. Miller was stationed in Plattsmouth he was at one time raising money to procure a house of worship for the Church. He went into a saloon, kept by a German, with his subscription. When he entered, the saloon-keeper made a very polite bow, stepped behind the bar, and asked him what he would take. Brother Miller said: "I am raising money to build a church, and I have a subscription here, and I have called to see how much you will give."

"What church?" said the saloon-keeper.

"The Methodist church."

"Te Metodist, te Metodist church, eh? Te Metodist dey drink no beer; dey drink no whisky; dey play no billiards. T—m te Metodist church. Me give tem no cent."

On February 17th and 18th I held quarterly meeting at Seward. Seward at this time was a thriving village of some three hundred inhabitants, and was the head of the circuit. The people came from the various appointments on the work to the meeting. Brother A. J. Combs, a young man with a soul all on fire for souls, was the pastor. Brother Combs has long since entered upon his reward. The revival flame had swept over the entire circuit. At every appointment the people were clothed with panoply divine. Some came thirty-five miles to the meeting. To a soul filled with the Holy Ghost the distance to church amounts to nothing at all. The pastor, in announcing the quarterly meeting, requested those coming from a distance to bring their own bedding, as there were but few members in Seward, and sleeping apartments were scarce. The Masonic Hall was used as a bedroom, and was filled with men during each night of the meeting. Brothers Beatty and Davis provided meals for large numbers, each feeding from thirty-five to forty, and providing sleeping apartments for the women. At every service the house was packed to its utmost capacity with devout and attentive listeners. After the sermon on Sabbath morning I was called a few blocks away to marry a couple. This I did while the collection was being taken. Then I returned to the Church, and administered the sacrament. The meeting throughout was one of great power. Many souls were converted, and the Church greatly quickened. It was a Pentecost from the beginning to the end.

In the month of February, 1872, a revival of religion took place at the Haynes School-house, in Butler County, under the labors of Rev. William Worley, assisted by Rev. Joshua Worley and Rev. James Query. Here a class was organized, and on the 20th day of the following December I held a quarterly meeting at this school-house. This was the first quarterly meeting ever held in this neighborhood. Near where this school-house stood now stands the beautiful village of Garrison. Brother Haynes lived in a "dug-out" a mile and a half away. On Saturday, when about to leave for the meeting, his wife, who was unable to attend, said to him: "Bring all to supper who will come, but do not invite any one to stay all night; and, above all, do not invite the presiding elder." Brother Haynes disregarded the instructions of his excellent wife, and took the presiding elder home with him to tea.

This disregard of his wife's request gave the good sister great distress of mind for a little while. When the elder entered the "dug-out," Sister Haynes was greatly confused, and attempted to stammer out an apology; but the elder instantly came to her relief by saying: "O, sister! a sod-house may be a palace if we have Christ with us." They were from the East, and had been used to much better things, and their present surroundings were humiliating to them in the extreme. Many years afterwards Sister Haynes said to the writer: "The look the presiding elder gave me, and the words he spoke, at once banished all my false pride." Then the thought of the elder's staying over night with them was another source of great anxiety and trouble to the heart of the good sister. What to do with him, and where to put him to sleep, were indeed perplexing questions. Just at this juncture, however, Brother Haynes greatly relieved the burdened heart of his much-distressed wife by saying that arrangements had been made for the elder to stay at a neighbor's, who lived in a *frame house*. All went to service on Saturday night; but the party living in the frame house did not put in an appearance, and the only thing for Brother Haynes to do was to invite the elder to go home with him. As Sister Haynes neared her rude "dug-out," she was greatly surprised to see a gentleman walking in company with one of her sons, carrying a valise. A nearer approach revealed to her the awful fact that the gentleman was the identical and much-dreaded elder. The elder, seeing how wonderfully confused the good sister was, endeavored, as much as possible, to relieve her embarrassment, and earnestly prayed that his stay might prove a benediction rather than an annoyance and trouble to the kind family. How much these brave men and women, in the earlier settlement of the State, suffered, not only for the necessary comforts of life, but from chagrin and humiliation as well!

The year before I was appointed to the district, while stationed in Lincoln, at the request of my presiding elder I went out and held a quarterly meeting for him on the Oak Creek Circuit. The meeting was in a private house on the bank of Oak Creek, near where the village of Raymond now stands. The good man and his wife who kindly opened the doors of their house for the meeting were not Christians. At the close of the afternoon service, on Saturday, I was cordially invited to make my home with them during the meeting. I accepted the kindly invitation, and was most pleasantly entertained by them until Monday morning. That first pleasant visit with that kind family will never be forgotten. It ripened into the warmest and most lasting Christian friendship. Though not Christians themselves, they were quite free to talk on the subject of religion. On this subject they were more than ordinarily communicative. We had several pleasant conversations on religion during my stay. On Monday morning, while my horse was being harnessed and brought to the door, I again spoke to the lady on religion. She said: "I would like to be a Christian. My husband would like to be a Christian. We have talked the matter over many times, and we expect to become Christians some day. But if we were to become Christians, we could not join your Church."

"Why not?" said I.

"Because," said she, "it is contrary to the rules of your Church for its members to dance."

"Yes, that is true," said I. She continued:

"My husband and I do not think there is any harm at all in dancing. We go to our neighbors', and have a pleasant, social dance almost every week, and we do not think there is anything wrong in it. So, of course, we could not join your Church."

I said to her: "Sister W., you get religion, and you may dance." She looked at me with surprise. I continued: "You get religion, and you will have no desire to dance." This closed the conversation. I thanked her and her good husband for their kindness, stepped into my buggy, and drove home.

At the next Conference I was appointed presiding elder of the district. Just one year from the time I held the above meeting, I went out and held another in the same neighborhood. In the meantime a small, frame school-house had been built. It was about a half mile from where the meeting was held the year before. In this school-house I held the quarterly meeting; and on Sabbath night that man and his wife were both happily converted to God, and they have been faithful and consistent members of the Church ever since. Brother C. C. White has held honorable positions in Church and State. In 1880 he was one of the lay delegates of the Nebraska Conference to the General Conference, and was an active and influential member of that body. He is alive to all the great interests of the Church. He has taken an active part in educational matters, and his deep interest is manifested by the thousands of dollars he has contributed for the promotion of Christian education in the State. I have often heard Sister White refer to the conversation we had during that meeting at her house on Oak Creek, and she has since said to me: "When you said, 'Get religion and you will have no desire to dance,' I did not believe a word you said. I did not believe you would tell a willful falsehood, nor did I believe you would willfully misrepresent, but thought you were very greatly mistaken. From the very moment I was converted I have had no desire whatever to dance."

If we are in the Church, and the desire to dance is still strong, it seems to me we have not got what Christ has for us. If Christ can not give us something better than the world gives, then it seems to me our religion does not amount to very much. Before I was converted I was passionately fond of dancing. It was the most fascinating amusement I ever engaged in. There is something about the dance and cards that is wonderfully bewitching; and yet as dearly as I loved cards, and as passionately fond of dancing as I was, the very moment I was converted the desire for these things left me, and—to the praise and glory of God I say it!—never once has it returned. When God, for Christ's sake, converted my soul, he gave me something infinitely better than the world ever gave.

I once heard the late Bishop Clark relate the following: "A most gracious revival of religion was in progress in one of the charges in Cincinnati. Night after night a young lady of wealth and fashion was seen at the altar for prayer. She was a leader in the fashionable circles of society in the city. She manifested great earnestness and was in deep mental distress, and yet could get no relief. I said to her: 'Are you willing to give up all for Christ?' 'Yes,' was the prompt reply. I knew she was passionately fond of dancing, and said: 'Are you willing to give up dancing?' She replied: 'I can be a Christian and dance.' I said: 'I am afraid you will not get religion until you are willing to give up the ball-room.' The next night after this conversation I knelt in front of her at the altar. She raised her head, and, smiling through her tears, said: 'I do n't want to dance now!' The desire for the dance left her, and she became as eminent a worker in the Church as she had previously been a leader in the fashionaable circles of the world."

Let Christ come into the heart in his fullness, then old things pass away and all things become new. Our nature's rapid tide is turned back, and all our affections flow out after God.

CHAPTER XVIII.

FURTHER ACCOUNT OF DISTRICT WORK.

MARVELOUS GROWTH — PRIVATIONS AND TOILS OF THE PREACHERS—THE CHRISTMAS-BOX — A TOUCHING INCIDENT—THE CONFERENCE OF 1873—BISHOP ANDREWS—CONFERENCE OF 1874 — BISHOP BOWMAN — DR. J. M. REID—CONFERENCE OF 1875—BISHOP GILBERT HAVEN—HIS TRIUMPHANT DEATH—REV. GEORGE WORLEY.

THE Conference year which closed March 23, 1872, had been a year of unparalleled success. The most wonderful spiritual victories had been gained all along the line. The toils and sacrifices of the ministers and their families were crowned with the most brilliant achievements. The hardships endured by these heroes and heroines in planting the Church along the frontier, in the sparsely-settled neighborhoods, are known only to themselves, to God, and "the Church of the first-born." What a grand reward awaits these pioneer heralds of the cross! Some of them have already entered upon their reward. They have gone home, and they rest from their labors, but their works follow them. They built not on other men's foundations; they laid the foundations of the Church in this new land at a time that "tried men's souls;" and others are now building on the foundations laid by these pure men and women, and cemented by their tears of suffering and sorrow. It requires neither nerve nor pluck to go to an appointment where there is a fine church, a fine parsonage, a fine membership, and a fine salary. Any ordinary man can go to an appointment like that. But it takes a man of nerve and pluck and indomitable perseverance—a man of the Pauline and Bishop Taylor type—to go where none of these things exist, and, by his faith and heroic labors, create from raw material the fine church, the fine parsonage, the fine membership, and the fine salary. This work the pioneers of Nebraska did. They counted not their lives dear unto themselves, nor the lives of their families, so that they might finish the work they were commissioned by the Master to do. Paul did not want to "build upon another man's foundation," nor do work where everything was "made ready to his hand." He swam rivers, climbed mountains, crossed oceans; was stoned, beaten with rods, imprisoned, wrecked upon the stormy sea time and again,—all that he might carry the gospel into "the regions beyond," and plant the standard of the cross where it never before had been planted. So these early pioneers carried the gospel into "the regions beyond," and planted the standard of the cross upon entirely new terri-

FURTHER ACCOUNT OF DISTRICT WORK. 271

tory; and where it was first planted, that standard still proudly waves to-day.

In 1872, Ulysses first appeared upon the Conference Minutes. The pastor appointed to this charge was impecunious—he had scarcely anything at all; but he went to work like a true Methodist preacher, laid out a circuit over a hundred miles around, organized a number of new classes, and although he had no means to procure himself a horse, having good feet and long legs, and a heart overflowing with love for God and souls, he traveled his work the whole of the year on foot. God was with him. The revival flame swept over the entire circuit, and he returned one hundred and forty members, including probationers, an increase of one hundred and sixteen during the year. Many of the preachers on the district that year did just as heroic service for the Master as Brother Reed.

We do not disparage the work of those who came after the vanguard, and are building upon the foundations they found laid and "made ready to their hand." Theirs, too, is a big work, and they, too, will receive a great reward. God " shall reward every man according to his work." But I have sometimes thought that among the multitudes that shall gather around the great white throne in the last day, those who shall stand nearest the throne, be most like the Master, have the brightest crowns, the loveliest palms, and have accorded to them the highest praise and the greatest honors, will be those who can present the longest list of sufferings for the Master, and can say, "We suffered all this for thee."

At that time there was no "Woman's Home Missionary Society" in operation. The pioneers along the frontier seldom received assistance from the East. That society to-day is doing a noble work in furnishing supplies to God's great spiritual army at the front. The picket-lines are exposed to peril and suffering now, just as they were twenty years ago. The only difference is, the lines are a little farther to the West. Some out on these picket-lines have received aid that has brought joy and gladness to their hearts, and cheer and sunshine into their homes.

One incident may be cited to show what this society is doing, and what it may continue to do. The narrative is by a minister's wife on the frontier, and was published in *The Woman's Home Mission*.

"I remember a day during one winter that stands out in my life like a boulder. The weather was unusually cold; our salary had not been regularly paid, and it did not meet our needs when it was. My husband was away traveling from one district to another much of the time.

"Our boys were well; but my little Ruth was

ailing, and, at best, none of us were decently clothed. I patched and repatched, with spirits sinking to their lowest ebb. The water gave out in the well, and the wind blew through the cracks of the floor.

"The people in the parish were kind, and generous too; but the settlement was new, and each family was struggling for itself. Little by little, at the time when I needed most, my faith began to waver. Early in life I was taught to take God at his word, and I thought my lesson was well learned. I had lived upon the promises in dark times, until I knew, as David did, who was 'my Fortress and Deliverer.' Now a daily prayer for forgiveness was all that I could offer.

"My husband's overcoat was hardly thick enough for October, and he was obliged to ride miles to attend some meeting or funeral. Many a time our breakfast was Indian cake and a cup of tea without any sugar. Christmas was coming; the children always expected their presents. I remember the ice was thick and smooth, and the boys were each craving a pair of skates.

"Ruth, in some unaccountable way, had taken a fancy that the dolls I had made were no longer suitable; she wanted a large, nice one, and insisted on praying for it. I knew it was impossible; but, O, how I wanted to give each child its present! It seemed as if God had deserted us;

but I did not tell my husband all this. He worked so earnestly and heartily, I supposed him to be hopeful as ever. I kept the sitting-room cheery with an open fire, and tried to serve our scanty meals as invitingly as I could. The morning before Christmas James was called to see a sick man. I put up a piece of bread for a lunch— it was the best I could do—wrapped my plaid shawl around his neck, and then tried to whisper a promise, as I often had, but the words died away on my lips. I let him go without it. That was a dark, hopeless day. I coaxed the children to bed early, for I could not bear their talk. When Ruth went I listened to her prayer; she asked for the last time most explicitly for her doll and for skates for her brothers. Her bright face looked so lovely when she whispered to me, 'You know I think they'll be here early tomorrow morning—early, mamma," that I thought I could move heaven and earth to save her from disappointment. I sat down alone, and gave way to the bitterest tears.

"Before long James returned, chilled and exhausted. He drew off his boots; the thin stockings slipped off with them, and his feet were red with cold. I wouldn't treat a dog that way, let alone a faithful servant. Then, as I glanced up and noticed the hard lines in his face, and the look of despair, it flashed across me that James had let go too! I brought him a cup of tea, feeling sick and dizzy at the very thought. He took my hand, and we sat for an hour, neither uttering a word. I wanted to die and meet God, and tell him his promise was n't true—my soul was so full of rebellious despair. There came a sound of bells, a quick step, and a loud knock at the door. James sprang to open it. There stood Deacon Pike. 'A box came for you by express just before dark. I brought it around as soon as I could get away. Reckoned it might be for Christmas. At any rate, they shall have it tonight. Here is a turkey my wife asked me to fetch along; and these other things, I believe, belong to you.' There was a basket of potatoes and a bag of flour. Talking all the time, he hurried in a box, and then, with a hearty good-night, rode away.

"Still, without speaking, James found a chisel and opened the box. I drew out at first a thick, red blanket, and we saw that beneath was full of clothing. It seemed at that moment as if Christ fastened upon me a look of reproach. James sat down, and covered his face with his hands. 'I can not touch them!' he exclaimed. 'I have n't been true just when God was trying me to see if I could hold out. Do you think I could not see how you were suffering, and I had no word of comfort to offer? I know now how to preach the awfulness of turning away from God.' 'James,' I said, clinging to him, 'do n't take it to heart like this. I've been to blame. I ought to have helped you. We will ask Him together to forgive us.' 'Wait a moment, dear; I can not talk now.' Then he went into another room. I knelt down, and my heart broke. In an instant all the darkness rolled away. Jesus came again, and stood before me; but now with the loving word, 'Daughter!' Sweet promises of tenderness and joy flooded my soul, and I was so lost in praise and gratitude that I forgot everything else. I do n't know how long it was before James came back, but I knew that he too had found peace. 'Now, dear wife,' said he, 'let us thank God together;' and then he poured out words of praise— Bible words, for nothing else could express our thanksgiving. It was eleven o'clock. The fire was low; and there was the great box, and nothing touched but the warm blanket we needed so much. We piled on some fresh logs, lighted two candles, and began to examine our treasures. We drew out an overcoat. I made James try it on. Just the right size! and I danced awhile around him, for all my light-heartedness had returned. Then there was a cloak, and he insisted on seeing me in it. My spirits always infected him, and we laughed like foolish children. There was a warm suit of clothes also, and three pairs of warm woolen hose. There was a dress for me, and yards of flannel; a pair of Arctic overshoes for each of us, and in mine was a slip of paper. I have it now, and mean to hand it down to my children. It was Jacob's blessing to Asher: 'Thy shoes shall be iron and brass, and as thy days, so shall thy strength be.' In the gloves—evidently for James—the same dear hand had written: 'I, the Lord thy God, will hold thy right hand, saying unto thee, Fear not, I will help thee.'

"It was a wonderful box, and packed with thoughtful care. There was a suit of clothes for each of the boys, and a little, red gown for Ruth. There were mittens, scarfs, and hoods; down in the center a box; we opened it, and there was a great wax doll. I burst into tears again, and James wept with me for joy. It was too much; and then we both exclaimed again, for close behind it came two pairs of skates. There were books for us to read—some of them I had wished to see; stories for the children to read; aprons and underclothing; knots of ribbon; a gay little tidy; a lovely photograph; needles, buttons, and thread; actually a muff, and an envelope containing a ten-dollar gold piece! At last we cried over everything we took up. It was past midnight, and we were faint and exhausted even with happiness. I made a cup of tea, cut a fresh loaf of bread, and James boiled some eggs. We drew up the table before the fire. How we enjoyed our supper! And then we sat talking over all our life, and how sure a help God had always proved.

"You should have seen the children next morning! The boys raised a shout at the sight of their skates. Ruth caught up her doll, and hugged it tightly without a word; then she went into her room, and knelt by her bed. When she came back she whispered to me, 'I knew it would be here, mamma; but I wanted to thank God just the same, you know.' 'Look here, wife; see the difference!' We went to the window, and there were the boys, out of the house already, and skating on the crust with all their might.

"My husband and I both tried to return thanks to the Church in the East that sent us the box, and have tried to return thanks unto God every day since. Hard times have come again and again; but we have trusted in him, dreading nothing so much as a doubt of his protecting care. Over and over again we have proved that 'they that seek the Lord shall not want any good thing.'"

This family represents many on duty to-day along the picket-lines of the great Northwest. I have known families like the above—pure, noble men and women, God's saints on the earth—to whose very door want had come; but there was no Woman's Home Missionary Society to help them.

During the year the membership on the Lincoln District increased ninety per cent, and the Sunday-schools and church and parsonage-building enterprises increased at the same ratio. Other districts of the Conference were abreast with Lincoln.

The Conference year ending March 24, 1873, was also a year of marvelous growth. The mighty wave of emigration from the East continued to roll into the State, and on to the western counties where land could be homesteaded. The Conference met this year at Plattsmouth. The reports were all exceedingly gratifying. Every presiding elder reported great progress on all lines of Church work. Great revivals had taken place, and hundreds had been converted and gathered into the Church. In sod churches, sod school-houses, sod dwellings, dug-outs, and in the tented grove, God's saving power had been most signally displayed in the conversion of sinners and the sanctification of believers. The plains and hills of the beautiful prairies were made to resound with praises to Almighty God.

At this Conference we first met Bishop Andrews. At first sight we feared we should not like him. These fears, however, were very soon dissipated. His kind and genial manner, his great interest in the welfare of all the preachers, his deep sympathy with them in their privations and sacrifices, won the hearts of all. We all felt that Bishop Andrews was the right man in the right place. How wonderfully we have been blessed as a Church in our superintendents! The bishop lived for a number of years in Des Moines, Iowa; and, while his home was in the West, he was, like Paul, " in journeyings often, in labors more abundant;" and since his return to the East his labors have been none the less arduous and unremitting. No class of men in the Church are harder worked than the bishops and the presiding elders. We never called on the bishop for extra work but he willingly responded, and we drew on him often.

At Weeping Water a good stone church was finished January 13, 1874, under the successful labors of Brother A. L. Folden. Bishop Andrews came over and dedicated it, and raised the necessary amount to liquidate all debts. The good people of that city who were there at that time well remember the dedicatory services. Although the dedication was on week-day, and the weather bitter cold, the house was packed to its utmost capacity, and the services throughout were most interesting. Some of the members gave more than they thought they were able to give. I really thought so myself. They deprived themselves of many of the necessaries of life that they might have a church in which to worship God. I have no doubt but God has rewarded them for their liberality. Many gracious revivals of religion have taken place in that church, and hundreds of precious souls have there been converted to God.

The next winter the bishop was with us, and dedicated the church at Syracuse; then went with us to Seward, and dedicated the church there, which had been built by Brother Folden also. Nearly all the churches built in Nebraska while the bishop resided at Des Moines were dedicated by him.

At the Plattsmouth Conference a resolution was adopted respectfully requesting the bishops to change the time of the sessions of the Nebraska Conference to the fall of the year. The request was complied with, and the next Conference year was eighteen months long.

The fourteenth session of the Nebraska Conference met at Omaha, October 1, 1874, Bishop Thomas Bowman presiding. On Sunday morning the bishop preached a masterly sermon. His subject was, "The Tyndall Prayer-test." Brother S. P. Van Doozer had given to the bishop and the cabinet some remarkable answers to prayer during the year by members of the Church who lived in the district scourged by the grasshoppers. The bishop used these with telling effect and power in illustrating his sermon on Sunday morning.

The Conference year had been one of great trial, both to preachers and people. The grasshopper scourge was upon us. In addition to the destructive grasshoppers, the crops had been cut short by the dry weather and hot winds; so what the grasshoppers did not eat, the hot winds, to a great extent, destroyed. There are a few days almost every year when we feel the hot winds from the south, but we have never known a year in which there were so many days with hot winds from the south as there were in 1874. The hot winds felt just as though they came from a furnace. It did no good whatever to use a fan. If you did, it was blowing hot air into your face. Many farmers that year became discouraged and left the State. Some of them never returned; others, after years, returned, greatly regretting that they were so foolish as to have left the State. Those who remained and were industrious have become independent, and many of them affluent.

Dr. J. M. Reid, missionary secretary, came with the bishop to this Conference. He was greatly moved when he heard of the privations and sufferings of the people. He said to the writer: "I wish I had known the condition of

FURTHER ACCOUNT OF DISTRICT WORK. 283

affairs in your Conference sooner. If I had, I could have secured some more missionary money for you from the Contingent Fund; but I can't do it now." He placed in my hands twenty-five dollars, saying: "This is from a Christian lady of New York City. She wants you to give it to five of the most needy Methodist preachers' wives in your district." I think he gave the same amount to the other elders. I said to him: "What is the lady's name? I should like to know the name of the generous, Christian lady who makes this donation to the wives of my preachers, and I am sure the wives of the preachers would be glad to know." "That does not matter. She does not care to have her name known," said he. I felt certain in my own mind that it was the Doctor's generous and big-hearted wife that had made the gift. I gave five dollars each to five of the most needy preachers' wives on my district, and they received the present with grateful hearts. I often wished that the giver knew just how much good that donation did; it was a real benediction to these toil-worn, self-sacrificing women. The giver will most assuredly receive her reward.

A full account of the grasshopper scourge may be found elsewhere in this book.

The next Conference was held in Lincoln, beginning September 15, 1875, Bishop Gilbert

Haven presiding. The good bishop has long since gone to his reward. His death was a shock to the whole Church, and the whole Nation as well. His fame was not only national, but worldwide. His departure from earth was triumphant. Among his last words were: "I am floating! I am surrounded with angels!" Like the sainted Cookman, one of his dearest friends, he went "sweeping through the gates, washed in the blood of the Lamb."

The four years from 1871 to 1875 were years of great spiritual and numerical prosperity. During these four years the appointments in the Conference increased from sixty-four to one hundred and six, and the membership from five thousand one hundred and fifty-three to nine thousand and fifty-six.

In my report to the Conference, I said: "We must remember, however, that the strength and influence of a Church does not always depend upon her numbers. She may be numerically strong, but weak in influence and spiritual power. If the spirituality of the Church does not keep pace with her numerical strength, we may well fear and tremble. 'Onward!' should be the rallying cry of every Christian. Every mountain of faith and joy climbed by the Christian points to a still higher mountain beyond for him to climb, and every mountain summit thus gained increases his power with God and men; and he should remember with joy that, however high the mountain of faith and joy may be to which he has attained,

'Still there's more to follow.'

The Church has not only grown in numbers but in spiritual power."

I can not close this chapter without a personal reference to Rev. George Worley. Brother Worley was one of the most successful, devoted, and self-sacrificing local preachers it has ever been my privilege to know. I first met him in 1869. While on the district, I employed him at different times as a supply, and no preacher ever did more effective work. Revival after revival swept over the different charges he traveled. His crown will not be a starless one; and his pure-spirited and large-hearted wife will have a crown, methinks, that will flame with as many brilliant stars as that of her husband. James, their son, has for years been one of our successful missionaries in China; William and Thomas are both honored ministers in the Church at home—the former a member of the North Nebraska Conference, the latter of the Nebraska Conference. I shall never forget the many kindnesses received from Brother and Sister Worley. All honor to such fathers and mothers in Israel! On the fifth day of March, 1890, at the ripe age of seventy-two, from her home in Garrison, Nebraska, Sister Worley bid adieu to earthly friends, and passed in triumph to her heavenly home. A few moments before her happy spirit took its upward and eternal flight, she repeated one verse of her favorite hymn:

"O would my Lord his servant meet!
  My soul would stretch her wings in haste,
Fly fearless through death's iron gate,
  Nor feel the terrors as she passed."

CHAPTER XIX.

FURTHER ACCOUNT OF DISTRICT WORK—
CONTINUED.

APPOINTED TO OMAHA DISTRICT—COLUMBUS—OSCEOLA—
RISING CITY—DAVID CITY—THE WORK IN OMAHA—
CONFERENCE AT FALLS CITY—BISHOP FOSTER—AP-
POINTED THE SECOND TIME TO NEBRASKA CITY DIS-
TRICT—A REMARKABLE MEETING—WEST NEBRASKA
MISSION FORMED—DR. T. B. LEMON—DIVISION OF THE
CONFERENCE.

AT the Conference of 1875 we were appointed by Bishop Haven to the Omaha District. The district extended as far west as Columbus, and embraced territory on both sides of the Platte River. Columbus first appeared as an appointment in the Minutes of the Nebraska Conference in 1867, Joel Warner the pastor. At the end of the Conference year seven members were reported. At this Conference the appointment was dropped from the list, and did not appear again until 1871. At this Conference it appears again in the Minutes as one of the appointments, with L. F. Whitehead as pastor. For some years the growth of the society was very slow.

When we took the district in 1875, Columbus

was the most western appointment, was a small town, and our Church was very weak; but that little town has grown to a city, and that little, weak Church to a strong one, and it is now one of the leading stations of the North Nebraska Conference. Osceola, the county-seat of Polk County, just south of Columbus, was then a small village, with only a few houses. Among the first settlers at this point were Rev. James Query, H. C. Query, Wm. Query, G. W. Kenyon, and J. F. Campbell.

Rev. James Query was a local preacher in the Methodist Episcopal Church, and, if I am rightly informed, preached the first sermon ever preached where Osceola now stands. Brother Query preached in private houses and school-house in Polk County long before a circuit was organized. Under his faithful labors many revivals took place, and many souls were saved. His crown of rejoicing in the heavenly world will not be without stars. On the foundations laid by him others are now building.

In 1875 we had a small society here, but no Church. J. H. Mickey, L. J. Blowers, and Brother Campbell were at the front, leading on the little band of Christians. These noble men are still at the front, just as zealous, devoted, and active as ever. It is not surprising that, with such men to lead a city and Church, Osceola should be one of the most enterprising cities, and the Methodist Episcopal Church one of the best in the State.

Our quarterly meetings at Osceola were always "seasons of refreshing from the presence of the Lord." I shall never forget them.

The place where Rising City now stands was then a farm, owned and cultivated by Albert Rising. Brother Samuel W. Rising came to Nebraska in 1870, and pre-empted the land adjoining the city of Rising, where he still lives. His sons took land adjoining their father's; the city was located on their land, and named in honor of them. They are all active members of the Methodist Episcopal Church. Often while traveling the district I was hospitably entertained by these large-hearted Christians, and I shall never forget their kindness. We now have a splendid church and a large and flourishing society at Rising City.

David City was then in the Omaha District. It is situated upon the beautiful table-land near the center of Butler County. It was designated as the county-seat in 1873, at which time it was nothing more than a broad expanse of level prairie. I passed over the spot where the city now stands long before there was a single house.

The first sermon ever preached here was in 1871, and, I think, was preached by Rev. D.

Marquette in the private house of Captain A. F. Coon. At the same time a class was organized, composed of a few members. In 1876, under the labors of Rev. A. J. Combs, a small church was built, and on the 5th day of March I preached the dedicatory sermon, and consecrated the house to the worship of Almighty God. This church was afterwards enlarged, and at length gave way to the present elegant structure. The dedication took place in grasshopper times. While taking up the collection, a man, standing away back by the door, said: "If I thought the grasshoppers would not come and destroy my crops again next year, I would give twenty-five dollars." I said in reply: "That is just the thing to do in order to keep the grasshoppers away;" and then I quoted the words of Malachi: "Bring ye all the tithes into the storehouse, that there may be meat in mine house, and prove me now herewith, saith the Lord of hosts, if I will not open you the windows of heaven, and pour you out a blessing that there shall not be room enough to receive it. *And I will rebuke the devourer for your sakes.*" He gave the twenty-five dollars, and the following year the grasshoppers did but little harm.

At that time the outlook for Methodism in Omaha was not the most hopeful. Dr. L. F. Britt was appointed pastor of the First Church.

This church had been laboring for years under a constantly accumulating and burdensome debt, and was just ready to succumb to the fearful pressure when the Doctor took charge. The property all passed into the hands of the creditors during the year, and the society was left without any property, save the furniture of the church and parsonage. But, notwithstanding the deplorable condition of the finances, and the gloomy outlook generally, under God the Doctor had a gracious revival of religion, and seventy-five members were added to the Church. The next year, under the leadership of Dr. H. D. Fisher, a new lot was purchased, a frame building was erected, and the First Methodist Church started anew; and to-day this church has one of the most beautiful and imposing structures in the city.

Although the sad effects of the grasshopper raid were felt all over the Conference, the year was one of prosperity on all lines of Church-work.

The next Conference met at Falls City October 4, 1876, Bishop Foster presiding. On Sunday morning the bishop preached from Gal. iv, 4, 5: "But when the fullness of the time was come, God sent forth his Son, made of a woman, made under the law, to redeem them that were under the law." His theme was the fulfillment of prophecy touching the advent of Christ. When he announced his subject we were not a little disappointed, and said: "Well, is it possible he is going to preach to us on that threadbare subject?" It was a subject we had all gone over time and again in our text-books, and we did not care to hear a sermon on the old, dry theme. But the bishop had proceeded but a short time until we were perfectly satisfied with the theme selected. That familiar subject was presented in a new light. It was clothed with a beauty and power such as we had never seen or heard. The discourse was a perfect chain of argument from the beginning to the close, and at the same time was glowing with fervent heat. It was "logic on fire" all the way through. He made a statement at the outset that shocked many for the moment, and seemed to savor a little of the braggadocio. He said in substance: "I intend to make an argument to-day that hell can not overthrow." And when he reached the climax, and had driven and clinched the last nail in his argument, every one in the vast congregation felt he had made good his promise. A citizen of Falls City, whom I had known well for years, heard the bishop until he was about two-thirds of the way through, when he left the house. He afterwards said to one of the members of the Conference: "I had no idea you had such arguments to prove the truth of Christianity. I remained as long as I could. A very peculiar feeling came over me, such as I had never felt before, and I was obliged to leave the house before the bishop closed." Poor man! It seemed he did not know what was the matter. We knew; he was smitten by the mighty power of the Holy Ghost. He was convicted by the Holy Ghost "of sin, and of righteousness, and of judgment." Whether he ever yielded and gave his heart to God or not, we never learned.

At the end of one year we moved back to Lincoln, where we had a house of our own, and I traveled the district from this place. This necessitated my being absent from home much of the time, and the year was one of great toil and exposure.

At the next Conference, which met at the Eighteenth Street Church, Omaha, October 11, 1877, we were appointed to the Nebraska City District. This was my second term on this district, having traveled it from 1861 to 1865. I was again on old territory, although the most of the people were new and strange.

I shall never forget a quarterly meeting held at Highland, a few miles west o Peru. With great care and much prayer I had prepared a sermon especially for the unconverted, and I hoped to be able, under God, to reach their hearts.

Saturday afternoon we had a good congregation composed of members of the Church, and I preached a sermon appropriate to the occasion. Sunday morning came. The weather was forbidding, and a storm was evidently brewing. A goodly number were at the love-feast, and we had an excellent meeting. The meeting had hardly commenced when it began to rain, and the rain increased throughout the whole service, and at the close was literally pouring down. From the way the storm raged we knew very well that all were present that could come. But then my sermon was not appropriate for the congregation at all. It was for sinners, and all present were Christians. It would not do for me to preach to the unconverted alone, when there was not a single unconverted person present in the congregation. For the life of me I could not think of a single thing to preach that would in any way be appropriate. I thought of the advice in our excellent Book of Discipline, "Always suit your subject to your audience," and for a moment my brain fairly whirled. Silently I breathed an ejaculatory prayer to God for light and help. I opened my satchel, took out my portfolio, and ran hurriedly over some skeletons of sermons, when my eyes fell upon one from the text, "Ye are complete in him." Something seemed to say: "That's the sermon for you to preach." Afterwards I knew well that voice was the Holy Spirit. I looked over the sketch, and almost instantly the whole sermon rose vividly before my mind. It stood out beautifully in bold relief before me. I was satisfied. I said to myself: "This is what God wants me to preach from." The opening services over, I announced my text, and began to talk. As I proceeded with the subject my soul warmed. My mind was wonderfully illuminated, and my heart strangely fired. My tongue was as "the pen of a ready writer." O how easy it was to talk! It is always easy when under the divine afflatus—when the Holy Ghost inspires, and warms, and fires. It was all of God, and it was marvelous to me and to others as well. Having talked about forty minutes, I saw to my right a man whispering to his wife. I did not know what it meant. I afterwards learned that he was trying to get his wife to go with him to the altar and seek for heart-purity. Presently he arose, slipped around just in front of me, and fell upon his knees at the altar. Then I said: "If there are any others here to-day who are not satisfied with their religious experience, and desire 'full salvation,' come to the altar while I continue to talk." Instantly his wife followed, and in a few moments the railing all around the altar was filled. I continued to talk for about ten minutes, then we had an hour of prayer and song and testimony. Such a precious hour! Its memory lingers with me to-day. A number on that stormy day received the witness that "the blood of Jesus Christ cleanseth from all sin."

The General Conference of 1880 formed the West Nebraska Mission, which included the greater part of the Kearney District. Dr. T. B. Lemon had served the Kearney District as presiding elder for two years, and no man was better acquainted with the needs of that vast and rapidly growing territory than he. He was appointed superintendent of the mission, which position he held until the mission was organized into the West Nebraska Conference in 1885. The touch of the Doctor's molding hand was felt throughout the entire western part of the State.

The same General Conference passed an enabling act, granting the Nebraska Conference the privilege of dividing during the next four years, by a majority vote of the members, and the bishop presiding concurring.

At the Conference held in York, beginning September 14, 1881, the following resolution was adopted by a vote of 39 to 32:

"*Resolved*, That under the enabling act of the last General Conference, we deem it wise at this time to divide the Nebraska Conference into the

Nebraska and North Nebraska Conferences, the Platte River to be the boundary-line."

The most of the members of the Conference living north of the Platte River voted against the division. The question had been agitated for a number of years, and it was thought best not to delay the matter longer. Time has proved that the action of the Conference was eminently wise.

CHAPTER XX.

GRASSHOPPER INCIDENTS.

Their Origin—Depredations in All Ages—An Atheist renounces his Atheism—Wonderful Answers to Prayer—A Touching Incident—Another Atheist changed — Annie Wittenmyer—Assistance from the East—Mrs. M. E. Roberts—Reflex Influence of Work done for Others—Man's Weakness and God's Power.

THE year 1875 is memorable in the annals of Nebraska. Those who lived in the State at that time will never forget it. That year the State was visited with what is known as the "grasshopper plague." The grasshoppers, which were so destructive to the crops, were a species of locust. They appeared first in 1874, but were more destructive in 1875, and they did more or less damage in 1876 and 1877. They were natives of the high and dry regions of the Rocky Mountains, north of latitude forty-three. Here, whenever the conditions are favorable, they lay their eggs, and the young are hatched in such vast numbers as utterly to astound those who have never had any experience with them. They can not long endure low and moist regions combined with extreme and sudden changes of temperature, and for this reason Nebraska can never become the permanent habitation of the grasshopper. In the spring of 1877 millions of them were hatched out, then followed rains and sudden changes of temperature, and in a little while they nearly all disappeared, having done very little damage to the crops.

History informs us that in all ages, the locusts, of which the grasshopper is a species, have committed great depredations. Locusts were one of the plagues sent upon the Egyptians. "Moses stretched forth his rod over the land of Egypt, and the Lord brought an east wind upon the land all that day, and all that night;" . . . "and the east wind brought the locusts. They covered the face of the whole earth, so that the land was darkened; and they did eat every herb of the land, and all the fruit of the trees which the hail had left; and there remained not any green thing in the trees, or in the herbs of the field, through all the land of Egypt." (Exodus x, 13–15.) "And the Lord turned a mighty strong west wind, which took away the locusts, and cast them into the Red Sea" (verse 19).

They came with the wind, and disappeared with the wind. So with the grasshoppers of Nebraska. They came with the strong wind, and disappeared with the same. They travel only when the wind is strong and in the right direction. Rising high in the air, with their wings spread, the wind carries them along with but very little effort on their part.

Mr. Volney, in his "Travels in Syria," gives an account of the awful ravages of the locusts: "Syria partakes, together with Egypt and Persia, and almost all the whole middle part of Asia, in that terrible scourge. I mean those clouds of locusts of which travelers have spoken; the quantity of which is incredible to any person who has not himself seen them. When these clouds of locusts take their flight in order to surmount some obstacle, or the more rapidly to cross some desert, one may literally say that *the sun is darkened by them.*" Dr. Adam Clarke quotes from Baron de Tott, who gives a similar account of them: "Clouds of locusts frequently alight on the plains of the Tartars, and, giving preference to their fields of millet, ravage them in an instant. Their approach darkens the horizon, and so enormous is their multitude, it hides *the light of the sun.* They alight on the fields, and there form a bed of six or seven inches thick." The graphic description, given of the grasshoppers, by these travelers, agree with the accounts given by Moses and Joel, and are in harmony with our observation and experience in Nebraska. In 1874, in the high and dry regions above referred to, they were hatched by the mill-ious, and when large enough to migrate, they left their native land and swooped down upon the green fields of Nebraska, destroying almost every green thing. They came in such vast numbers that they appeared, at times, like a cloud. I have seen large fields of corn completely destroyed in a few hours, and immense wheat-fields eaten up in a day. Sometimes they would settle down upon a field of corn so thick, they would completely cover every stalk from the root to the tassel; the ground beneath would be perfectly black with them, and in places they would be from one to four inches deep. Large fields of corn, just beginning to ripen, which at noon appeared green and beautiful, before sundown would be entirely destroyed, and nothing remain but the naked stalks. And woe be to the gardens they entered! A garden-patch was their delight. Turnips, radishes, beets, carrots, and everything in the bulb line was entirely destroyed. The inside of these vegetables was all eaten out, and nothing but the skin, or rind, remained. Tansy, red-pepper, and onions were their peculiar favorites.

Sometimes the women would tie up their cabbage and cauliflower with paper sacks and cloths, in order to save them, but these wrappings could no more stop their ravages than a straw could dam up the Mississippi River. They would eat through the paper and cloth almost as quick as you could penetrate them with a sharp knife. Every green thing gave way before them. The awful description given by the Prophet Joel of the locusts of his day, most aptly illustrates the grasshopper scourge of Nebraska in 1875. He likens them to a mighty nation. "A nation is come upon my land, strong and without number, whose teeth are the teeth of a lion. He hath laid my vine waste, and barked my fig-tree: he hath made it clean bare, and cast it away; the branches thereof are made white." (Joel i, 6, 7.) The above is a most fitting illustration of the grasshopper plague. They were indeed "without number." Their teeth were more to be dreaded than "the teeth of a lion." Not only were green fields and beautiful gardens "made clean bare," but orchards and hedges were stripped of their foliage, peeled, "made white," and withered and died. The prophet continues his graphic and awful description of the locust plague: "The field is wasted, the land mourneth; for the corn is wasted: the new wine is dried up, the oil languisheth" (verse 10). "A day of darkness and of gloominess, a day of clouds and of thick darkness." "A fire devoureth before them; and behind them a flame burneth: the land is as the garden of Eden before them, and behind them a desolate wilderness; yea, and nothing shall escape them" (ii, 2, 3). "Before their face the people shall be much pained: all faces shall gather blackness" (verse 6).

I have seen with my own eyes, many beautiful farms, which were as the "garden of Eden" before they came, but in a few hours after they came, were "a desolate wilderness." I have looked upon the people whose hearts were "much pained," and whose faces "gathered blackness," at this mighty army of robbers. Many a strong man's heart sunk within him, as he saw in a day, the last vestige of his crop destroyed, and the living for himself and family for the next year swept away.

An atheist, living some miles north of Lincoln, had his entire crop destroyed by these marauders. He had a large family. Their crop was their only dependence for a living that year. Many of his neighbors had suffered the same fate. The prospect for an abundant harvest never had been better. But the grasshoppers came like a cloud, settled down upon their fields and gardens, and in a few hours all was destroyed. The heart of this atheist sank within him, and his face turned deathly pale. Shortly after the dreadful calamity, he said to some of his neighbors, in a voice tremulous with emotion: "I believe there is a God, and if God don't help us, I don't know what we shall do." His atheism and infidelity at once left him, and it was said by his neighbors that he became a firm believer in the Christian religion, and never afterwards was he heard to utter a single word against the existence of a God or the truth of the Christian religion. The grasshopper scourge led many to see, as never before, how weak and helpless man is, and how utterly dependent he is upon a higher power. The people were greatly humbled. They felt that "vain is the help of man." They were led to see clearly their dependence upon God, and prayed more earnestly than ever; and the result was, many wonderful revivals of religion. The people never were more devoted than when the country was devastated by the grasshoppers. Our quarterly meetings were seasons of wonderful power, and God overruled this great scourge for the people's welfare. Great material prosperity is not always conducive to deep piety. Financial crashes, material reverses, and failure of crops are often the best things that can possibly befall a people. Along with panics, financial reverses, and the failure of crops have swept gracious revivals of religion.

Brother S. P. Vandoozer, presiding elder of the Covington District, related the following incident to Bishop Bowman and the cabinet during the Conference held in Omaha, in 1875: "A pious family, members of the Methodist Episcopal Church, lived in the bounds of his district. They were firm believers in the power of prayer. About twelve o'clock, one beautiful day in August, the grasshoppers settled down upon their field of corn. The corn was black with the devouring insects. The wife was at home alone. She knew very well if they remained a few hours the corn would be entirely destroyed. This corn was their only dependence for a living for the year. When she saw them settle down upon the corn, she went into the house, kneeled down, and prayed. She told God that the corn was their only hope for a living that year, and earnestly asked him, for the sake of his Son, to cause the grasshoppers to leave, and while she prayed her faith took hold on God, and she said to herself: 'They will leave.' She arose from her knees, went out of the house, and there the grasshoppers were, eating away like ravenous wolves devouring their prey. Her faith began to waver, and she went back into the house, fell upon her knees and began again to pray, and while she prayed was enabled to grasp the promise, 'Ask of me whatsoever thou wilt, and I will give it thee.' She said to herself: 'They certainly will go.' She arose, went out and looked, and lo! they were still there, eating away as ever. She watched them a little while and her faith began the second time to give way. She rushed back into the house, fell upon her knees the third time, and began to pray more earnestly than ever that God might remove the scourge, and as she prayed, she again grasped the promise with an unyielding grip, and said: 'They will go.' She arose, went out and gazed for some moments upon the destroyers. Although there were no signs whatever of their leaving, her faith did not waver in the least. She said to herself, as she looked upon the destroyers, and listened to the crackling of the corn as this mighty army made way with it: 'They will leave, they will leave.' In a very little while they began to rise, slowly at first, then more rapidly, then all of them, like a mighty cloud, arose and passed away. While the neighbors' crops all around them were entirely destroyed, their field of corn was unharmed. It stood alone in the neighborhood, a monument of the mighty power of prayer." The next day Bishop Bowman preached on "The Tyndall Prayer-test," and during the sermon related the above incident, while tears rained from many eyes, and loud shouts of "Glory to God" were heard all over the congregation.

That year, two families living near where Fairmont now stands, with many others, had lost their entire crop by the grasshoppers. They were poor, and had come to Nebraska for the purpose of getting themselves homes. They took homesteads near the railroad. For many weeks they had lived on short rations. The time came when the last cake was baked and the last mouthful eaten. There was no meal in the barrel and no oil in the cruse, and no money or anything else with which to buy more. If God did not feed them by a miracle, as he did Elijah of old, they must starve. Elijah's God was their God, and in him they trusted. At family prayer that morning they laid their wants before God, and asked him to come to their assistance and supply their needs. That day, R. R. Randall, now a member of my Church, from whom I obtained all the facts connected with this incident, was in charge of a railroad excursion from the East. Among the excursionists was a lady who was a blatant atheist. She denied the existence of a God, denounced the Scriptures, and ridiculed the idea that God answers prayer. She was loud in her profession of atheism, and proud of her infidelity. A hot box compelled the engineer to stop the train in sight of the houses of these poor families about noon the same day they had eaten the last mouthful of provisions. While waiting for the box to cool, the children of these families came out to the train. They were thinly clad, and their garments were patched until they were like Joseph's coat of many colors. The passengers got out of the coaches and gathered around the children, and began to ask questions. The children told them the artless story of their poverty. They said they had eaten the last mouthful of provisions that morning, and that their parents had prayed for God to send them help, and they expected God would answer their parents' prayers. The hearts of the excursionists were touched, and tears were seen in many eyes, as they listened to the simple story of the children. A collection was at once taken, and it was by no means a meager one. The passengers did not hunt for the smallest piece of money they had. Silver and gold and greenbacks were poured out in abundance, and the little girls, with their aprons full, returned with joy to their homes. The infidel lady witnessed the touching scene with the deepest interest and the greatest emotion. And when all was over, the hot box cooled, and the train about to move on, Brother Randall said to her: "What do you think of that? Is there a God, and does he answer prayer?" She broke down, the tears came to her eyes, and she said: "I never saw anything like it. There must be a God, and he certainly answers prayer." Her atheism and infidelity at once took wings and flew away, and the belief in a God who hears and answers prayer took possession of her heart. To-day, as in Elijah's day, God answers prayer.

I held a quarterly meeting during the grasshopper scourge, at Brother Fair's, in Fillmore County. It was in August. The weather was very hot and dry. There had been no rain for weeks. Everything was burning up with the heat. What the grasshoppers did not eat, it seemed the intense dry weather would destroy. On Saturday night, at family prayer, I prayed that God might send a shower of rain upon the dry and parched earth. About midnight one of Brother Fair's boys awoke and said to his father: "Pa, it is going to rain." "What makes you think so, my son?" said the father. "Because the preacher prayed for rain, and I know it will rain." How wonderful is a child's faith! If we all had the faith of children we would have many more signal answers to prayer than we have, and many more wonderful demonstrations of the Divine power. Sure enough, true to the child's faith, the rain came. Early next morning the rain literally poured down, and the people and all nature rejoiced after the refreshing shower. A child's faith, how simple and beautiful it is!

"Mamma," said a little child, "I prayed for God to forgive me, and he heard my prayer."

"How do you know?" said the mother.

"Because I asked him."

A wife had long been praying for her unconverted husband. At times her distress of spirit was so great that, when about her household duties, her troubled countenance was sad to behold. One day her little girl of seven summers, seeing her arise from her knees with the same weary, anxious face, ran up to her and said: "Mamma, won't God say yes?" and receiving no answer, she asked again: "Mamma, why won't God say yes?" A light flashed upon the woman's troubled soul. Had she prayed in faith and humble trust in the Redeemer? Then she said: "Lord, increase my faith;" and then she offered the prayer of faith, and then her glad soul rejoiced in the salvation of her husband. Her little child had taught her how to offer the prayer of faith. From the children we learn many lessons. How true, "A little child shall lead them!"

About this time, Mrs. Annie Wittenmyer visited Lincoln. She was the first corresponding secretary of the Ladies' and Pastors' Christian Union of the Methodist Episcopal Church, and was at this time laboring in the interest of this society. She was afterwards president of the National Woman's Christian Temperance Union. The active part she took in hospital work during the Civil War, in administering to the wants of the sick, wounded, and dying soldiers, her great talents, deep piety, and untiring energy in almost every good work, won for her a national reputation. Many in the great day of eternity will have reason to praise God for Annie Wittenmyer. While in Lincoln, we had the privilege of entertaining her as a guest at our own home a short time. And, although she was with us but a few hours, and sat but once at our table, that delightful visit will never be forgotten. We let no time run to waste while she was present, for we wanted to get all the information from her we possibly could. We asked her a great many questions, which were answered with the greatest pleasure. She was past fifty years old before she did any work in public. She gave us a most interesting account of her maiden speech. It was delivered at a camp-meeting in the East. She was so frightened that two ministers, one taking hold of her right arm and the other her left, had to assist her in getting upon a bench, where she stood and talked for over an hour to the people. To her it was a memorable occasion, and would never be forgotten. I said to her:

"We ministers sometimes have what we call liberty, and sometimes we do not. How is it with you? Do you always have liberty when you speak?"

"O no!" was the reply. "About two-thirds of the time I *trail*, and about one-third of the time speak with satisfaction to myself. Sometimes I do more good, however, when I trail than I do when I speak with ease and satisfaction."

"How is that?" said I.

"Well, I will tell you. About a year ago

Brother Cookman, pastor of one of our Churches in New York City, requested me to speak to his people. I complied with the request, and had a most delightful time. Brother Cookman was pleased, his people were pleased, and I was pleased. We were all delighted. Some months afterward he requested me to come again and talk to his people, and I went. This time, however, I had a very hard time. I trailed all the way through my speech. When I went into the parsonage, after the service, I said: 'Well, Brother Cookman, I had a hard time to-night; I am afraid I did not do your people any good at all.' 'O yes, Sister Wittenmyer, you did my people more good to-night than you did when you were here before. When you were here before, my people said: "O, that is Sister Wittenmyer; nobody can talk like her!" and they went away from the church discouraged, feeling as though they never would try to do anything, because your effort was so far superior to any effort they might attempt to make; but to-night they said, "Why, almost any one could do that well!"'"

I remember once trying to preach in Lincoln on Sunday night. I felt it was the most complete failure I had ever made in my life. I left the church chagrined and mortified. A few months afterward I met a man in Omaha who heard me preach that sermon. He referred to the sermon and the text, and said: "Under that sermon my daughter was awakened and converted, and has been living a faithful Christian ever since."

A minister was called unexpectedly one evening to preach in a pulpit not his own, and announced as his text, "Will a man rob God?" He left the church in deep depression, with a sense of utter failure. Sixteen years afterward, when on a voyage, a stranger accosted him, and, calling him by name, said: "I am heartily glad to see you! A sermon you preached sixteen years ago—or, rather, the text—was the means of my conversion. I went to church, when I heard you announce as your text 'Will a man rob God?' I was a young man, from a Christian home, just going abroad to commence my life-work. I was meaning some time 'to be obedient to the heavenly vision.' That text revealed God to me; it brought me face to face with God." He saw God, and then and there was saved. A public speaker does not always know when he is doing the most good. What to him is a complete failure, in the hand of God may be a perfect success.

The finances of the society for which Sister Wittenmyer was laboring were not in the best condition at that time, and when she referred to the matter I said: "Don't you get discouraged sometimes?"

"O no," was the prompt reply. "You would not get discouraged either if you had seen what I have seen. Let me give you an incident," said she: "Our society was in debt some three hundred dollars. We ladies planned a course of lectures, in order to pay off that debt. We secured several of the best and most noted lecturers in the field, and, after the course was delivered, we were eight dollars worse off than when we began. We felt badly. A number of the ladies were disheartened. One day some of us were talking over the matter, and wondering how we were to liquidate the indebtedness, when Brother Hughes came up, and we told him what we had been talking about and what we wanted. He said: 'Why don't you ask God to send you the money?' 'Sure enough; we had not thought of that. We will ask God to send us three hundred dollars.' 'Ask God to send you a thousand!' said Brother Hughes. So we agreed together to pray for a thousand dollars. A few months afterward the two New York Conferences were in session. I spoke to the New York East Conference one night, and the next night addressed the New York Conference. At the close of the meeting, as I walked down the aisle, Brother Remington met me, and handed me a check for one thousand dollars for our society. There was the answer to our prayers. I could give you other incidents similar to this. No, I do not get discouraged."

The people of the East were very kind, and money and clothing in large amounts were given to aid the grasshopper sufferers. Some six hundred dollars were sent to me during the year, which amount I gave to the most needy on my district. An emporium was established in Lincoln, where large quantities of clothing were stored, divided, given, and sent to the destitute. I knew of many families on my district who were very needy. Mrs. Davis and I requested Mrs. M. E. Roberts to help us in selecting clothing for these needy ones. We spent the day in doing this, and Mrs. Roberts afterwards declared that it was the most delightful day's work she had ever done. She is always happy when she can help others. While engaged in this work she felt conscious she was rendering invaluable service to the suffering poor. Nothing brings such rich joy to the heart as the work of benefiting others. All that is done for humanity has a reflex influence. While it goes forth to benefit those intended, it comes back with a richer blessing to the benefactor. Many know from experience the truth of the Savior's words, "It is more blessed to give than to receive."

Many of the preachers of my district were living on a mere pittance. They were struggling hard with poverty—barely able to keep the wolf from the door. I knew well their needs. Flannels and muslins and calicoes were carefully divided, that all might share equally, and certain garments were carefully laid aside for Brothers A and B and C. While carefully assorting the goods, Sister Roberts came across a beautiful pair of lavender kid-gloves, and, holding them up in her hand, said: "O see here, what a lovely pair of gloves I have found! To whom shall we give them?" We thought of Sister A and then of Sister B. We suggested first one and then another. "Lavender kid-gloves! lavender kid-gloves! For whom would they be appropriate?" We were at a loss to know. What did grasshopper sufferers need of lavender kid-gloves? We discussed the matter *pro* and *con* for some time, but could not decide who should have them.

Sister Roberts afterward said: "We were a little like the Sanitary Commissioners in the South during the war. Among the many things sent to relieve the wants of the suffering soldiers was a box of paper collars. The commissioners were very much perplexed to know what to do with them. For whom they would be appropriate they knew not. Finally they sent them back, saying: 'We have fried them, and boiled them,

and baked them, and we can not do anything with them; so we send them back to you.'"
Whatever became of the lavender kid-gloves I do not know to this day; but we could find no earthly use for them.

In the grasshopper plague we have an illustration of the wonderful influence and power of little things. A snow-flake is a little thing. Who cares for one snow-flake? But a whole day of snow-flakes, drifting over the fences, blocking up the roads, and gathering upon the mountain-sides, to crush in awful avalanches, who does not care for that? A spark of fire is a little thing. Who cares for a spark of fire? A drop of water may extinguish it; a touch with the foot or hand may put it out. But drop that spark of fire in the grass on a dry and windy day, and soon it becomes a rolling wave of flame; and fences and hay-stacks, and barns and houses melt away before the devouring element. One of the most fearful of all things is a prairie-fire on a dry and windy day. It sweeps everything before it, and its track is marked by desolation and gloom. A grasshopper is a little thing. Who cares for such a tiny insect? But millions on millions of grass-hoppers, flying like a cloud, and settling down upon fields and gardens, literally covering everything, who does not care for them? A woman whose corn had all been destroyed by them said:

"I would not have felt so badly if a drove of buffaloes had entered the field and eaten up my corn; but to have it all destroyed in a few hours by such insignificant things as grasshoppers is really aggravating."

The grasshoppers brought gloom and sadness to many a home and many a heart, and we have no desire at all to see them again; yet, under an overruling providence, they were not without profit to many of the people. Man's weakness and God's power were seen in a light never before manifested. Without the intervention of Almighty God, man is at the mercy, in spite of all his knowledge and power, of a little, insignificant insect. Many were led to cry out with David: "I will lift up mine eyes to the hills, from whence cometh my help. My help cometh from the Lord, which made heaven and earth."

CHAPTER XXI.

BEATRICE.

LOCATION—FOUNDED IN 1857—EMIGRANTS ON A MISSOURI STEAMER ORGANIZE A COLONY—BEATRICE IN 1861—ALBERT TOWLE—GOVERNOR BUTLER—FIRST HOMESTEAD— FIRST METHODIST PREACHER—FIRST QUARTERLY MEETING — INDIANS — TERRIBLE MASSACRE — THE GREAT CHANGE.

BEATRICE, the county-seat of Gage County, is one of the beautiful cities of Nebraska, and is situated on the banks of the Blue River, one of the lovely streams of the State. It is forty miles south of Lincoln, the capital of Nebraska, and some seventy miles west of the Missouri River. It was founded in 1857, and named Beatrice in honor of Judge Kinney's daughter. It is supposed that the name was originally derived from the beautiful woman whom Dante has immortalized in his poems, and the object of his devotion. One of the most beautiful of women, she was the emblematical personification of divine wisdom. It was the thought of her lover that a being so pure and lovely could not stay long on the earth. God seemed to have created her for one of his angels, and at the age of twenty-four years took her to himself in heaven. The name, Beatrice, suggests beauty, purity, and wisdom. Whether the city of Beatrice can claim all these admirable traits or not, is a question. One thing is certain, however, it can claim the first-named—beauty. Its location can not be surpassed in loveliness, and we may truthfully say: " Beautiful for situation, the joy of the whole ". people, is Beatrice.

In the spring of 1857, a steamer weighed anchor at St. Louis, Missouri, floated out into the center of the Mississippi River, and, with her prow set for the head-waters of the Missouri, began slowly to move up against the mighty current of the "Father of Waters." On board of that steamer were some three hundred passengers,—many of them the deluded followers of Brigham Young. Their faces were turned to the "city of Zion," located in a safe retreat amid the mountain fastnesses of the far-away West. Others were looking to the plains of "bleeding Kansas," while quite a number had their eyes fixed on the new and inviting Territory of Nebraska.

The Missouri River is full of snags and sand-bars, and is a very dangerous stream to navigate. As this steamer moved slowly up the turbid and treacherous stream, nearing Kansas City, she struck a sand-bar, stuck fast, and remained for some time. This was not the first time, however, the steamer had grounded, yet this was the most serious accident of the kind on that memorable voyage. While the boat lay upon that sand-bar, and the weary hours passed by, to break the monotony and relieve the restlessness of the passengers, a colony was organized, from among the passengers, for the purpose of locating in Nebraska. That organization framed a constitution and by-laws, and thirty-five persons signed the written agreement. Among the signers of that instrument were Albert Towle, J. B. Weston, Judge John F. Kinney, and others who have since occupied positions of trust and honor in the State. This colony located, platted, and named the city of Beatrice.

As stated elsewhere, in 1861 I was appointed to the Nebraska City District, which comprised all the territory south of the Platte River; and Beatrice was one of my appointments. I first visited the place in 1861. At that time there was a blacksmith-shop, a store, kept by Joseph Saunders, with about as many goods as two or three men could carry in their arms, and three or four dwelling-houses. During my first visit to the place I was kindly entertained by Brother Albert Towle and his estimable wife, and ever afterwards met a royal welcome at their hospitable home. Their house was always the home of the Methodist itinerant. They worked hard and made sacrifices for the Church. To them, more than any other two perhaps, is due the credit and honor of laying the foundations of the Church in the city of Beatrice. Although Brother Towle was not a member of the Church, he was as moral and upright in his walk as any who were members; and when he came to die gave assurances to his family that he was prepared to go. Sister Towle told the writer that her husband said to her not long before he passed away that perhaps he had made a mistake in not joining the Church, and if he had his life to live over again he would connect himself with the Church. While I believe there are many good Christians out of the Church, and many who have lived and died Christians who never belonged to any Church organization, still I believe it is far better for us personally, and our influence for good will be much greater if connected with the Church than otherwise. The Church was instituted for our benefit, and we ought to avail ourselves of her sacred privileges. It is not only a great privilege to be identified with the visible Church, but it is, at the same time, a duty to make that public "confession before men" on which Christ, the head of the Church, has laid so much stress. "Whosoever therefore shall confess me before men, him will I also confess before my Father which is in heaven."

Brother Towle was familiarly known as "Pap." Every body called him "Pap," and every one loved him almost as a child loves its affectionate parent. He was postmaster from the organization of the place until the day of his death, and had he lived, would, without doubt, still have held that position. His name, and that of his amiable wife, are embalmed in the hearts of a grateful people.

The following story is told on David Butler, who afterwards became governor of the State: During the war he was recruiting officer and came to Beatrice for volunteers. He stopped at "Pap's cabin," which was a favorite resort in that early day. In the evening, as he was talking with Mr. Towle, the young men began to come in, and each one saluted him as "Pap." About ten had gathered in when Mr. Butler asked Mr. Towle to take a walk. They walked some distance and sat down, when Mr. Butler began explaining how badly the Government was in need of troops, and hinted about the size and ability of the "boys" of his family. Mr. Towle listened attentively to all that was said, and seemed very greatly interested. When Mr. Butler had discussed the matter sufficiently he asked him if he would not spare some of his boys, and Mr. Towle said he would spare all the boys he had.

"How many boys have you, Mr. Towle?"

"Why, bless you, man, mine are all daughters, and I have not a boy to my name," said Mr. Towle.

The first quarterly meeting on the Beatrice Circuit, in 1861, was held on Cub Creek, some four miles, if I remember correctly, north-west of Beatrice. I reached the village Friday evening, and staid over night at Brother Towle's. On Saturday morning, Brother Towle ordered out his two-horse wagon, and Sister Towle, three of the daughters, some of the neighbors, and myself, got in and rode out to the quarterly meeting. The meeting was held in a grove on the farm of Brother Kilpatrick. He had made ample arrangements for the meeting, and we were most royally entertained during the meeting at his cabin. Brother Kilpatrick long ago passed to his home in the skies. That first quarterly meeting on the Beatrice charge will never be forgotten.

In 1879, Brother Towle passed peacefully away to his heavenly home, and ten years afterwards was followed by his beloved wife, both honored and respected by all.

The first homestead ever taken under the "United States Homestead Law" was near the city of Beatrice. To Daniel Freeman belongs this honor. His claim was on Cub Creek, four miles west of Beatrice, and not far from where I held the quarterly meeting above referred to.

The Homestead Law was enacted in 1862, and Mr. Freeman took his claim January 1, 1863, the day the act went into effect. His patent is numbered 1, and is recorded in Volume I, on page 1, of the Records of the General Land Office at Washington.

At the third session of the Kansas and Nebraska Conference, held at Topeka, Kansas Territory, April 15–19, 1858, Beatrice was placed on the Conference Minutes as one of the appointments of the Nebraska City District, and left to be supplied. At the next session of the Conference, held in Omaha, Nebraska Territory, April 14–18, 1859, no members were reported. At this Conference J. W. Foster was appointed pastor. During the year Brother Foster organized a class at Beatrice, one at Blue Springs, and at various other points on the circuit organized classes.

For a number of years the growth of the Church at Beatrice, as well as at other points, was slow. In 1870 a small stone church was erected, and on November 13th of that year I had the honor and privilege of preaching the dedicatory sermon, and of consecrating the house to the worship of Almighty God. Brother William Presson was the successful pastor at the time. The dedicatory services throughout were attended with the divine presence and power, and the people were greatly rejoiced in having a beautiful and comfortable church in which to worship God. In 1881, after having been on district-work for ten successive years, I was appointed to the Beatrice Station, and served the Church two years. During the first year God gave us a most gracious revival of religion, and over one hundred and thirty were converted.

In 1886, under the labors of Brother W. K. Beans, the present beautiful edifice was erected, and named "Centenary Methodist Episcopal Church of Beatrice." Soon after, the West Beatrice Church was built; and now there are two thriving Methodist Churches in this rapidly growing city. Other denominations have been very active, and have kept pace with the growth of the place.

In 1864, while holding a quarterly meeting on the Brownville Circuit, word came that the counties west of the Blue River were being raided by the Indians, and that men, women, and children were being slaughtered indiscriminately. It was reported that the Indians had reached Beatrice, the village had been burned, and the settlers who had not fallen victims to the merciless and bloodthirsty savages, were fleeing as fast as possible to the Missouri River. The report created intense excitement at the meeting, and many felt like starting at once for the defense of the frontier settlers. It was soon ascertained, however, that, while the Indians were driving everything before them as they moved towards the east, and were massacring the whites wherever they could reach them, they had not harmed Beatrice. The people in and around the town were greatly alarmed, and the excitement was at white heat. The settlers from the West came pouring into the village, and a strong corral was made around the old mill, where the frightened refugees remained for ten days. A company of men was organized, and started out to meet the murderous Sioux. This company of brave pioneers met a band of these savages on the Little Blue, and defeated them. The battle was a sharp and severe one, and two honored and highly respected citizens of Gage County, M. C. Kelley and J. H. Butler, fell mortally wounded. Although Gage County paid dearly for the relief and safety of her neighbors, the result was the Indians were panic-smitten, and instead of pushing their way further eastward, began at once to retreat to the west, and Beatrice was saved from their ravage. This raid, made upon the settlers all the way west of Beatrice to Fort Kearney, was one of the most complete and destructive ever made in the State. The raid was previously arranged with all the Indians along the route for two hundred miles, the exact time set, and to every settlement a band of Indians allotted. This was during the war, and it was thought that this awful massacre was instigated by white men—white men with hearts as dark as any that ever beat in the breasts of the most cruel Red-men of the plains.

The 7th day of August, 1864, was the day set for the simultaneous attack of every settlement west of Beatrice to Fort Kearney. It was the Sabbath, and many of the people had gathered together at the different stations along the road, and at different places in the different settlements for religious worship. No fear of the Indians disturbed the peaceful hearts of the settlers. The sun rose in splendor, poured his genial light over the beautiful prairies, and all nature rejoiced. On that calm and lovely morning the noble pioneers who had come to Nebraska to procure for themselves homes, felt just as secure as they had in their old homes in the East. Little did they dream that the day begun so bright should close so dark. Every station and settlement was attacked within ten minutes of the first, so perfect was the execution of this most carefully planned and cold-blooded massacre. The Indians appeared at the stations as they were in the habit of doing, and as usual were warmly received and kindly treated by the whites. Then, without a moment's warning, they began to shoot down their helpless victims, mutilating their bodies, burning their houses, and carrying away all they could.

I have no plea whatever to make for the Indians in their cruel and dastardly work, for many of their atrocious crimes are without a single palliating circumstance. Yet I am compelled to say that, in many instances, the treatment of the Indian by the white man has been just as cruel as the treatment of the white man by the Indian. I would indeed be glad if I could say only Indian hands have been stained with human blood; but alas! I can not. The hands of many white men have dripped with the innocent blood of the Indian. The white men who instigated the above massacre were just as guilty as the Indians who executed it.

A white man, in cold blood, without the least provocation whatever, shot and instantly killed an Indian squaw near where the city of Lincoln now stands, leaving her husband, the Indian brave, to pass on alone without any redress whatever. A party of Mormons, passing through St. Joseph, bought a cow that they might have a supply of milk, while crossing the plains to Salt Lake, for a sick child. Reaching Jefferson County, the cow gave out, and they had to rest a day or two for her to recuperate. They resumed their journey; but she soon gave out again, and they were compelled to leave her to shift for herself on the hills and plains of Nebraska. Soon after, this cow was found by a band of thirty Pawnee Indians. Thinking she was an estray, they killed her, and while removing her hide, a rough white man came along with a mule-train. He was a freighter, reckless and daring. Some of these old freighters were as tough as some of the "cow-boys" on the plains are at the present time. Seeing what had been done, he made a demand of the Indians who had killed the cow. They refused to comply with the demand, but instead offered thirty dollars, all the money they had, and really more than the animal was worth. Then they offered their best pony, which was refused, and the man went on his way swearing vengeance upon them, and declaring he would have the Indians' scalps. He secured a party of men, went in pursuit of the Indians, and, when he overtook them, again pressed his demand. . A parley ensued, then a bloody fight, in which one Indian and one white man was killed. News was sent to Fort Kearney that the Pawnees had made an attack upon the whites. The troops were ordered out, and before the matter was settled, the Government had expended one hundred and forty thousand dollars. In too many instances the white man has been the aggressor.

In 1861 the country between Beatrice and Nebraska City was very sparsely settled. For many miles east of Bear Creek there was not a single house. Over this dreary and desolate region I traveled to and fro four times a year for four years. It was a dismal ride, and I always greatly dreaded it. The scream of the prairie-snipe and the bark of the coyote often startled me as I sat in my buggy half asleep, while my bronco pony jogged wearily along the dim and but little traveled road; and ever and anon a herd of beautiful antelope would be seen grazing upon the hillside or skipping over the prairies. But this scene has greatly changed. The scream of the snipe and the bark of the coyote have long since died away, and the antelope is no longer seen playing upon the hillsides and along the valleys of this beautiful country. Instead of these is heard the bleating of sheep, the lowing of cattle, and the neighing of the horses; and rich and finely-cultivated farms cover all this once dreary and desolate region.

CHAPTER XXII.

YORK.

Location—First Settlers—First Grave in the County—Methodist Class organized—David Baker—Buffaloes invade the County—Friendship of the Early Settlers—W. E. Morgan—First Quarterly Meeting—Other Churches—Appointed to York Station, 1883—Great Revival—The Little Girl and the Dark Cloud—Second Year—Another Great Revival—The New Church—Subscription—Third Year—Church completed—Dedication by Bishop Warren.

YORK is the county-seat of York County. It is a lovely city, situated in the beautiful valley of Beaver Creek, and is the geographical center of the county. When first located it was called "York Center."

The first settlements made in York County were in 1861, shortly after the location of the territorial road from Nebraska City west, to a point on the "California Trail," forty miles due east of the present city of Kearney. It was known by the early freighters as "The Nebraska City Cut-off." Ranches were established along this road at different points. These ranches were the hotels along this public highway, kept for the benefit of travelers and freighters over the plains. Five of these ranches were established in York County shortly after this road was located. The first one established was by Benjamin F. Lushbaugh, United States Indian Agent of the Pawnees. It was near the west line of the county, situated on Porcupine Bluffs, and was known as "Porcupine Ranch." Afterwards the "Jack Smith Ranch," the "McDonald Ranch," the "Antelope Ranch," and the "Jack Stone Ranch" were established at different points in the county. At these "pioneer hotels" the weary traveler over the plains found rest and refreshment.

The grave of the first white man in the county may be seen near where the old "Jack Smith Ranch" stood. The victim was an overland stage-driver. When he reached the ranch he was under the influence of bad whisky; was shamefully abusive, and threatened the life of the ranch-keeper. For this purpose, he went to the stage, secured his revolvers, returned to the ranch, and drew a bead on Mr. Smith. Mr. Smith saw his danger, and shot first, the ball entering the driver's forehead, killing him instantly. Mr. Smith was exonerated in the course he pursued, as he acted entirely in self-defense. Although a drunkard fills the first grave in York County, to the praise and honor of the people be it said, York County has been freer from intoxicants, and less evil has resulted from the use of the vile stuff, than in almost any other county in the State. Her temperance principles have long been known, far and wide, and the result has been, the very best class of citizens have been attracted to the county.

The first permanent settler in York Precinct was Mr. David Baker. In August, 1869, he, with his family, pitched their tent on the banks of Beaver Creek, under the spreading branches of a beautiful old elm-tree, not far from where the city of York now stands. In this tent the family made their home for three months, during which time Mr. Baker erected the first frame house in the precinct, hauling the lumber from Nebraska City, a distance of over one hundred miles.

The city of York was founded in 1869 by the "South Platte Land Company." The site was taken as a pre-emption claim by A. M. Ghost and Mr. Sherwood for the company. In the spring of 1870 the town was represented by one sod-house and the little frame building which had been occupied by Messrs. Ghost and Sherwood when the site was pre-empted.

The first Methodist class was organized at the house of David Baker in the spring of 1871, and was composed of the following persons: David Baker, Elvira Baker, J. H. Bell, Thomas Bassett, L. D. Brakeman, Ella Brakeman, Sarah M. Moore, Thomas Myres, John Murphy, Mary Murphy, S. W. Pettis, and Mrs. Shackelford. Brother Baker was the leader. At Brother Baker's house the class was regularly held; and here the traveling preacher always found a royal welcome. The home of Brother and Sister Baker was always open to new-comers, and Father and Mother Baker were household names in every settler's cabin in York County for many years. In 1872 the writer had the privilege of sharing their hospitality, and, after remaining over night with the kind family, in the morning Brother Baker ferried me over Beaver Creek in a sorghum-pan. The stream was high and could not be forded, and there was no bridge, so the only way of crossing was in this unique boat. All the early settlers know very well what a sorghum-pan is. Some, however, may read these pages whose information is not so extensive; so for their benefit I will explain the nature of the little vessel in which I sailed the first time across the raging Beaver. At that day almost all the farmers raised a species of sugar-cane called sorghum. Out of this they made molasses, which they used for sweetening purposes. The juice was pressed from the cane-stalks, and then boiled to a syrup in pans from three to ten feet long; the bottom and ends were of sheet-iron, and the sides of plank. They were from one to two feet wide, and the sides from twelve to eighteen inches high. In these sorghum-pans the juice was placed; a fire was kindled underneath, and the liquid was boiled to its proper thickness. Brother Baker's pan resembled somewhat an Indian canoe, and in it I was safely carried over the swift-flowing stream.

On November 30, 1888, Sister Baker, in the eighty-third year of her age, went up to join her husband, who had preceded her to the skies some years before. I was requested to be present and preach her funeral sermon, but was unable to comply with the request of the kind friends. She was buried from the Methodist Episcopal Church on Sunday, December 2, 1888, Rev. W. K. Beans officiating. The founders of the Church in York County are passing away. "They rest from their labors, and their works do follow them."

In 1868 there were a few settlers in different parts of the county, and the most of them were very poor, and some were in destitute circumstances. They had come to secure homes under the "Homestead Law," and had but very little with which to begin. In August of this year the county was visited by large numbers of buffalo. This was the last appearance of these animals in any considerable number. The coming of these buffaloes at this time seemed providential; for these destitute pioneers were without meat, and the prospect was that they would have to remain without meat during the coming winter. When these cattle of the prairies appeared, the settlers were not slow in availing themselves of the privilege of laying in an abundant supply for the season. Though coarser-grained than the beef from the American cattle, the beef from the buffalo is sweet, palatable, and healthful.

The settlers at that time thought nothing of going twenty miles to visit a neighbor. A new settler was hailed with delight, and the neighbors would go ten or fifteen miles to assist him in erecting his sod-house, and give him a warm and honest welcome. The stranger at once became acquainted and felt at home. Such hearty good-will was irresistible, and no sooner did the new settler see it than he took the contagion, and was as jolly, free, and friendly as the rest. Solomon's proverb holds good the wide world over, and has been verified in every age: "A man that hath friends must show himself friendly." Friendship of the true type was beautifully manifested among the earlier settlers of the State. Would that the same social, benevolent, free-and-easy spirit were manifested now!

York first appeared as an appointment in 1871 upon the Minutes of the Nebraska Conference. It was in the Beatrice District, and was left to be supplied. Near the close of the year

Rev. W. E. Morgan was employed by the presiding elder, Rev. J. B. Maxfield, to supply the work until Conference.

At the Conference of 1872, York was placed in the Lincoln District. I was the presiding elder and W. E. Morgan pastor. The mission embraced the whole county. Over this vast territory Brother Morgan traveled, enduring great hardships and privations, that he might give to the people in the sparse-settled neighborhoods, scattered over the country, the bread of life, and lay deep and broad the foundations of the Church. To his untiring labors and bold advocacy is due largely the strong temperance sentiment which has always prevailed in the county. The little society of which he was the first pastor has grown into one of the strongest and most desirable stations in the Nebraska Conference.

On the 7th of June, 1872, I left my home in Lincoln, and sallied forth in my buggy, drawn by a span of spirited ponies, for my first quarterly meeting at York. Recent heavy rains had left the roads in very bad plight. The streams were badly swollen, many of the bridges were washed away, and the mud was deep, making travel exceedingly slow and difficult. Late in the evening I reached Beaver Crossing, and was most kindly entertained at the hospitable cabin of Brother and Sister Jones. Brother Jones and family afterwards moved to York, and while stationed in that city were, for three years, among my most faithful parishioners. The next day I pushed on to York, and held the first Quarterly Conference ever held in the place. At this Conference plans and specifications for the new church were adopted, and arrangements made for pushing the work to a speedy completion. The church was soon finished and dedicated, the Rev. Minor Raymond, D. D., of Evanston, Illinois, officiating.

At the close of the Quarterly Conference, in compliance with the kindly invitation of Brother and Sister Morgan, I rode out to their homestead, and spent a most pleasant night with them in their new frame-building. The sod-house had just been superseded by this neat and beautiful frame cottage. Possessing, in no small degree, one of the usual weaknesses of a Methodist preacher, I remember well how I enjoyed the excellent fried chicken Sister Morgan gave us for breakfast Sunday morning. After a hearty and very enjoyable meal, we hurried away to the nine o'clock love-feast, where, for an hour, we had a genuine, old-fashioned feast of love. Then came the preaching, then the collection, then the sacrament of the Lord's Supper, and then the reception of members into the Church. Representatives from various parts of the county were present. The people at that time thought nothing of going twenty or thirty miles to attend quarterly meeting. The services were held in the new frame building belonging to the Burlington and Missouri River Railroad Company, and used for a land-office. This building stood on the west side of the square. Here I met Judge D. T. Moore, Milton Sovereign, and their estimable wives, and they also, for three years, were among the most faithful of my parishioners while pastor of the York Station.

The Presbyterian Church was organized in July, 1871; the Congregational Church in May, 1872. At a later period, the Baptist and Christian Churches were organized. All now have elegant church-buildings and large and flourishing societies. The citizens of York are altogether the best church-going people it has ever been our privilege to become acquainted with. The intelligence and piety of the people are far above the average, and it is one of the most desirable of places in which to live.

The Nebraska Conference Seminary was founded, in 1879, by the Nebraska Conference, and located at York, a full account of which may be found in chapter xxiii, of this book.

We were appointed to the York Station by Bishop Wiley, September 10, 1883. My predecessor, Brother G. A. Smith, had left the charge in an excellent condition. I found peace and harmony, and the Church in good working order. There were two hundred and seventy-one members enrolled on the Church record. We had no church-building at that time. The first church built had long since become too small for the congregations, and had been sold, and our people were worshiping in "Bell's Hall."

Mrs. Davis and I entered upon our labors, as we always do, with an intense desire for the salvation of souls. During the first three months I preached every Sunday morning to the Church what I called in my own mind, although I did not announce them as such, awakening sermons, showing the members their great privileges and responsibilities as well. In the evening, I preached to the unconverted, and more especially to the young, what I called in my own mind awakening sermons, designed to produce conviction and show them the great need and importance of salvation. At the end of three months it seemed to me the Church was ripe for a revival; in fact, a revival was already in progress. A number had already been converted, others were under deep conviction, while many others were thinking seriously of the important matter. On the 6th day of January I began special revival services, preaching every night, and holding social meetings every afternoon. During the first two weeks of the meeting twelve persons were converted. Slowly but steadily the meetings increased in interest and power, and almost every night new interest was manifested. The third week twenty-eight were converted. Then I appointed a day of fasting and prayer, and earnestly exhorted all to observe that day. I also appointed a meeting the same day in the hall, at two o'clock P. M., and announced that I would preach on the subject of "Consecration." Dr. Thomson dismissed the college, and requested all to observe the day as a day of fasting and prayer to Almighty God for the outpouring of the Holy Ghost upon all the people, and urged all to attend the services in the afternoon. At precisely two o'clock I went to the hall, and as I entered I was astonished, and at the same time very greatly delighted, and it seemed that a new inspiration came upon me. I was moved and thrilled through and through at the sight. I found the house packed from the door to the pulpit with devout worshipers. Leading business men of the city had left their stores and offices and various places of business, and had come to worship God; the president of the college and members of the faculty, and many of the students were there, all waiting and anxiously looking for the heavenly anointing. I took for my text Exodus xiii, 2, "Sanctify unto me all the first born;" and I had "liberty." Every Methodist preacher knows well what that means.

The power of God came upon the preacher and the congregation, and the Holy Ghost carried truth to the hearts of the people. At the close of the sermon I said: "Now, all who wish to consecrate themselves wholly to God—to make an unconditional and eternal surrender of all to the Lord Jesus Christ—come to the altar." In less than one minute the altar was crowded. They were kneeling four tiers deep, filling all the space between the platform and the seats. I saw others pressing their way forward, anxious, but unable to reach the altar. I called upon them to kneel down in the aisles. The aisles were filled. Then I called upon the people to kneel right where they were sitting. Nearly every person present knelt. The whole house was an altar. Such a scene! I shall never forget it. Its precious memory is with me to-day, and will linger with me, methinks, forever. Then we prayed. The bending heavens touched the congregation,

> "Heaven came down our souls to greet,
> And glory crowned the mercy-seat."

Many that were there will remember that scene forever. That night thirty were at the altar, and some twenty were clearly converted. It was the crowning day of the meeting—the great day of the feast. God puts his seal of approbation on these days of fasting and prayer. We continued the meetings about six weeks, and the result was one hundred and thirty-two conversions, and the whole Church wonderfully quickened in faith and power.

Then we turned our attention to instructing and building up the young converts. The converts were of all ages, ranging from the man fifty years old in sin down to the little child. The students in the college shared largely the benefits of the meeting. The members of the faculty took an active part in the revival, and aided in the work. Many young men and women were wonderfully saved, and became mighty factors in bringing others into the kingdom of Christ. A little girl only thirteen years old was very clearly converted; her experience was most beautiful and touching. A few days afterward I met her on the street, and she looked very sad. Gloom was in every lineament of her face. Looking up to me very imploringly, she said: "O, Brother Davis, a dark cloud has come over me, and I feel so bad! Can you tell me what to do to make the cloud go away?" "O yes," said I; "you go and pray, and ask Jesus to take away the cloud, and it will go away." Her countenance changed in an instant; she looked relieved, and thanking me very kindly, with a light step bounded away down the street. A day or so afterward I met her. Her face beamed with joy, and, with a glad heart, she said: "Brother Davis, I did just what you told me to do. I went and prayed, and asked Jesus to take away the cloud, and the cloud went away; and I have been so happy ever since!" O the wondrous power of prayer! He who feeds the ravens when they cry, hears the children when they pray.

> "Prayer makes the *darkened cloud withdraw;*
> Prayer climbs the ladder Jacob saw—
> Gives exercise to faith and love,
> Brings every blessing from above."

Are you tempted? Pray, and the tempter will flee from you; for

> "Satan trembles when he sees
> The weakest saint upon his knees."

Do clouds gather heavy, thick, and dark about you? Pray, and the clouds will rift, the sunlight of glory will come streaming down into your soul. Does faith waver? Pray, and it will grow strong, and on its mighty pinions you will rise above all doubts and fears. A praying Church is a happy Church, a safe Church, a conquering Church. Such a Church we had at York.

The Conference year closed with very gratifying results. I was returned to York Station by Bishop Mallalieu in 1884. I began the year with another revival of religion in view. In all my pulpit preparations, pastoral visiting, preaching, and Church work, I had this object constantly in mind, and I worked continually to this end.

On the 4th of January I began revival services. From the very beginning sinners were converted. In fact, long before the extra meetings began souls were saved. Twelve had already been converted; one or more had been converted every week for a number of weeks before the extra meetings began. The tide of spiritual power rose rapidly from the very commencement. On the 27th day of January I announced another fast-day. That day I preached on "Christian Perfection." It was another memorable day. A number came into the light of "perfect love," and are witnesses to-day to Christ's wondrous power to "save to the uttermost." The result of this meeting was one hundred and twenty-six conversions, and the realization of "full salvation" on the part of many members of the Church.

At the close of the meeting we began to talk up the matter of a new church. All seemed to think the time had come when we ought to build. The first thing we had to do was to decide on a location; and of all questions this is the most difficult and delicate question to handle. Some members of the Board wanted the church built on the lots where the parsonage stood. These lots had been given by the "South Platte Land Company" for church purposes, and it was thought by some that, in view of this fact, and the eligibility of the location, the church ought, in justice, to be built here. They were very strong in their convictions on this matter. Others thought the church ought to be built on "East Hill," near where the college building stood, and they were just as strong in their convictions. The Official Board was nearly equally divided. After discussing the matter *pro* and *con* in a number of meetings, a compromise was at length reached, and the Board decided to build on the corner of Sixth Street and Nebraska Avenue. There were at first a few criticisms of this action. A faint murmur from a few was heard, but this murmur in a very little while died away. The action of the Board in locating the church where it did was eminently wise, and has never since been called in question. Perfect harmony prevailed, and the church stands to-day just where it should stand—right in the center of the city. The Board decided to build a church not to cost more than twelve thousand dollars, and not to begin work until ten thousand dollars were subscribed.

On the 26th day of April I took for my text Nehemiah ii, 10: "We his servants will arise and build." At the close of a short talk from these words, I called for subscriptions for the new church. I stated the decision of the Board—not to begin work till ten thousand dollars were subscribed. I asked the congregation for eight thousand dollars, and said: "If this congregation will subscribe eight thousand dollars, I think I can get the other two thousand dollars pledged in a week or two, and then work will begin on the new church." When I asked for eight thousand dollars from the congregation present, some laughed right out. They thought the request absurd and the most preposterous. I, however, felt confident. that the eight thousand could be raised. I had been working the matter up for several days, and had over four thousand dollars in sight. I had felt the pulse of many, and knew there was a very healthy feeling in the community touching the subject. I closed the morning service with over nine thousand dollars subscribed. The matter was presented again in the evening, and the day's work closed with ten thousand three hundred and sixty dollars pledged. It was the best subscription, taking the number and ability of the people into consideration, I had ever known. The people were jubilant. Smiles were on all faces, and tears of joy in many eyes. It was a "red-letter day" for York. The enthusiasm over the new church-building was at white-heat. In a few days afterward men were at work on the building, and when Conference came the church was well under way.

We were returned to York by Bishop Andrews for the third year. The collecting of money for the new church, and looking after matters connected with the building, occupied a great deal of my time during the first part of the Conference year. Work on the building was pushed; the basement was completed, and we took possession and informally dedicated it to the worship of Almighty God December 6th. I took for my text on the occasion Psalm lxxxiv, 1: "How amiable are thy tabernacles, O Lord of hosts!" The room was full, the interest deep, and the attention the most profound. It was easy to preach to such a congregation. I have often said: "If a preacher can not preach in York, he can not preach anywhere." The members of the Church bear the preacher right up to the very throne of God on the mighty wings of prayer and faith. God wonderfully helped his weak servant in delivering the message of salvation. The glory of the Lord filled the house, and the first day's service in the new church was indeed most precious. It was the augury of the good things to come.

The audience-room was completed and ready for dedication February 27th, when Bishop H. W. Warren was present and preached the dedicatory sermon. His text was Isaiah lx, 17: "For brass I will bring gold, and for iron I will bring silver, and for wood brass, and for stones iron." The sermon was just such as Bishop Warren could preach. The house was packed to its utmost capacity with a most appreciative and intelligent audience. Over thirteen hundred were present at the morning service. We needed seven thousand dollars to remove all indebtedness. In a very little while over eight thousand dollars were subscribed, giving us a margin of one thousand dollars. The subscriptions were taken in notes bearing seven per cent interest. Dr. C. F. Creighton preached at night, and a most eventful day for York closed. It was another "red-letter day."

The official Board had determined to build a church costing twelve thousand dollars. We now had a church costing eighteen thousand dollars, and virtually out of debt. God's seal of approbation seemed to rest upon pastor and people from the moment the work began until "the head-stone was brought forth with shoutings, crying, Grace, grace unto it!"

During our three years' pastorate three hundred and thirty-five souls were converted, and the membership more than doubled. We left the charge with over six hundred members. Our success was due wholly to the fact that God was with pastor and people. We leaned not upon our own strength nor "unto our own understanding." These three years were memorable in our ministry. They will never be forgotten. They will be remembered with pleasure and delight when we reach the plains of glory. We expect to meet and to live forever with the good people of York.

CHAPTER XXIII.

METHODIST EDUCATION IN NEBRASKA UNIFIED.

Methodist Schools in Nebraska during the Past—
The Nebraska Wesleyan University.

BISHOP NINDE said, in an address delivered before the Educational Convention, held in Lincoln in the spring of 1889: "Nebraska has solved the great problem of the unification of Methodist education."

This question has baffled the minds of the greatest educators and divines in our Church for the past one hundred years. This great problem—one of the most perplexing of all educational problems—Nebraska has been the first to solve.

Up to 1887, the history of Methodist education in Nebraska had been anything but satisfactory. Up to that time the efforts of the Church along the line of education had been a succession of failures and the most disastrous defeats.

Against the multiplication of weak and sickly institutions of learning, our Discipline for many years has contained a standing protest. In section 2, paragraph 344, may be found the following recommendation: "And it is also recommended

METHODIST EDUCATION UNIFIED. 353

that no fewer than four Conferences unite in support of a college or university, and the Conferences are earnestly advised not to multiply schools, especially of the higher grade, beyond the wants of the people or their ability to sustain them." The wise men of our Church, who have given the above sensible advice, knew well that it takes immense sums of money to build up a successful university; and where two or more schools of high grade are attempted to be built up under the patronizing territory of three or four Conferences, all of them must of necessity be weak and sickly. But, notwithstanding this urgent request from the highest authorities of the Church, weak and sickly institutions of learning have gone on, multiplying and dying, all over our land; and the work of folly goes on to-day as in all the years of the past. The result has been that many warm friends of Christian education have become discouraged and utterly disheartened, and at many points Methodist education and the Methodist Episcopal Church have received a blow from which they will probably never fully recover. This process, for years and years, went on in Nebraska, just as in all other States.

The late Dr. John Dempster at one time had his eye on Nebraska as a suitable place to found a theological institute. This great and good man was among the first who felt deeply impressed with the conviction that there should be a seminary for young ministers. He began to devote himself to this work, and in 1847 he founded and opened the Biblical Institute at Concord, N. H. For seven years he labored faithfully as an instructor, during which time he traveled extensively and collected funds for the institution. After having, by his tireless zeal and indomitable energy, placed the institution firmly on its feet, and having seen it securely fixed in the affections of the preachers, he resigned his place to become a pioneer in the West. About this time, Mrs. Eliza Garrett, of Chicago, Ill., a lady of wealth, was arranging to devote her property for a theological school. The Doctor visited her, and through her munificent donations, opened a preliminary school at Evanston, which afterwards became the Garrett Biblical Institute. Having founded this school, and seen it firmly established, he began to look for a suitable place to found the third. His great heart was not satisfied with what he had already done. His yearning spirit was turned further West. He was exceedingly anxious to accomplish still more along the line of ministerial education. In 1858 the town of Oreapolis was founded, at the mouth of the Platte River, just north of the city of Plattsmouth. The design of the parties in locating this town was to make it a great educational center, and to build up a second Evanston. They confidently expected that Oreapolis would not only become a great educational center, but would be the eastern terminus of the Union Pacific Railroad, and the metropolitan city of the Great West. Liberal propositions were made to the Church by the town company.

At the Kansas and Nebraska Conference, held in Omaha in the spring of 1859, the Committee on Education, of which the writer was a member, submitted as part of its report the following, which was adopted:

"Your Committee on Education, to whom was referred the communication of John Dempster, in reference to the establishment of a Biblical institute at Oreapolis, would report:

"That they have carefully considered the propositions therein contained, and recommend the adoption of the following resolutions:

"1. *Resolved*, That we will cordially and heartily co-operate with the friends of ministerial education generally, and with Dr. John Dempster in particular, in the great work of founding and sustaining a Biblical institute, for the education of our junior ministry in the Missouri River valley, to be located at Oreapolis, N. T.

"2. *Resolved*, That the thanks of this Conference be tendered to Dr. Dempster for the noble and generous donation he has tendered to said institute, and for his efficient and devoted labors in the cause of ministerial education in our Church, and that he be cordially invited to join this Conference.

"3. *Resolved*, That it is the opinion of this Conference that said institute may with confidence expect as many as ten students from the Missouri Valley at its opening, as proposed by Dr. Dempster, in the autumn of 1860.

"4. *Resolved*, That this Conference respectfully memorialize the Territorial Legislature of Nebraska to grant the trustees of said institute a charter, with the usual franchises securing the control of the same in perpetuity to the Methodist Episcopal Church.

"All of which is respectfully submitted.

OREAPOLIS SEMINARY.

"Your Committee on Education, to whom was referred the charter of the seminary at Oreapolis, and the communication of John Evans in regard to the same, have had the same under consideration, and recommend the passage of the following resolution in reference thereto:

"*Resolved*, That we will co-operate with the friends of education in the establishment of said seminary at Oreapolis, and that we will exercise the control of said institution provided for in its charter in the appointment of trustees.

"All of which is respectfully submitted.

CASS COUNTY UNIVERSITY.

"Your committee, to whom was referred the charter of the university to be located in Cass County, N. T., and the communication from its Board of Trustees, have had the same under consideration, and respectfully report:

"That in view of the establishment of the institute and seminary at Oreapolis, and the great importance of concentrating our efforts upon one great leading enterprise in Nebraska, as a central educational point; in view of the liberality of said Town Company in not imposing onerous obligations upon the Conference as conditions of their large donation; and in view of the necessity of the theological as well as the literary and scientific departments being established in connection with a university to make it really such, we recommend the passage of the following resolutions:

"1. *Resolved*, That we accept the trust imposed upon us by the terms of the charter of said university in filling its Board of Trustees.

"2. *Resolved*, That we will cordially unite with the friends of education in exerting our best efforts to build up and sustain said university."

The following year a brick building, eighty feet in length, and three stories high, was erected, and a school of seminary grade opened. The school ran with encouraging success for awhile. But the location was bad, the town was not a success, the school became a failure, the property never came into the hands of the Church, and the whole scheme fell to pieces. The seminary, the Biblical Institute, and the Great University proved to be only the idle dreams of their projectors. Good men often make great mistakes. *Humanum est errare.*

In 1864, Professor J. M. McKenzie founded a seminary and normal institute at Pawnee City. The name of this school was "Nemaha Valley Seminary and Normal Institute." In the spring of 1865 the Nebraska Conference passed a resolution, recommending this institution of learning to the favorable consideration of all our people. While it never became the property of the Conference, it was largely patronized by our people.

This school, under the efficient management of Professor McKenzie, did good work for awhile, but, for the want of adequate means and patronage, soon ran its course, and died.

In 1866, under the leadership of the Rev. H. Burch, the people of Peru and Nemaha County raised several thousand dollars for the founding of a Methodist school at Peru. A building eighty feet long, forty feet wide, and three stories high, was erected. This school was incorporated under the style of "Peru Seminary and College," and its friends earnestly desired the Conference to adopt it, and take it under its absolute control. The Conference, however, was not willing to comply with the request of the trustees, unless they would modify their charter so as to reduce the grade of the school to a seminary. This they were not willing to do. The trustees then offered the property to the State, on condition that it be made a normal school. The offer was accepted, and a State normal school was founded, which has had increasing success ever since.

In 1879 two propositions were presented to the Conference; one from Osceola, and one from York. The proposition from York was accepted, and a school of seminary grade was at once started. Soon after this, the North Nebraska Conference founded a school at Fullerton. This school lived but a little while.

METHODIST EDUCATION UNIFIED. 359

Rev. Edward Thomson was appointed principal of the York Seminary. The new seminary started out under favorable auspices. Its friends were hopeful, and to them the future of the institution was exceedingly bright. Their expectations were sanguine in the extreme; they contracted debts, and these debts accumulated yearly.

In 1883 the grade was changed from that of a seminary to college, with a full classical curriculum. The future of the college was as hopeful as that of the seminary. Students increased. The college grew in favor with the people. Withal, each year swelled the indebtedness of the college, and the trustees had many a fearful grapple with them. Midnight often found them wrestling with the fearful problem: "How shall we meet these accumulating obligations?" Then, worn down in body and mind, they would retire to dream over the gloomy situation.

Central City College, only about forty miles away from York, was founded by the North Nebraska Conference. Here were two rival institutions, within forty miles of each other, each jealous of the other's success, and both struggling for existence.

Meanwhile, the Mallalieu University was founded at Bartley; but, like the others, was without financial bottom.

In the fall of 1886, Bishop Fowler was to preside at the Nebraska Conferences. Some of the friends of education saw very clearly the precarious condition of all our schools of high grade in the State. It seemed evident to the close observer of educational matters that the death of them all was only a question of time. Not one was on a firm financial basis. While Bishop Fowler was on his way to the North Nebraska Conference, he was met by Dr. C. F. Creighton and Dr. R. N. McKaig. Dr. McKaig was then president of York College. Dr. Creighton was pastor of Saint Paul, Lincoln.

The gloomy outlook of our educational matters, the want of sympathy between the friends of these local institutions, and the demand that something be done, both for the sake of education and religion, were laid before the bishop.

Dr. Creighton proposed that all our educational interests in the State be consolidated, and that we build up one great educational institution. After listening to the above facts, and the proposition of Dr. Creighton, the bishop arose and said, with stirring emphasis: *"This is the greatest work you have in Nebraska. Now what do you want me to do?"* Meantime, Rev. J. M. Phelps, presiding elder of the Omaha District, came in, and the bishop gave him the matter in substance, and Brother Phelps assented to the wisdom of such a plan, and agreed to stand by it. This was the unification of Methodist education in Nebraska in its incipiency.

That month, September, 1886, all the annual conferences in Nebraska—namely, the Nebraska, North Nebraska, and West Nebraska—at their sessions appointed a joint commission of ministers and laymen for the purpose of unifying the educational interests of the Church in the State, and the founding of a university.

That commission met in the city of Lincoln, December 15, 1886, and remained in session three days. Bishop Thomas Bowman and Bishop H. W. Warren were present part of the time. The following plan of unification was agreed upon:

PLAN OF AGREEMENT

FOR THE UNIFICATION OF OUR COLLEGES IN A UNIVERSITY IN NEBRASKA.

First. That trustees, to be hereafter appointed, secure a charter for a university, to include, as contributory or allied institutions, the schools and colleges at present or hereafter coming under the control of the Methodist Episcopal Church in Nebraska.

Second. That all schools or colleges, which are now or may hereafter become the property of the Methodist Episcopal Church in Nebraska, shall be under the control of the university trustees; but all the property, real, personal, or mixed, shall be held and controlled by their own local Boards of Trustees.

Third. The first Board of University Trustees shall consist of seven trustees, from within the boundaries of each Conference in Nebraska, to be appointed by this commission, and approved by the several Conferences to which they belong, and that hereafter the trustees shall consist of seven persons from each and every Conference, elected in four annual classes by their respective Conferences. The persons thus elected by the several Conferences shall constitute the local Boards of the several colleges within the bounds of their respective Conferences.

These several local Boards of Trustees to hold and control the property of each college as above provided, and each local Board may nominate so many additional members as each separate Conference may determine to elect who, in addition to said local Board, shall perform the duties of said local trustees.

Fourth. Duties of the university and college trustees:

(a) The university trustees to have and hold all property belonging to the university proper, and to manage the affairs of the same.

(b) To determine the course of study, text-books to be used, systems of grading, and to do all such other work as appertains to the general educational interests of the allied colleges; providing that each college elect its own faculty and arrange for its own internal discipline.

All other powers remain with the local Boards of Trustees as defined by their charters and by-laws.

Fifth. Any school or college existent, or that may come under the charter of the university, shall be entitled to retain its college name, to acquire property to be held for the benefit of such college, to teach regular preparatory and collegiate studies, as far as the end of the sophomore year of the university course, and to confer academic and normal degrees. The colleges of the university shall have the same courses of study, use the same text-books, and students of one college shall be entitled to enter the same grade and rank in any college of the university, on certificate of standing, without examination.

Amendment to Article V:

The clause in Article V of the above, which reads "as far as the end of the sophomore year," etc., shall be understood to be so interpreted that any college of this university may be graded in its classical curriculum in every detail, so that its classical senior year of graduation shall not be graded higher than the end of the sophomore year of the classical course of the university.

The following addition was adopted:

The Board of Trustees shall make the grade of the university equal to that of any Methodist university in the United States.

York, Central City, Bartley, Omaha, and Lincoln were all applicants for the university. On the second ballot, Lincoln was selected as the place for its location. The friends of York worked hard to secure the location, but failed, and they returned home sadly disappointed. The trustees in their haste unwisely passed a resolution declaring York College independent of the "Plan of Agreement." They soon saw, however, their great mistake. The cry of disloyalty was at once raised, and the trustees realized that they were losing the sympathy of people and preachers throughout the Conference. They then changed tactics and wheeled into line. A resolution was passed by the Board rescinding the action whereby it had declared York College independent of the "Plan of Agreement." But the college was loaded down with a debt of sixteen thousand dollars; the trustees were sued, and were about to be sold out by their creditors, and their property sacrificed. Rather than have this done, they sold the property themselves, paid off their debts, and closed the school. It was a sad day for York College. The noble men who had stood by her in her darkest days felt most keenly the loss. The money spent on the York College, however, has not been lost. Forth from that college have gone students and an influence, the salutary effects of which will be felt in many parts of the land through all time.

The university was located at Lincoln, within a radius of three and one-half miles from the United States post-office. A beautiful site was selected on an elevated position. From this elevated position the city of Lincoln and the whole surrounding country can be distinctly seen. Chancellor Creighton took Chaplain McCabe to the highest point on the campus before the building was completed, and then said to him: "Chaplain, look around." The chaplain took off his hat, gazed with delight in every direction, and, taking a long breath, inflated his lungs with the pure air of Nebraska, then said: "Methodism always gets ahead."

At another time the chancellor took Bishop Joyce to the same spot, and, after the bishop had taken in the situation, said: "Would n't we be jealous if some other denomination had this?"

The campus contains forty-four acres. In the center stands the university building, which is four stories high, one hundred and sixty-eight by seventy-two feet, built of brick, and trimmed with red granite from Colorado, and is one of the most beautiful and imposing structures in the West. The building cost seventy thousand dollars. Of this amount the city of Lincoln paid fifty thousand dollars, and the balance was paid from the sale of lots donated to the university.

Along all lines great victories are not gained without great conflicts, and the Nebraska Wesleyan University is not an exception to this rule. The parties who gave the site required the trustees to give bonds in the sum of ninety thousand dollars, that the building should be ready for occupancy by the first of October, 1888, and should cost not less than fifty thousand dollars. A few of the trustees, individually, gave the required bond. Work began, but time and again stopped for the want of means. The matter weighed heavily on the mind of Dr. Creighton. The cloud at times grew awfully dark. Often at the hour of midnight he would crawl out of bed, get down upon his knees, and pray for God to come to their help.

Lots were sold for one-fourth cash, the balance on one, two, and three years' time. Some of this paper was negotiated to Eastern parties. The banks in Lincoln offered to take this paper at a discount of twenty per cent, and the personal indorsement of the trustees. The trustees declined this offer. Again the work stopped. The Board met. The outlook was dark in the extreme. The trustees looked ominously at each other. Some said: "The thing is a failure." Bishop Warren was present, and listened with deep interest to the long and weary discussions. Finally the bishop said: "I will give you a thousand dollars." The chancellor said: "That will not relieve us." "What do you think I ought to do?" "Give us ten thousand dollars," said the chancellor.

The bishop replied, "I will take five thousand dollars worth of lots and five thousand dollars of your paper, on condition that you sell the remaining collateral," amounting to over ten thousand dollars. Dr. Creighton sold that paper within a week, and telegraphed the bishop asking if he (Dr. Creighton) should draw on him for the ten thousand dollars. The bishop replied affirmatively, and Dr. Creighton drew the money. The financial credit of the university from that hour was at par. The trustees breathed easy; the clouds began to break and roll away; work on the building was pushed, and on the twenty-fifth day of September, 1888, the Nebraska Wesleyan University was informally opened. A handful of students, with a few friends of the institution, met in the library hall, on the third floor of the building. Dr. W. G. Miller, president of the Board of Trustees, and presiding elder of the Lincoln District, conducted the religious services. Chancellor Creighton delivered a short address, and the writer followed with a brief sketch of the history of Methodist education in Nebraska. The few who were privileged to be there will probably never forget that memorable occasion. The formal opening of the university took place in the university chapel, October 24th, when Bishop John P. Newman delivered an able and exceedingly interesting address on the occasion, and Chancellor Creighton gave his inaugural, which was an able review of the history of the university up to that time. Governor John M. Thayer followed with a well-timed impromptu address, and one of the greatest educational enterprises of the Methodist Episcopal Church was inaugurated.

It will be observed by the "Plan of Agreement" that the Nebraska Wesleyan University is the property of all the Annual Conferences of the Methodist Episcopal Church in the State. Second, that the university includes, "as contributory or allied institutions, the schools and colleges at present or hereafter coming under the control of the Methodist Episcopal Church in

Nebraska." Every academy and college that shall hereafter become the property of the Church in Nebraska will be part of this great university.

The wisdom of this plan will appear if we take into view a few facts:

First. The age in which we live is one of the most intense mental activity. One high in authority in our Church said in a letter to the writer some time ago, touching this matter: "We are in great need of the best possible workmen, with the best possible training. Not a shred of Christian faith will survive that can not be defended on the hottest field, and we are compelled to go into the death-struggle for the Church with strong, scholarly men, who can command the attention and confidence of the people. This makes it necessary for us to have the best possible training-schools. Our university must be second to none on the earth. If we can make her the peer of the best, so that our graduates shall be honored among any company of college men, then we can expect to retain our hold upon the confidence and patronage of the public. I am sure we shall come far short of this if we go into the fight with little, poor colleges, that have only the name and not the appliances of colleges. The freshman and suphomore years can be taught by drill-masters, whose salaries need never be large; but in the junior and senior years, where a number of elective studies are furnished by our best universities, thus enabling the students to start somewhat towards their particular line of life, we, too, must furnish these elective studies, under competent professors, or we must stand aside and let others do the work. All this requires money. It needs no argument to prove that Nebraska Methodism is not capable of running three schools of such magnitude and character; but if she will combine all her money and energies on one she may compete successfully with the schools anywhere in the land."

This is just what Nebraska Methodism has done. She has founded a university with a grade equal to that of any Methodist university in the United States, and is uniting her money and energies in building up this great institution.

Second. Academies at different points in the State are already projected, with the view of becoming parts of the university. These will multiply with years, and thus feeders to the university will be constantly increasing. At these academies the bulk of education done by the Church in the State may be accomplished, and will be done at the lowest possible expense. Not more than ten out of every one hundred who pass through the academy ever go through the university; those who desire to do so, however, can receive the greater part of their education at the academy, where the expense will not be great, and only the last two or three years need necessarily be spent at the university, where they will have all the appliances of a university of the highest grade.

Third. The students who shall graduate from the Nebraska Wesleyan University will never be ashamed of their *Alma Mater*. From her halls of learning they will go forth to be honored among any company of college men in the land.

Fourth. Men who, under God, have been blessed with wealth, and desire to consecrate that wealth to the building up of Christ's kingdom, want to place it where it will yield the largest returns for God. They are not willing usually to give their money to weak and sickly schools, whose existence is merely an experiment.

Those who have money they wish to consecrate, and desire to place it where it will yield the largest income, will make no mistake in endowing the Nebraska Wesleyan University. Here is an institution of learning that will grow in usefulness and power with the centuries.

There are consecrated men of means who are looking around to see where they can make the safest and most profitable investment for the Lord. Should the eyes of any such chance to fall upon these pages, they may rest assured that the Nebraska Wesleyan University furnishes a place for the safest and most profitable investment.

METHODIST EDUCATION UNIFIED. 371

Fifth. Already this university, although only a little over two years old, has more property than all the schools connected with the Methodist Episcopal Church in Nebraska combined, and all the schools run by private members of the Church, from the organization of the Territory, in 1854, to the present time. Why this phenomenal growth? Why the wonderfully encouraging outlook of this university? Because she has behind her all the preachers and all the members of the Methodist Episcopal Church throughout the entire State.

Every Methodist preacher throughout Nebraska is an unpaid agent, to advertise, send students, and raise money for the building up of this institution of learning. Two hundred miles wide, and four hundred miles long is pre-empted forever for one Methodist university; namely, the Nebraska Wesleyan University.

Methodism in Nebraska to-day has thirty-five thousand two hundred and sixty-one members, including probationers; and three hundred and fifty-four traveling preachers, including supplies.

On the same ratio of increase as during the past few years, Methodism in the State in ten years will have seventy-five thousand members, and seven hundred traveling preachers. Then there will be seven hundred unpaid agents working in all parts of the State for this university.

From more than seven hundred points in the State will flow streams of students and wealth to our great educational center; and these streams of students and wealth will multiply as the years roll on. If I were to utter a prediction, that I feel in my heart will be fulfilled if Methodism is true to the trust imposed on her, as to what this university will be in ten years from now, I should probably be called an enthusiast. No Methodist institution ever had such a propitious start.

CHAPTER XXIV.

METHODISM'S DISTINCTIVE DOCTRINE REVIVED.

WHAT THE DOCTRINE IS—THE GREAT REVIVAL.—HISTORY OF THE BENNETT CAMP-MEETING.

THE peculiar and distinctive doctrine of the Methodist Episcopal Church—that which distinguishes her from all other Protestant Churches—is the doctrine of entire sanctification, as a work wrought by the Holy Ghost subsequent to conversion. Our Board of Bishops, in their "Episcopal Address," on the first page of our excellent book of Discipline, say: "In 1729 two young men in England, reading the Bible, saw they could not be saved without holiness; followed after it; and incited others so to do. In 1737 they saw likewise that men are justified before they are sanctified; but still holiness was their object. God then thrust them out to raise a holy people." These words are quoted by our bishops, as they tell us, from John and Charles Wesley. Further, in this same address, they say: "We believe that God's design in raising up the Methodist Episcopal Church in America, was to reform the continent, and spread Scriptural holiness over these lands."

"Holiness unto the Lord" was the rallying cry of John Wesley. These inspiring words became also the rallying cry of the founders of American Methodism. On the banners of the Church these burning words were written by the "Fathers," and then these banners were boldly flung to the breeze. Under the clean-cut, powerful preaching of this doctrine, wonderful revivals were witnessed in many parts of the land. The Church grew and spread mightily. As we neared the close of the first century of American Methodism, however, the tide of spirituality in the Churches had gone down to a very low ebb. All felt the demoralizing influence of the Civil War. The leaders of the hosts of our Zion saw and felt it most clearly. They felt, too, the need of a more complete and thorough consecration of all to God. The bishops, in their Address to the General Conference of 1864, said: "It becomes us, dear brethren, to humble ourselves in the dust in view of our manifold sins, individual and National. We are yet, it may be feared, a haughty and rebellious people; and God will humble us. There can be no good reason to expect the restoration of order and unity until we properly deplore our sins, and return to God with deep self-abasement and fervent prayer. A gracious revival of religion—deep, pervading, and permanent—is the great demand of our times. We beg you, brethren, turn your most thoughtful and prayerful attention to this demand. Let God, our Heavenly Father, behold us in tears and confidence before his throne, pleading night and day, through the Redeemer, for the outporing of the Holy Ghost upon the Church, the Nation, and the world. This is our only hope; let our faith command it, and it shall be." The Address of the bishops stirred the hearts of many, and both preachers and laymen began to feel their great need. The following year there was quite an awakening upon the subject of holiness. A camp-meeting was held on the Bridgeton District, New Jersey Conference. The presiding elder, Rev. Charles H. Whitecar, had charge of the meeting, and entire holiness was made quite prominent. The meeting was one of great interest and power. Many went down into the cleansing fountain, and returned to their homes to tell the wondrous story of Christ's cleansing power. The influence of that meeting was wide-spread. Remarkable revivals followed, " and the whole district was in fact ablaze." The following year, 1866, another meeting was held on the same ground, which was still more successful. " The result was, the ground was literally fire-swept. It flamed with the glory of God." Many ministers and laymen went down into the pool, were cleansed, and wondrously endued with power. The tidings of these meetings spread far and near. They became the topic of conversation, not only in our Church, but in other Churches as well; and a devoted Christian belonging to a sister Church uttered the following prophecy: It was publicly declared "that within four years camp-meetings would be held over this land for the promotion of holiness, and that in that very section there would be a great gathering of God's people of different names in this interest." The next year the first National Camp-meeting for the Promotion of Holiness was held at Vineland, and the above prophecy was literally fulfilled.

A public call for a meeting of ministers and laymen, favorable to holding a camp-meeting for the promotion of entire sanctification, was made, to meet June 13, 1867, at the Methodist Bookroom, 1018 Arch Street, Philadelphia. The call was signed by Rev. A. E. Ballard, presiding elder, and twelve others.

At the appointed time many ministers and laymen, with hearts all aglow with heaven-fire and holy zeal, assembled. Rev. George Hughes, in his "Days of Power," gives the following description of that first council:

" Hallowed memories cluster around the council-chamber, at 1018 Arch Street, Philadelphia.

The morning of June 13, 1867, will never be forgotten. It was an auspicious morning. A holy atmosphere seemed to pervade the room. The rustle of angel's wings was almost perceptible to mortal ear. The presence of the Triune God—Father, Son, and Holy Ghost—was distinctly apprehended. Every face was bright; every spirit was joyous. Never did good men grasp more warmly each other by the hand Brother Osborn was there, ready to stand in his lot, and never more satisfied that this was of God. The time-honored Dr. Roberts, of Baltimore, occupied his place, his countenance glowing with delight, and his soul magnifying the Lord Jesus exceedingly. Rev. John S. Inskip shouted aloud the praises of God as he grasped each fraternal hand; he was full nerved for the battle. The presiding elder, Rev. A. E. Ballard, genial, kind spirited, determined, was in the company.

"The beloved disciple—our own ascended brother, Rev. Alfred Cookman—with his saintly face and dignified mien, was ready to be consecrated on this altar. Close to him was Rev. Andrew Longacre, who was his bosom companion, glorying only in the cross, and saying none other thing than that the blood of Jesus cleanseth from all sin. Lovely were those brothers in their lives, even as David and Jonathan; and in death they were not divided. We can not give a full list. It was not a large meeting as to numbers, but it was composed of united, earnest men, disposed to assume the responsibilities of the occasion, with a single eye to the divine glory.

"The meeting being called to order, Rev. Dr. George C. M. Roberts, of Baltimore, was elected chairman, and Rev. John Thomson secretary. The president then led in prayer. He poured out his soul in thankfulness that he was permitted to see that favored hour. He was like a patriarch talking with God. He knew the way of access. He grasped firmly the horns of the altar. He pleaded for divine aid. He invoked wisdom and strength. He made his plea on the ground of Christ's atoning blood. He put forth a hand of faith; it took fast hold of the promise. The answering tokens were given.

"Rev. J. S. Inskip followed in prayer. His voice was tremulous with emotion. His soul was feeling the mighty responsibilities of the occasion. His vision was expanded to compass the thrilling interests involved in the action of that day. He was earnest in supplication for divine guidance. He besought the Lord not to carry his servants up hence unless his presence should go with them. The prayer was divinely indited. The adorable intercessor, pleading on his behalf, even with groanings that could not be uttered, was in his servant's prayer. That hour of communion with

Heaven will never be obliterated from the memory of those privileged to be present. The 'Master of assemblies' was there. The cloud, big with blessings, was just overhead. A solemn awe rested upon the whole company. A divine hush was upon every spirit. The wealth of eternity was in every bosom. The joy of the Lord was the strength of the little assembly. Some found relief in tears; others praised the Lord aloud. O, how glorious it was to be there! Undying praises to the Lamb!"

Under these circumstances the great holiness revival was inaugurated. Ten hundred and eighteen Arch Street, Philadelphia, was the Jerusalem upper room to that spirit-baptized band of holy men. Forth from that little room rolled a wave of revival flame that soon girdled the globe.

At that council arrangements were made for holding the first camp-meeting for the promotion of holiness. The meeting was held at Vineland, beginning Wednesday, July 17th, and closing Friday, July 26, 1867. On this first meeting God put his seal of approbation. The meeting was crowned with wondrous success. Hundreds went down into the cleansing fountain, and large numbers were clearly converted. At the close, the people, by rising to their feet, expressed the earnest desire to have another meeting of similar character the following year. A committee was appointed for the purpose of carrying into effect the desire of the people. The next meeting was held at Manheim, with the same happy results; and every year since similar meetings have been held. Chaplain McCabe once said: " You ought to attend one holiness camp-meeting before going to heaven." A holiness camp-meeting is in fact about as near heaven as one can get in this world.

In the spring of 1871, Bishop Ames invited Rev. J. S. Inskip and his wife to accompany him to his spring Conferences. The kindly request was cheerfully complied with. They accompanied the bishop, kindling a mighty fire of holiness at every Conference, and creating a wonderful thirst for purity in many hearts.

The Nebraska Conference met at Lincoln, March 29, 1871. Brother and Sister Inskip were present. On the first day the following paper was read, and unanimously adopted:

"WHEREAS, We have learned with great pleasure of the labors of Brother and Sister Inskip with the various Conferences of the West during the last few weeks; and *whereas*, our hearts are in deep sympathy with them and the great special work in which they are engaged; therefore,

"*Resolved*, That we do most cordially welcome them to our Conference, and would most respectfully request that Brother Inskip take charge of our morning meetings and such other social religious exercises as may be held during the session of the Conference."

A meeting of about one hour each morning before the Conference business began, was conducted by Brother and Sister Inskip. These were meetings of wondrous power. We had never seen anything like them before. Brother and Sister Inskip told their experience of entire sanctification. They spoke with rapture of the new-found joy and marvelous power of holiness. Sister Inskip's singing was the most thrilling. Under its heavenly strains all hearts were melted. There was no lounging around the doors before the Conference sessions opened. Ministers and laymen flocked to the morning meetings. Many were fully saved, and the desire for holiness was planted in many hearts.

The following year, arrangements were made for holding a camp-meeting for the promotion of holiness at Bennett. Rev. W. B. M. Colt, of the Oak Creek Circuit, and Rev. C. A. King, of Schuyler, were both in the experience of full salvation, and were the leaders in arranging for and conducting this meeting.

A beautiful grove near Bennett was selected, the ground was prepared, and on Tuesday, August 13, 1872, the first meeting for the promotion of holiness in the State of Nebraska began. The attendance was not large, but the meeting from the very beginning was marked with unusual manifestations of divine power. At every meeting souls were saved. Many were converted and many wholly sanctified. On each succeeding day the tide of spirituality rose higher and higher, and the culminating point was reached on the Sabbath, which was the great day of the feast. The overshadowing presence of the Shekinah was felt by all throughout the entire day. During the love-feast, which lasted one hour and five minutes, one hundred and five testimonies were given, and the congregation sung fifteen different times. We had never witnessed anything like this. It seemed that it was Pentecost repeated. The whole day was one of power. At this meeting Mrs. Davis and myself and our daughter Allie, all sought and found the great blessing.

I had been under conviction for heart-purity for some time, and went to this meeting with somewhat confused ideas touching the doctrine, and with a religious experience not at all satisfying. Under the clean-cut preaching of the doctrine, and the many ringing testimonies, we were led to the most rigid and thorough heart-searchings. The spiritual conflict with me was long and severe. I was at that time presiding elder of the Lincoln District. To go down in the straw at the altar as a seeker of holiness was indeed humiliating. What would the people of my district think of me? Would they think that I had been preaching all these years without religion? Would they not say: "During all these years you have been a hypocrite?" What would the preachers say? What effect would such a step have upon my future appointments in the Conference? These and many other questions confronted me; but I had little difficulty in disposing of them all. Then the enemy said: "Are you willing to be called one of the sanctified ones? Are you willing to have the people say, 'He thinks himself holier than we?' Are you willing to take the odium that will attach to you if you seek this blessing?" All these questions I answered in the affirmative, as they came, one by one. The final test was applied. The last great question came. It was a staggering one: "Will you publish to the world the great doctrine of holiness?" I hesitated. The question was pressed home to my heart with increasing force and power. Still I hesitated. It was a hard question to answer, and involved grave responsibilities. The conflict went on in my mind for two days or more. No one on the ground knew anything about it. It was a secret but mighty conflict with the powers of darkness, a hand-to-hand grapple with the arch-fiend of hell.

Again the question came: "Will you fling to the breeze the banner of holiness, and under that banner will you march?" Still I hesitated. But finally I said, as I lay with my face in the straw: "Yes, Lord, I will." The battle was ended, the enemy completely routed, the victory gained; and there came into my heart a wonderfully sweet peace. There was no great ecstasy; no rapturous joy; no great emotion. But a sweet quiet reigned within. "The peace of God which passeth all understanding" took possession of my soul. God said to his ancient people: "O that thou hadst hearkened to my commandments! Then had thy peace been as a river, and thy righteousness as the waves of the sea." I saw and knew the meaning of that passage of Scripture as never before. Look at the majestic river as it sweeps onward, calm and unruffled, to the ocean, with scarcely a ripple upon its surface. There may be disturbing elements on either side of that river. Along its banks cities may be burned, bloody battles may be fought, raging epidemics may sweep away thousands of the people; but the river, undisturbed, moves onward amid all these scenes, "the same yesterday, to-day, and forever." "Men may come and men may go, but I go on forever." It is a beautiful emblem of the peace which takes possession of the saved soul. There may be disturbing elements all along the Christian's pathway; there may be disturbing elements in the home, in business matters, in the Church, in the community. But away down in the soul is the settled peace, the great calm; and this peace, this undisturbed calm, flows on amid all these disturbing elements, the same day after day, and year after year.

> "It sweetly cheers our drooping hearts
> In this dark vale of tears;
> Life, light, and joy it still imparts,
> And quells our rising fears."

Isaac Watts's hymn, altered by John Wesley, also beautifully expresses it:

> "The men of grace have found
> Glory begun below;
> Celestial fruit on earthly ground
> From faith and hope may grow.
>
> Then let our songs abound,
> And every tear be dry;
> We're marching through Immanuel's ground,
> To fairer worlds on high."

At this first camp-meeting for the promotion of holiness "The Nebraska State Holiness Association" was organized, and every year since a camp-meeting for the promotion of holiness and the conversion of sinners has been held; and on every one of these meetings God's seal of approbation has been placed. Not one has been barren of success. I am sorry I have not at hand a full list of the names of those who took an active part at that first meeting, and who were the charter members of the Association. The following were among the number: Rev. W. B. M. Colt, Rev. C. A. King, Rev. George S. Alexander, Rev. George Worley, Rev. Thomas Crowder, Rev. H. Burch, Rev. H. T. Davis, Professor J. M. McKenzie, Hon. C. C. White, Caleb Worley.

At the fifteenth session of the Nebraska Conference, held in Lincoln, beginning September 15, 1875, the following paper was adopted:

"WHEREAS, There is a growing interest among the people on the doctrine of entire sanctification, as held and taught by the founder of our Church; and *whereas*, we believe the National Association for the Promotion of Holiness are safe and successful teachers of the same; therefore,

"*Resolved*, That we, as a Conference, invite them to hold a camp-meeting among us at their own convenience during the summer of 1876, and that we pledge our co-operation to make such a meeting a success."

The National Association accepted the invitation, and fixed June 27th as the time for the meeting to begin. The officers of the State Holiness Association searched diligently and widely for a suitable place, and after careful and thorough search, the grounds at Bennett were selected for the meeting. A large outlay was made in digging wells, fitting up the grounds, and preparing for the coming great occasion. The meeting began at the appointed time. Only two members of the National Association could be present—Rev. S. H. Henderson and Rev. J. B. Foote. These two men, however, were equal for the occasion. They came in "the fullness of the blessing of the Gospel," and their preaching and teachings were "in demonstration of the Spirit and power." The work at this meeting was thorough, the convictions were deep, the conversions clear, and the sanctifications unmistakable. Then another remarkable feature of this meeting was the speed with which the work was done. The people of God had gathered such a head of divine power, and were so strong in faith that all they had to do was to "ask and receive." Sinners were converted and believers wholly sanctified almost as soon as they reached the altar. At one meeting the altar was crowded with seekers. Two rows of seats, reaching clear across the tabernacle, were filled. During one season of prayer every seeker, save one or two, was saved. A cloud of glory seemed to settle down upon the congregation, and a shock of divine power was felt by all present, such as is seldom the privilege of any to feel. Brother Foote said to the writer: "I never saw or felt anything like it in my life." Over the entrance to the grounds, in large letters, were printed on white canvas the words, "Holiness unto the Lord." This motto made a wonderful impression upon nearly all who came upon the grounds. As the people passed under this banner they seemed to feel that they were treading upon holy ground. An ungodly man, who was clearly converted at one of the meetings, said : "Just as I passed under that banner, on which were inscribed the words, 'Holiness unto the Lord,' I was most powerfully convicted." That man was just as powerfully converted, and left the grounds rejoicing in a Savior's love. A mysterious and hallowed influence was felt all over the grounds, that even the most ungodly could not possibly resist. A very wicked man, after being in one of the meetings a short time and witnessing the stirring and happy scenes, walked silently away, and as he passed out of the grounds, said to a friend: "My God, I wish I was a Christian !" A Christian lady came upon the grounds on Monday. Afterwards she said to me, in substance: "The moment I entered the encampment I was awed into reverence. It seemed that just above the grounds, all through the branches of the tree-tops, innumerable angels from the skies, robed in white, were hovering." It did seem at times that we could almost see these heavenly visitants, hear their sweet melody, and feel our cheeks fanned by their snowy wings. The results of this meeting were far more glorious than we had most sanguinely hoped. Two other meetings were held by the National Association—one in 1877, and the other in 1879. At each of these meetings the same divine power was manifested, and the same gracious results reached. At the last named meeting the State Holiness Association purchased from Mr. Roggencamp the Bennett Camp-grounds. Here on these hallowed grounds for eighteen years scenes have been witnessed that have delighted the angels in heaven, rejoiced believers on earth, and enraged the demons in hell.

At one of these meetings an old man, sixty years of age, said: "I came one hundred and fifty miles on horseback to attend this meeting and seek holiness, and I praise God I have got what I came for. I am more than rewarded for my long and weary ride." From this sacred encampment have rolled forth waves of holy influence that have touched, not only distant points in our own State, but have reached and permeated distant places in many other States as well. Many, we have reason to believe, will praise God forever for the Bennett camp-meetings.

It is the duty of every one who is converted to tell to the world what the Lord has done for his soul. It is the duty of every one who has been wholly sanctified, in a meek way to declare that fact to the world. David said: "Come and hear, all ye that fear God, and I will declare what he hath done for my soul." Paul says: "With the heart man believeth unto righteousness, and with the mouth confession is made unto salvation." John says: "They overcame him by the blood of the Lamb and the word of their testimony." We are to confess to the world just what Christ has done for us; no more, no less. In making this confession, however, great care should be taken lest we *seem* to boast of our superior piety. Holiness is a term that is odious to many, because they associate with it superior sanctity, and back of that hypocrisy. So it becomes us to be very judicious in our testimonies. Christ commands us to be "wise as serpents and harmless as doves."

While it is our duty to be pronounced upon this subject—to stand up for the doctrine—we should not always be harping upon our experience. There is great danger of our becoming spiritually proud. Many well-meaning people actually become so before they are aware of it. There is danger of our becoming men of "one idea," of our becoming fanatical. Bishop William Taylor says: "There is only one step from sanctification to fanaticism." And alas! too many take that fatal step.

DISTINCTIVE DOCTRINE REVIVED. 391

There is danger of our becoming too tenacious touching the use of terms. Some have pet phrases, and in describing the great work wrought in the soul by the power of the Holy Ghost, they always use the same set phrase, and consider it almost an unpardonable sin, or at least a lack of moral courage, to vary in the least from their set terms and pet phrases. Mr. Wesley was not a stickler for any set terms. He says: "I have no particular fondness for the term *perfection;* it seldom occurs, either in my preaching or writings. It is my opponents who thrust it upon me continually, and ask me what I mean by it. That it is a Scriptural term, is undeniable. Therefore none ought to object to the use of the term. But I still think that perfection is only another term for holiness, or the image of God in man. 'God made man perfect,' I think, is just the same as 'he made him holy.'" (Vol. VI, p. 535.)

"The moment a sinner is justified, his heart is cleansed in a low degree; but yet he has not a clean heart in the full proper sense till he is *made perfect in love.*" (Vol. V, p. 284.)

In March, 1761, in his journal he says: "I met again with those who believe God has delivered them from the *root of bitterness.*"

And again says he: "Abundance have been convinced of sin; very many have found peace with God, and in London only, I believe, full two hundred have been brought into *glorious liberty.*"

In his journal of June, 1765, he says: "Many others are groaning after *full salvation.*"

In writing to Miss H. A. Roe, in 1776, he says: "Certainly before *the root of sin is taken away,* believers may live above the power of it."

In writing to Mrs. Crosby, in 1761, he says: "The work goes on mightily here in London. I believe within five weeks, six in one class have received remission of sins, and five in one band received a *second blessing.*"

"This morning before you left us, one found peace and one *the second blessing.*" (Journal, June, 1763.)

In writing to Miss Jane Hilton, in 1774, he says: "It is exceedingly certain that God did give you the *second blessing,* properly so called. He delivered you from the *root of bitterness;* from inbred sin, as well as actual sin."

It is clear, therefore, that John Wesley was not a stickler for any set phrase. He used a great variety of terms in describing the work of holiness—"perfection," "holiness," "perfect in love," "glorious liberty," "the root of bitterness taken away," "second blessing," "full salvation "—all these he used, and these are all Scriptural terms.

John, the beloved disciple, uses the phrase

"perfect love." "Herein is our love *made perfect*. . . . Because as he is, so are we in this world." (1 John iv, 17.)

"*Perfect love* casteth out fear; because fear hath torment. He that feareth is not made *perfect in love*." (Verse 18.)

Paul used the term "holiness." "Follow peace with all men, and *holiness*, without which no man shall see the Lord." (Heb. xii, 14.) Paul used the phrase "fullness of the blessing of the gospel of Christ" (Rom. xv, 29), and "full assurance of faith." (Heb. x, 22.) From these, doubtless, Mr. Wesley got the phrase "full salvation." Paul used the phrase "second benefit." "I was minded to come unto you before, that ye might have a *second benefit*." (2 Cor. i, 15.)

From this passage, doubtless, came into use, by John Wesley and others, the words "second blessing."

Paul also used the phrase so often used by Wesley, "root of bitterness." "Follow peace with all men, and holiness, without which no man shall see the Lord. Looking diligently lest any man fail of the grace of God; lest any *root of bitterness* springing up trouble you." (Heb. xii, 15.)

So, then, these terms, "full salvation," "perfect love," "second blessing," "delivered from the root of bitterness"—all are Scriptural and all are legitimate.

There is danger, too, of our becoming censorious and dogmatic.

Whenever Satan can succeed in switching us off on any one of these lines, our influence and power for usefulness is to a great extent crippled.

Against all these dangers we should carefully guard. More and more every day do I see the great importance of *living holiness*.

Mr. Punshon, the great English divine, in giving his estimate of Rev. Alfred Cookman, says: "If I would write down my impression of Alfred Cookman's character, I find myself at a loss; for I can scarcely convey my estimate of him in sober words. I have been privileged to meet with many gifted and godly men in different lands, and in various branches of the Catholic Church. I speak advisedly when I say that I never met with one who so well realized my idea of complete devotedness. When some pagan questioners asked a Christian of old about the religion of Jesus, and were disposed to ascribe its spread to its loftier thought and pure truth, the Christian made for answer: 'We do not speak greater things, *but we live.*' This life, wherever it is embodied, is the highest power. And it was felt to be so in the wide sphere in which Alfred Cookman was permitted to testify for the Master whom he loved. There are men of sterling worth, who manage to hide their excellences from their fellows, living amongst men unappreciated, because they have no witness,—like some bird of rare plumage, of whose beauty the world knew not until they caught the luster which flashed from its parting wing. He was not one of these. His life was a perpetual testimony that God can come down to man, and that man can be lifted up to God. It was impossible to doubt that, 'swift-like, he lived in heaven.' There were many who objected to his doctrine; there were none within the range of his acquaintance who failed to be impressed, and few who failed to be influenced by his life."

What is needed more than any one thing is, not " to speak greater things, *but to live.*" What we want in order to speedily capture this world for Christ is, " living epistles " of Christ's power to save from all sin—" known and read of all men." Theodore L. Cuyler has well said : " The sermons in shoes are the sermons to convert an ungodly world."

No irregularities of an injurious tendency, so far as I am aware, have ever developed in the National Association ; and no such irregular tendencies have ever been developed at the Bennett holiness meetings. At times they have cropped out, but have been checked at once. In other holiness associations, however, such irregularities have been developed, and have brought the most blessed and desirable of all the doctrines of the Bible into disrepute. This hallowed Bible doctrine has suffered very greatly from the inefficient, inexperienced, and fanatical teachers of independent holiness associations. This fact led the New England Conference, at its session in the spring of 1889, to adopt the following resolutions. These resolutions were signed by Dr. Daniel Steele, a member of the National Holiness Association, and other leading members of the Conference:

"The New England Conference at its recent session passed the following resolutions in regard to holiness associations, signed by Dr. Daniel Steele and other leading members of the Conference:

"*Resolved*, That as pastors we will not organize nor associate ourselves with holiness associations in our charges; but we will continue in our regular ministrations, to unfold, defend, and enforce this important doctrine in due proportion to our other doctrines, so that there shall be no occasion for any of our members to resort to meetings not under our pastoral direction, and to incompetent teachers, whose unguarded instructions may be disastrous to spiritual life.

"*Resolved*, That we advise our people not to organize or to associate themselves with so-called holiness associations, independent of the Church and of their pastors. We believe that the meetings of such associations are often the occasion of jealousy and ill-feeling; that they tend to division in the Church; and that they unjustly reflect upon the unfaithfulness of the Church and the pastors to the doctrines of the Church."

These resolutions were not intended as a reflection on the profession of holiness, but on the independent holiness associations, which have developed irregularities, which tend to greatly injure the doctrine, and that are not warranted in God's Word.

As Methodists, we ought not to need independent holiness associations. Holiness is the distinctive and peculiar doctrine of the Methodist Episcopal Church. As loyal Methodists, then, let us fling the banner of holiness to the breeze. Let it float out and wave over every Church and every society. Let it be lifted so high that all the world can see it. Then let us avoid the extravagances and vagaries which have destroyed the usefulness of so many who have professed this doctrine. Above all, let us have the experience—the indubitable consciousness that the blood of Jesus Christ cleanseth from all sin—then the "beauty of holiness" will shine out in all our words and looks and acts, and then the world will be attracted to it as certainly as the needle is attracted to the pole.

CHAPTER XXV.

THE DISTINCTIVE DOCTRINE EXAMINED.

IN the last chapter an account was given of the great holiness revival, which rolled like a mighty tidal wave over our entire country, the blessed results of which Nebraska has had her share.

In the present chapter I desire to carefully examine this Bible and distinctive Methodist doctrine; and I hope to make it so simple and plain that the smallest child can understand it. If understood, none can reasonably object to it.

It is really wonderful how much is said in the Bible on the subject of perfection. God said to Abraham: "I am the Almighty God; walk before me, and be thou perfect." (Gen. xvii, 1.) Moses said to the Israelites of old: "Thou shalt be perfect with the Lord thy God." (Deut. xviii, 13.) "There was a man in the land of Uz, whose name was Job, and that man was perfect and upright, and one that feared God and eschewed evil." (Job i, 1.) David says: "Mark the perfect man, and behold the upright; for the end of that man is peace." (Psa. xxxvii, 37.)

Christ says, in his beautiful and inimitable Sermon on the Mount: "Be ye therefore perfect, even as your Father which is in heaven is perfect." (Matt. v, 48.) Paul said to the Colossians: "Stand perfect and complete in all the will of God." (Col. iv, 12.) He constantly pointed believers to the beautiful heights of perfect love. He had a longing desire to lead them up to this high plain. The height of his ambition was to "present every man perfect in Christ Jesus." He said to the Corinthians: "Be perfect." (2 Cor. xiii, 11.) The "central idea of Christianity," says Bishop Peck, "is perfect love." It is the sun, around which all the satellites revolve, and moving around this great center they rejoice in its broad, warm, genial, and life-imparting smile.

The design of the great scheme of human redemption was to bring man from a state of sin and pollution to a state of purity and happiness. "Christ gave himself for us, that he might redeem us from all iniquity, and purify unto himself a peculiar people, zealous of good works." (Tit. ii, 14.) And the design of the gospel is not accomplished in us until we are raised to this high, holy, and happy state, where our peace flows like a river, and our righteousness is as the waves of the sea.

In all ages there has been the most bitter opposition to the doctrine of holiness. There are many reasons for this. Holiness, or Christian perfection, is the most unrelenting, untiring, uncompromising, and powerful enemy the empire of Satan has; hence he puts forth every effort within his power to make the doctrine distasteful to men, in order that he may break its influence and power, and thereby save his own kingdom from wreck and ruin. In referring to the doctrine of Christian perfection, Mr. Wesley says: "This is the word which God will always bless, and which the devil peculiarly hates; therefore he is constantly stirring up both his own children and the weak children of God against it."

Another reason why so many object to the doctrine of holiness is because it is not rightly understood. There are multitudes in the Church who know but little about the doctrine of Christian perfection, as taught by John Wesley, the standard authors of our Church, and the Bible. If the doctrine were thoroughly examined, and thoroughly understood, I am confident the objections, to an extent at least, would give way.

Many object to the doctrine because of the inconsistencies of those who have professed it. We must admit that many who have professed holiness have not lived up to their profession, and that the doctrine has suffered very materially from its inconsistent and unwise advocates. Their profession and their acts have not been in harmony

DISTINCTIVE DOCTRINE EXAMINED. 401

at all. I think, however, that a careful examination of the matter will convince any unprejudiced mind that the proportion of inconsistent professors of holiness is no greater than the proportion of inconsistent professors of justification. It must be admitted that many in all ages, who have professed only conversion, have not lived up to their profession, and the cause of religion has suffered greatly from such inconsistent professors. If, therefore, we discard the doctrine of Christian perfection because of the inconsistencies of many who have professed it, for the very same reason we must discard the doctrine of justification—in fact, for the very same reason we must discard all religion, and take our stand on the broad platform of infidelity. Are we ready to take this rash step?

I do not pin my faith to the actions of any man. No wise man, it seems, would do such a foolish thing as that. My faith rests on God's word alone. Let God be true, though every man may be a liar. To the law, therefore, and to the testimony. To the word of God, and not to the actions of men do we appeal. That Christian perfection is attainable, is proved to my mind beyond the shadow of a doubt by the many passages of Scripture quoted in the forepart of this chapter.

While the term "perfection," "holiness," and

"entire sanctification" each has a shade of meaning peculiar to itself, these terms are all used in the Scriptures interchangeably.

What is Christian perfection? To answer this question satisfactorily it will be necessary to treat the subject negatively—to show what it is not; and in showing what it is not, we may be able, perhaps, before we get through, to show what it is. Touching this doctrine, the ideas of many are vague and very much confused.

1. It is not absolute perfection. The highest, the brightest, the sweetest, the loveliest angel that ranges the fields of light and glory is not absolutely perfect. Absolute perfection belongs alone to God. God is absolutely perfect in degree; Christians are perfect in kind only.

2. It is not angelic perfection. Angels are a higher order of intelligences than men. Angels never make mistakes, never err, never commit blunders. Their love burns with an intensity, and their services are performed with a precision that are not possible for mortals. They have none of the infirmities of fallen human nature. While the sad effects of the fall cling to these bodies of ours, we do not claim that it is possible for us to be as perfect as the angels in heaven. But when this corruptible shall put on incorruption; when this mortal shall put on immortality; when these bodies, sown in dishonor and

weakness, shall be raised in power and glory, then we shall be perfect as the angels.

3. It is not the perfection Adam had before the fall. Before man fell, all his faculties and powers were perfect. His intellectual, physical, and moral powers were all complete. Sin has marred and dwarfed all these powers. With the intellect marred and dwarfed by sin, with all the physical powers impaired by evil, it is not possible, since these are the medium through which the soul now operates, to be as perfect as if these powers had never suffered from sin. So it is not claimed, nor does the Bible promise the perfection Adam had before the fall. We must be content, therefore, with the perfection taught us in God's Word. And God's Word does not promise to us absolute perfection, nor angelic perfection, nor Adamic perfection, but *Christian perfection.*

4. It is not a perfection of the head. Nowhere in all the range of God's Word is there a single promise that God will make us perfect in judgment. The only perfection promised in the Bible is the perfection of love. Mr. Wesley says: "Another ground of these and a thousand mistakes is the not considering deeply that *love is the highest gift of God.* There is nothing higher in religion—there is, in effect, nothing else." Christian perfection is the loving God with all the heart, and all the soul, and all the mind, and

all the strength. This is the highest spiritual mountain-peak that can be gained here on the earth.

5. Christian perfection does not imply a faultless life. We are commanded to be blameless, but not faultless. A simple incident will illustrate this: A mother gave to her little girl a handkerchief to hem. She gave the child a needle, thread, and thimble, and gave her directions how the work should be done. The child followed the mother's directions as near as she possibly could. She did her very best to do just as the mother told her. When the work was finished she took it to her mother. The mother examined it. Some of the stitches were long and some of them were short; some places the hem was wide, and at other places it was narrow, and at other places it was badly puckered. The work was not faultless, but the child was blameless. She had gone according to the mother's directions as near as possible, and had done the very best she could. The mother gave the child a smile of approval and a kiss of affection. With all the divine grace it is possible for us to have, we shall not be faultless, but we may be blameless. If we go according to God's directions just as near as we possibly can, though our acts may be very far from being faultless, we shall have the divine smile of approval and the infinite kiss of affection from

our loving Heavenly Father. We shall be liable to make mistakes, commit errors, and make blunders as long as we live in a body marred and dwarfed by sin. An error in judgment may lead to an error in act. God goes back of the act to the motive that prompted the act. It is the intent that makes the crime. A man may be a murderer without ever having taken the life of a fellow-being. He may have desired to do so; and that constitutes the crime. On the other hand, he may have actually taken the life of a man, and still not be a murderer. He may have accidentally taken the life of his fellow-being. Hence Christ says: "Judge not, that ye be not judged." The Bible nowhere promises us a perfection that will free us from mistakes. While Christian perfection does not admit of any sin, inward or outward, properly so called, it does admit of a consciousness of infirmities and shortcomings. The purest persons that walk the earth are conscious of mistakes, shortcomings, and great weaknesses. These they often deplore in the deepest humility. These innocent mistakes and infirmities all need the blood of atonement, and we rejoice and praise God that the blood of atonement covers them all, and more than meets every demand. Christian perfection admits of many infirmities, but not one sin.

6. It is not freedom from temptation. If you

expect to be saved from temptation in this life, you are expecting something you will never realize. The servant is not greater than his Lord. If it were possible for us to reach a point where we could not be tempted, we should be greater than our Lord was. "He was tempted in all points like as we are, yet without sin." It is no sin to be tempted. The sin lies in our yielding to the temptation. Mr. Dow says: "We can not prevent the buzzards flying over our heads, but we can keep them from making nests in our hair."

Here on earth is the battle-field; here we are waging a warfare. Can there be war without conflict? Can there be conflict without enemies? Of all persons on the earth, those who are the most holy are the most exposed to temptation. Those who are the most holy are placed in the front of the battle. God has chosen them as his vanguard. They are the ones who make assaults upon the enemy. If they are in the front, and lead in the charge, they are, more than any others, exposed to the fiery missiles of the foe. At the pure Satan will hurl his sharpest arrows. Against them he will level his heaviest artillery. One holy person cast down is better for the empire of Satan than a whole regiment of ordinary Christians. One who is now in heaven once said: "As certain as night follows day, so certain will the black angel persecution follow holiness." A man who had recently come into the experience of perfect love, under the ministrations of Rev. Mr. Caughey, the great evangelist, went to him and said: "I don't understand this. I never had such severe temptations in my life as I have had since I received this blessing." "O," said Mr. Caughey, "that is not at all strange. It takes ten devils to watch you now, where it took only one when you were in a weak and sickly state." The less religion Christians have, the less trouble they have with Satan. Satan is satisfied with weak, worldly-minded Christians, and seldom troubles them. If we have no severe temptations we may well suspect the genuineness of our religion. A man once said: "I am opposed to revivals on principle." Another one said: "I am opposed to this doctrine of holiness." Are not such men sound asleep? The devil can do almost anything with a man when he gets him fast asleep. A man once dreamed he was traveling, and came to a little church, and on the cupola of that church was a devil fast asleep. He went on a little further and he came to a log cabin, and it was surrounded by devils, all wide awake. He was surprised, and asked for an explanation. One of the little imps said: "I will tell you. The fact is, that whole Church back there is asleep, and one devil can take care of all the members and sleep at the same time; but here in this cabin are two holy, wide-awake persons, a man and woman, and they have more influence and power than that whole Church." The greater the effort put forth on the part of the Christian to live near God and save souls, the greater will be the effort on the part of Satan to hedge up his way and thwart all his commendable plans. Every step we take from here to the throne of God will be hotly contested by the devil.

Then God will have a tried people. Job said: "When he hath tried me I shall come forth as gold." (Job xxiii, 10.) David said: "Thou, O God, hast proved us; thou hast tried us, as silver is tried." (Psa. lxvi, 10.) Solomon says: "The fining pot is for silver, and the furnace for gold; but the Lord trieth the hearts." (Prov. xvii, 3.) God said of his ancient people: "I have chosen thee in the furnace of affliction." (Isa. xlviii, 10.) "I will refine them as silver is refined, and will try them as gold is tried; they shall call on my name, and I will hear them." (Zech. xiii, 9.) James says: "Blessed is the man that endureth temptation; for when he is tried he shall receive the crown of life." (James i, 12.) He does not say blessed is the man that *has* temptation, but blessed is the man that *endures*, that stands firm, is loyal to God during the fiery temptation.

That man will at last receive a crown, before the beauty and splendor of which the crowns of the kings and emperors of earth will pale and sink into utter insignificance.

It is said that Napoleon once ordered a coat of mail. When the artisan completed it, he delivered it to the emperor. The emperor ordered him to put it on himself. Then Napoleon drew his large navy revolver and fired shot after shot at the man in the armor. It stood the severe test, and the artisan received from Napoleon a large reward. So if we stand the severe tests that will be applied to us here, great will be our reward hereafter.

God's method with his children here is found in Daniel, twelfth chapter and tenth verse: "Many shall be purified, and made white and tried." That is God's method. Purified, made white, then tried. Many are purified, but when the tests are applied give way.

"A few mornings ago," said a lady, "I placed a clean, white platter in the stove-baker, to warm it. By accident the door was closed, and the dish became very hot. When I removed it a scum of grease had covered nearly the whole surface. The heat had brought it out. I was surprised to see so much filth on what had appeared a perfectly clean, white platter. I wondered if such a scum of sin would come to the surface if I should be tried as by fire. What a state that must be, when no spot will appear, though a white heat is applied to bring out the defects!"

7. Christian perfection is not regeneration. It is a state of grace above and beyond conversion. Paul said to the Christians at Corinth: "And I, brethren, could not speak unto you as unto spiritual, but as unto babes in Christ. I have fed you with milk, and not with meat; for hitherto ye were not able to bear it, neither yet are ye now able. For ye are yet carnal: for whereas there is among you envying, and strife, and divisions, are ye not carnal?" (1 Cor. iii, 1, 2, 3.) "Having, therefore, these promises, dearly beloved, let us cleanse ourselves from all filthiness of the flesh and spirit, perfecting holiness in the fear of God." (2 Cor. vii, 1.)

Christian perfection is the perfecting, the completing, of the work which was begun at conversion. To the Church at Rome, Paul said: "I beseech you, therefore, brethren, by the mercies of God, that ye present your bodies a living sacrifice, holy, acceptable unto God, which is your reasonable service." (Rom. xii, 1.) And to the Christians at Thessalonica he said: "The very God of peace sanctify you wholly; and I pray God your whole spirit and soul and body be preserved blameless unto the coming of our Lord Jesus Christ." (1 Thess. v, 23.) Be it remembered that the faith of these Thessalonian Christians had been spread abroad "in every place" throughout all "Macedonia and Achaia." They were noted everywhere for their faith and good works, and yet Paul prayed that they might be wholly sanctified. All the above exhortations were given to Christians, showing very clearly that the work of *entire* sanctification had not been accomplished in them. They were not made perfect in love; but their great privilege was clearly set before them, and they were earnestly exhorted to avail themselves of their high privilege.

"But," says one, "is not God able to convert and wholly sanctify the soul at the same time?" Most assuredly he is. But it is not a question of God's ability at all, but of our faith. We are justified by faith. We are also sanctified by faith. Paul, in his discourse before Agrippa, says we "are sanctified by faith." (Acts xxvi, 18.) Dr. Adam Clarke, in commenting on this verse, says we are taught, "not only the forgiveness of sins, but the purification of the heart."

We get just what we believe for. "What things soever ye desire when ye pray, believe that ye receive them, and ye shall have them." (Mark xi, 24.) When faith is genuine it is always distinct, and is put forth for a particular object. A very common question with our Lord was: "Believe ye that I am able to do this?"

Blind Bartimeus cried out to the Savior, saying: "Jesus, thou son of David, have mercy on me. Jesus answered and said unto him, What wilt thou that I do unto thee? The blind man said unto him, Lord that I might receive my sight. And Jesus said unto him, Go thy way; thy faith hath made thee whole. And immediately he received his sight, and followed Jesus in the way." (Mark x, 51, 52.) He got just what he believed for—eyesight. The leper said to Jesus: "Lord, if thou wilt, thou canst make me clean." This was his faith. Jesus said: "I will; be thou clean. And immediately his leprosy was cleansed." (Matt. viii, 2, 3.) He received just what he believed for—cleansing.

A father went to the Savior with his son possessed with a dumb spirit. That father felt only as a father could feel under such circumstances. His own loved boy was under the complete power and control of the devil. How his heart must have bled with grief at every pore! Many a parent's heart bleeds to-day because a son is under the complete power of Satan. With the deepest anguish of heart the father cried out: "If thou canst do anything, have compassion on us, and help us. Jesus said unto him, If thou canst believe; all things are possible to him that believeth." The father exclaimed: "Lord, I believe; help thou mine unbelief. And the spirit came out of him." (Mark ix, 23-25.) He obtained just what he believed for—the deliverance of his son from the possession of a dumb devil.

The Syrophenician woman believed for the deliverance of her daughter from the power of the "unclean spirit," and she received just what she believed for. The faith of all these persons was put forth for a distinct object, and they all received that for which they believed.

The blind man believed for eyesight, and received it. The leper believed for cleansing, and received it. The father believed for the deliverance of his son from the possession of the dumb devil, and the son was saved. The mother believed for the deliverance of her daughter from the unclean spirit, and the daughter was rescued from his toils, restored, and made pure. To-day, as eighteen hundred years ago, we get just what we believe for. If we believe for pardon, we get pardon. If we believe for perfect love, we get perfect love. If we believe for the anointing of the Holy Ghost to qualify us for work, we receive the anointing. If the penitent at the altar, seeking pardon, could believe for pardon and entire sanctification at the same time, I believe he would receive both. But I have never known one who, at that moment, could grasp all. Mr. R. P. Smith, in his "Holiness Through Faith," relates the following: "While addressing a company in one of the mission-houses in New York, I noticed a young woman much affected. I found after meeting she was an actress, who had been brought to the point of turning her back on all her past life; but she was unable to believe that such a sinner as she was could receive the grace that was set before her. To my explanation of the divine sacrifice for sinners, she only exclaimed: 'O yes, sir; I know that it is all true, but I can't believe that it is for *me!*' It seemed too great presumption for her to believe that all her sins were blotted out, and she at once placed in the family of God. I left her in this condition of mind—longing for salvation, and yet too faithless to believe that it was for her.

"Upon parting with the actress, I was introduced to a refined, matronly, Christian woman, who, I understood, was giving her life to this gospel work among the abandoned. Her whole heart was in her work with an energy and simplicity that I have never seen surpassed. Her joy was to spend her years in the midst of this moral leprosy, raising the cross among the dying souls around her. But even while thus laboring for Christ, she felt most deeply her need of some privilege greatly beyond her present experience. So in earnest was she that she had just passed a sleepless night of sorrow and prayer for the full and satisfying revelation of Christ, with the complete victory over her own will. She knew that her sins had been forgiven her, and that she truly loved Jesus. Work for Jesus was the most delightful thing in the world to her. She knew that there was in the gospel a redemption 'from all iniquity,' but she had not found it. She knew that Christ bore her sins that she might become dead to sin and alive to righteousness; but she had not attained to it. The secret of this unsupplied need was soon found. Full of faith for God's work in others, and up to a certain point in herself, she needed to open the door of her heart yet more widely that the King of Glory might come in. This dear saint, who had so often taught the lesson to anxious sinners of faith as the means of blessing, now saw that the very same lesson was to be learned by herself upon a different level. The very words that a few moments before had been said to the awakened actress—*trust in Christ for what her soul felt the need of*—were now to be applied to herself. Shortly after this interview, the actress found Christ, through faith, pardon for all her sins; and the missionary, upon her high level of Christian experience, also *found in Christ*, through faith, cleansing 'from all unrighteousness.' Faith in each grasped the promise." Each received just what she needed, and just what she believed for. From the very beginning to the highest summit of Christian attainment, faith is the channel of God's blessing, while unbelief is the bar. "So much faith, so much deliverance; no more, no less! If we would live up to the gospel standard of holiness, we must believe up to the gospel standard of faith." Christian perfection is a soul made perfect in love. A soul made perfect in love is a soul perfectly pure. A soul perfectly pure is a soul cleansed from all sin, inbred or birth sin, and actual sin. If you desire that perfect cleansing, believe for it and you will have it.

8. Christian perfection does not imply that we can not fall.

If "the angels which kept not their first estate, but left their own habitation," fell into sin, and are "reserved in everlasting chains, under darkness, unto the judgment of the great day;" if Adam in paradise fell; if Solomon, the best and wisest man that ever lived, fell,—we need not expect that we shall become so holy that we can not fall. The very highest possible state of grace attainable in this life will not exempt us from danger. So it becomes necessary for us to say to the purest men and women that walk the earth:

"O watch, and fight, and pray;
The battle ne'er give o'er;
Renew it boldly every day,
And help divine implore.

> Ne'er think the victory won,
> Nor lay thine armor down;
> The work of faith will not be done
> Till thou obtain the crown."

9. Christian perfection is not maturity. Purity is one thing, and maturity is another. They are just as distinct as day and night. Many jumble the two together. Christian perfection is purity. Purity is freedom from sin, and is the result of God's extirpating power. Maturity is the result of growth, and takes time. Purity is a work wrought in the heart instantaneously by the power of God. Maturity, being the result of growth, is gradual, and may go on indefinitely.

Some think if they are sanctified wholly, they can never grow any more, when in fact they are just prepared to grow rapidly. Purity removes from the heart that which hinders growth. Inborn sin is a hindrance to growth, just as weeds in the field are a hindrance to the growth of the corn. Remove the weeds, and the corn will grow more rapidly. Remove all sin from the heart, and you will grow in grace more rapidly than ever. Let the cleansing blood of Jesus Christ be applied to the heart by the Holy Ghost, and you will receive an impetus that will send you on your heavenly way with a speed that you never dreamed of before.

We are commanded to "grow in grace," but

not *into* grace. Grace must first be imparted before there can be growth. As in nature, so in grace; first life, then growth. Pardon is by faith, and is instantaneous. God does not pardon gradually. When God pardons a soul, it is a perfect work. All actual sin is forgiven, and will be remembered against that soul no more forever; and that work is done in an instant, in the twinkling of an eye. After pardon, then we may grow. Entire sanctification is by faith, and is instantaneous, just as pardon is.

A few years ago the wife of a distinguished minister was lying hopelessly ill. All was mist and uncertainty before her. She longed for the purity and peace promised in the holy Word, but her husband had always preached a gradual growth in grace, and completeness in Christ only at death, and she waited for that hour in dread uncertainty. "O that I could have complete deliverance from sin now, before that fearful hour!" she exclaimed. "Why not?" the Spirit suggested. She sent for her husband, and as he entered her sick chamber, she anxiously inquired: "Can Christ save me from all sin." "Yes; he is an almighty Savior, your Savior, able to save to the uttermost." "When can he save me? You have often said that he saves from all sin at the dying moment. If he is *Almighty*, don't you think he could save me a few minutes before death? It would take the sting of death away to know that I am saved." "Yes; I think he could." "Well, if he could save me a few minutes before death, don't you believe it possible for him to save a few hours, or a day before death?" The husband bowed his assent. "But," she said, with deep emotion and great earnestness, "I may live a week, or a month; do you think it possible for God to save a soul from all sin so long before death?" "Yes; all things are possible with God," he answered with deep emotion. "Then kneel right down here and pray for me. I want this full salvation now, and if I live a month, I will live to praise God."

He knelt beside her bed, and offered a prayer such as he had never offered before, and while he prayed the cleansing blood that makes whiter than snow was applied to her soul, and she was enabled to rejoice with joy unspeakable and full of glory. She lived a month afterwards to magnify the grace of God, and testify to that perfect love that casteth out fear. From the grave of his wife that husband went forth to preach Christ as a present Savior, able to save from all sin.

A wholly sanctified soul is just as pure a moment after the cleansing blood is applied as the soul of the man who has been wholly sanctified for twenty years. But the man who has been walking for twenty years under the cleansing blood, has an experience deeper, wider, richer, and far more extensive than the man who has just been fully saved. The difference is not in quality but in quantity. A drop of water may be just as pure as an ocean, but there is more in the ocean than in the drop. A soul cleansed of all sin is prepared to grow more rapidly than ever.

When crossing the Sierra Nevada Mountains in 1850, after traveling for some time, we reached a point where we supposed we saw the summit. A lofty mountain-peak rose in solitary grandeur before us. We said, and we rejoiced at the sight, "There is the summit." We started up the rough mountain-side, and after traveling for some three hours reached its summit. But to our surprise, and not a little disappointment, we saw rising far away above and beyond us another mountain-peak. We said: "Well, we thought this was the summit, but were very much mistaken. That's the summit away up there." We started, and after several hours of weary travel, we at length reached this mountain summit. But to our utter disappointment and astonishment we saw rising before us, higher up, and farther away, another mountain-peak. We made no more predictions. Again, after a short rest, we started, and after plodding through slush and snow for near a half a day, reached this mountain summit. Then away above and beyond us rose another. Mountain-peak rose above mountain-peak, higher, and higher, and higher. And thus it is with the religion of the Lord Jesus Christ, if we live up to all the light God gives us.

The Christian's pathway to the skies is an ascending pathway. Mountain-peak of joy and knowledge in divine things rises above mountain-peak, higher, and higher, and higher. Our experience may grow deeper, and wider, and richer, and grander. We go from a justified soul to a soul made perfect in love, from a soul made perfect in love to a soul glorified in body and spirit; then onward and upward, forever and ever.

10. Perfect love is not simply ecstasy. It is not simply a bubbling up of joy, overflowing the soul with rapturous delight. It is, however, always peace, always rest of soul, and sometimes the great tidal waves of joy roll over the heart, deluging the whole soul, and filling it with an unearthly rapture.

It is not always liberty in prayer, or in testimony, or in preaching. So if we do not always have great ecstasy, or great liberty in prayer or testimony or preaching, we are not to conclude that we are not saved. Christian perfection is not ecstasy, but purity; and we obtain purity, not by feeling, but simple faith in Christ.

> "O for a faith that will not shrink,
>   Though pressed by every foe,
> That will not tremble on the brink
>   Of any earthly woe!
>
> A faith that shines more bright and clear
>   When tempests rage without;
> That when in danger knows no fear,
>   In *darkness* feels no doubt!"

Unconditional surrender of all to Christ, and unshaken faith in his ability and willingness to save to the uttermost now, this very moment, will bring to the heart the consciousness of this great salvation. May every reader of these pages have this sweet, rich, glowing, and abiding experience!

THE END.

www.ingramcontent.com/pod-product-compliance
Lightning Source LLC
Chambersburg PA
CBHW022108290426
44112CB00008B/590